THE
CUSTOMER
CULTURE
IMPERATIVE

A LEADER'S GUIDE TO DRIVING
SUPERIOR PERFORMANCE

DR. LINDEN R. BROWN
AND
CHRIS L. BROWN

New York   Chicago   San Francisco   Athens   London
Madrid   Mexico City   Milan   New Delhi
Singapore   Sydney   Toronto

1 2 3 4 5 6 7 8 9 0   DOC/DOC   1 0 9 8 7 6 5 4 3

ISBN   978-0-07-182114-8
MHID   0-07-182114-7

e-ISBN 978-0-07-181982-4
e-MHID   0-07-181982-7

Library of Congress Cataloging-in-Publication Data

Brown, Linden R.
  The customer culture imperative : a leader's guide to driving superior
performance / by Linden R. Brown and Chris L. Brown.—1 Edition.
      pages cm
  ISBN-13: 978-0-07-182114-8 (alk. paper)
  ISBN-10: 0-07-182114-7 (alk. paper)
  1. Leadership. 2. Consumer satisfaction. I. Brown, Linden, author. II.
Title.
  HD57.7.B764 2013
  658.8'12—dc23   2013035619

McGraw-Hill Education books are available at special quantity discounts to use as premiums and sales promotions or for use in corporate training programs. To contact a representative, please visit the Contact Us pages at www.mhprofessional.com.

From Linden

To my wife and life partner, Marie-Noelle, whose tireless work in helping others—extended family, friends, and the wider community—reminds us every day what it really means to be customer-centric.

From Chris

To my best friend and wife, Stephanie, my personal role model for how to be customer-centric.

I also want to dedicate this book to my grandfather, grandmother, mum, and dad, who instilled in me from an early age a love of learning and the passion and drive to take on big challenges. They taught me that doing the right thing may sometimes be the hardest thing in the short term but always pays off in the long run.

Contents

Preface

This book is about creating, building, and maintaining customer-centric organizations and how leading companies have done it. It gives you a framework for assessing your business's customer-centricity and steps to strengthen it. From our detailed research of more than a hundred companies in 2007–2010 we became convinced that what's best for the customer is also best for the business. Those companies that have strong customer-centricity outperform those that don't. When we started our journey down this path we had a vision to spark and sustain a customer culture transformation in organizations around the world that inspires employees, delights customers, and rewards shareholders. In talking with business leaders over the past two years who have willingly given their time and experience for stories and cases for this book, we have realized that customer-centricity has a much higher purpose—a purpose that has benefits not only for customers and stockholders but also for employees, the community, and the planet. We would be so bold as to say that it can act as a transformation of the way business works for the betterment of society if enough organizations truly adopt a customer-centric culture as the enduring way in which they do business.

We believe that if more companies follow the lead of Virgin, Starbucks, Amazon.com, Zappos, Costco, and salesforce.com, where their purpose is beyond short-term profit and they enact their real vision of doing good for people (their customers, employees, and the wider community), a transformation will occur. This will result in more satisfied and less-stressed customers, happier and highly engaged employees who look forward each day to contributing to their company's higher purpose, fewer layoffs of highly competent people with the associated stress for their families, more effective innovation that produces products and services valued by customers and the wider community, . . . and a longer-term legacy. We believe this aspiration is worth striving for, and as leaders in organizations, large and small, we will all be far happier and will leave an enduring legacy for the generations to come.

Richard Branson puts it this way:

There is no greater thing you can do with your life and your work than follow your passions— in a way that serves the world and you.[1]

We have been inspired to write this book by many people. John Stanhope, chairman of Australia Post, has been a constant source of inspiration from our original research through today's understanding of what it really means to be customer-centric. We have been inspired by the remarkable insights and leadership of David Thodey of Telstra, Lance Uggla of Markit, Alex Bard of salesforce.com, Tony Collins of Virgin Trains, Arthur Rubinfeld of Starbucks, Ahmed Fahour of Australia Post, and Brian Hartzer and Jason Yetton of Westpac. Inspiration has come from what has been achieved by Richard Branson, Jeff Bezos, Howard Schultz, and Marc Benioff as today's pioneers in creating, building, and maintaining highly customer-centric organizations. We want to thank for their time and insight John Parkin, Liz Moore, and Rachel Sandford of Telstra; Mark Gilmour and Ian Grace of Virgin; Dr. David Cooke of Konica Minolta; Ryan Rampersaud of BlackRock; John Hooper of Ergon Energy; Grant Ellison of CommsChoice; Nic Cola and Kirsty Shaw of FairfaxMedia; Shane Morris and Nic Nuske of Australia Post; Mike McGrath and Peter Wheeler of PricewaterhouseCoopers; and Lex Dwyer of Corporate Fitness. All of these people have encouraged us in our research and contributed substantially to our understanding of customer-centricity and what it takes to get there.

We want to thank our colleague, Professor Philip Kotler, who was the first to read what has become Chapter 1 of this book and encouraged us to publish our work. Also Professor George Day reviewed our initial customer culture model and suggested the term "peripheral vision" for one of the key factors. Professor Malcolm McDonald, emeritus professor at Cranfield University, School of Management has been a constant source of encouragement and an enthusiastic supporter of our work.

Our work colleague and friend Debi Garrod has provided ongoing encouragement, ideas, and input for this endeavor and is a passionate believer in our purpose. She has been an inspiration in the customer-centric mindset and skills she brings to individuals and teams in organizations in the United Kingdom and the Middle East and has encouraged us to reveal who we are in the writing of this book. She has been particularly involved in engaging the Virgin Group in this research and conducting interviews with senior executives for this book.

Our business colleague and friend, Stephen Wilson, whom we affectionately call our "corporate thinker," has spent many hours reviewing our ideas and helped us clarify them so that they can be communicated and understood. Stephen has evangelized our cause and inspired us to persevere with our vision.

We owe a great debt of gratitude to our core research team members. Sean Gallagher, a self-proclaimed "learned optimist," brought a laser focus to the project and gave us "reality checks" to ensure we progressed with the best use of resources available to us. Lucas Coffeen managed the project and the information system to a timetable and could find any piece of relevant research, no matter how obscure its source. Hjalte Hojsgaard brought discipline to the team by asking the hard questions—and more often than not also providing the best answers. April Holland, a talented data analyst, assessment designer, and behavioral expert, helped us develop, test, and validate our customer culture measurement tool, the Market Responsiveness Index (MRI).

For their advice and contributions to our early research and initial testing of our tools, we want to thank Danielle MacInnis, Veronique Ellison, Ali Cassim, Peter Moore, David Morgan, Steve Fischer, Kirsten Gates, Alan Colvin, Steve Newman, Mary Ann Mercer, Nic Simon, Hugh Pattinson, Jason Krieser, Charlie Lawrence, Bruce Perrott, Shaan Tainton, and Darren Kane.

There have been many more people who have helped us shape our ideas along our journey. We particularly want to thank Dr. Roger Best, Doug Biehn, Seth Berman, John Konsin, Chris Zane, Cam Crawford, Greg Hudson, Marcus Weare, Dave Adams, Gordon Alexander,

Russell Morse, John Nanscawen, Nick Kurtis, Sean Mathieson, Ian Pollard, Mark Woodbridge, Stuart Lee, Richard Overton, Ben Wignall, Koshi Okamoto, Leslie O'Carmody, Alessandra Rasmussen, and Stuart Plane.

We also want to thank our friends Jerry Gleason and Donald Williamson, who reviewed our manuscripts along the way and provided insightful suggestions. They gave us continual encouragement and alerted us to new developments in Silicon Valley and innovations by some of the world's most iconic companies. We thank Scott Hamilton for helping us tell our story at conferences and workshops. Also, special thanks are due to Henry DeVries for sharpening our focus and helping us navigate and connect with the publication world.

We want to thank Donya Dickerson and Zach Gajewski at McGraw-Hill for receiving our book proposal with such enthusiasm and believing in the value of telling the world about our work. Zach brought focus and editorial skill to our manuscript in a way that led us to clarify our viewpoint and tell our story much more effectively. Also our thanks go to Scott Amerman for his copy-editing expertise. The whole team at McGraw-Hill has brought consummate professionalism to the project and for that we thank them wholeheartedly.

Finally, we owe an incalculable debt to our respective wives, Marie-Noelle and Stephanie Brown, for their unyielding support, patience, and endurance as we travelled through the seven years of this project.

Introduction

A customer-focused culture in organizations is not easy to really "get." Most business leaders would agree that the concept is not very tangible, not easily accessible, not readily measurable, and not easy for many to explain. Some think of it as good customer service, others as having satisfied customers, and still others as providing a good customer experience.

Most organizations would claim to have some level of customer focus. Their marketing and sales teams identify the needs of particular market segments and target them. Their customer service teams aim to offer prompt, relevant responses to customer problems. Few, however, have a culture in which the customer is at the heart of all decisions taken in all functions and units within a business. Few have shared values across the entire business that translate into behaviors in all functions that are aligned and committed to profitably creating superior value for customers. Few have a culture that delivers a customer experience that is consistently excellent along the whole service chain. To be truly customer-focused, you must have a customer culture.

Our aim in this book is to make customer culture tangible, accessible, measurable, and memorable so that it is easy to communicate and demonstrate for yourself and your team. We aim to link customer culture to strategy and business performance. We want you to see its value to you and your team and be able to implement it to your benefit and the benefit of your business.

We have come to realize that customer culture is a discipline—a set of attitudes, behaviors, and skills that can be developed, refined, and practiced to become habits that lead to better personal and business results. But, like physical fitness, it can be lost if it is not continually practiced and revitalized.

Each of us began our journey moving from customer focus to customer culture from different starting points. Linden's first business experience was operating a small pickled onion manufacturing company, Blue Banner Pickles, in Tasmania, purchased with his cousin, from an elderly couple who had started the brand 25 years earlier, in the 1940s. Linden next held marketing and sales positions in a wide array of industries, gaining ground-floor experience working with customers and learning what they truly wanted. His second start-up was the successful Overseas Shipping Services (OSS World Wide Movers) in Sydney, Australia, which further imbedded the importance to Linden of interacting with customers, understanding their emotional and rational needs, and delivering to them exactly the service that has been promised.

On reflection it was obvious that all staff members at OSS had developed the same mindset and collaborated to ensure the customer was satisfied and their expectations were met or exceeded. Both of these businesses still operate today, more than 40 years later. Linden went on to teach marketing at a number of university business schools and to consult with and educate business leaders and marketers in some of the world's largest corporations. It became clear from his corporate education experiences over many years that much of the learning was lost in large corporations because their corporate cultures worked against the concepts he was teaching—namely, a customer culture. This sparked his research and interest in what is required to develop a customer-focused culture and working with companies to help them build it.

Chris's business experience began with Hewlett-Packard (HP) in Australia when he delayed his commerce studies to accept a two-year full-time work internship in sales at the age of 19. After completing his marketing and finance degree he worked in sales and marketing roles with the world's largest wholesaler of computers, Ingram Micro. He later returned to HP, working in sales, product management, and subsequently became marketing director for Australasia and the South Pacific.

His experience in a predominantly business-to-business (B2B) environment brought home to him the value of deep customer relationships to creating customer loyalty and advocacy. In these roles Chris experienced firsthand the challenge of operating a customer-centric business as part of a large multinational organization. It became clear that the most successful parts of the HP business were those with the highest levels of customer understanding and alignment. The leaders of those businesses were both customer- and employee-centric; they cared deeply about customers being successful by using HP's products. This was the beginning of Chris's curiosity into what really makes businesses successful over the longer term. Business is about making profits, but how you make those profits is just as important. Are profits being made at the expense of your customers, or are they being made as a result of customer success? This question and the question of how leaders create more customer-centric businesses helped lead Linden and Chris toward the creation of MarketCulture Strategies.

Since 1988 MarketCulture Strategies, has helped leaders align their business culture with their market through an integrated process of culture assessment, management training, marketing skills training, and strategic planning. We are the developers of the Market Responsiveness Index (MRI) Benchmark tool, which enables executives to understand their level of customer- and market-centricity across the entire business. In short: we help leaders profit from increased customer focus.

From extensive research involving the review of more than 200 studies over the last five years, our own empirical research and direct work with more than 100 companies, we have found seven disciplines of customer culture that consistently predict enhanced, sustainable business results. Each discipline is linked to a particular strategy and drives predictable and measurable improvements in one or more business performance factors: customer satisfaction, sales growth, profit growth, profitability, innovation, and new product or service success. As you and your team gain these disciplines you will find "profit coming up through the floor." What's more, you will find very happy customers and fulfilled employees.

We explain what each of these seven disciplines comprise, their links to particular strategies, and how to implement them in your team or business by following a few clearly defined steps that will ensure embedding of a strong customer culture.

What's the Difference between Customer Focus and Customer Culture?

First we must distinguish between customer focus and customer culture. The term *customer focus* means different things to different people. It ranges in its meaning from "good customer service" to "identifying the needs of customers and delivering products and services that meet those needs" to "ensuring that the whole organization, and not just frontline service staff, puts its customers first"—meaning understanding customers' needs and doing what is right for the customer. In this last meaning, every department and every employee should share the same customer-focused vision. For this to occur, an organization must have a *culture* based on the belief that *what's best for the customer is best for the business.* It is this meaning of customer focus we call *customer culture.* In fact, we maintain that to have real customer focus you *must* have a customer culture.

Second, a *customer culture* is embraced by every individual, team, and business unit. It is embedded in people through orientation and induction, leadership, processes, rewards, key performance measures, a common language, and an expected way of doing things. What's more, customer culture is a discipline—a shared set of behaviors and skills that can be developed, refined, and practiced to become habits that lead to better personal and business results.

Third, customer culture is not the same as customer-compelled.[1] A customer-compelled company is one that responds to any and every request for improvements or new products and services that any and all customers say they want. This is usually impractical and unprofitable and does not allow the firm to focus on the customers it can best serve with superior value. Every business must have a clear strategy, value proposition, and target customers whose needs are understood and for whom superior value and experience are delivered. A strong customer culture is one that is clearly aligned to the company's strategy and understands and responds to the current and future needs of targeted customers. It includes the discipline and skills to know when particular customers or enquiries can't be met by the business and can better be served by competitors and to help customers to find a solution elsewhere. A customer culture is one in which people in a business interact with both customers and noncustomers in a way that shows they care—either by solving the customers' problem or by referring noncustomers to other companies that can meet their needs better.

Customer culture embodies shared values across the entire business that translates into behaviors in all functions that are aligned and committed to creating superior value for customers in a profitable way. A strong customer culture delivers a customer experience that is consistently excellent along the whole service chain. The ultimate aim is to have the customers make your business the center for everything they do for your particular offering. Then your customers will be advocates of your business and your products and services. You can't get to the ultimate unless you build the right culture—a *customer culture*.

Does a Customer Culture Matter?

It may sound like a simple question with an obvious answer, but after a lifetime of helping business leaders improve their level of customer culture we felt the question worth revisiting.

For most of us the answer to this question is intuitive: yes, customer culture matters! We are all customers, and when we reflect on our most fulfilling business relationships we sense these companies are focused on our needs and helping us to be satisfied and successful.

In fact the most successful companies on earth understand their own customers' needs better than the customers themselves through observation, rapport, and relationships. Steve Jobs of Apple famously suggested, "It isn't the consumers' job to know what they want."[2] Apple's ability to look at every aspect of the customer's experience in painstaking detail is legendary and has resulted in unprecedented success. It starts with the customer experience in an Apple store. It continues when you unpack your new Apple device. Then as you start to use it you feel that the designers have thought about your needs for easy use, visual appeal, and convenience and how you are likely to use it.

Although Apple provides great inspiration, it is an example of a company that was born with a unique, deeply innovative leader who embedded a customer culture. But, what about a company that must transform itself from an inward-looking culture to one that is externally focused and embraces the customer? We look at the companies that have done it and some of those that are still in the process of becoming customer-centric.

So why revisit the question *does customer culture matter*? First, we wanted to find hard evidence that a strong customer culture does indeed yield higher business performance than a weak customer culture. Second, if strong customer culture does drive superior results, then we wanted to build a measurement tool and approach for leaders to manage, develop, and track their level of customer culture.

Does customer culture really matter to *business performance*? Our answer is a resounding *yes!* After spending three years researching this question we have scientific evidence to show that it does matter. It has a deep impact on an organization's business performance and sustainability. In fact it is *imperative*. Customer culture is as fundamental to business performance as breathing is to living. It is the life force of your business. You only have a sustainable business if it is driven by a customer culture.

The purpose of this book is to show you, your team, and company what you need to do to build and sustain an innate customer culture. We will show you how to do it by giving you the method and framework for changing to, or strengthening, your customer culture. This will enable you to:

- Successfully shift and build the culture
- Create the engagement of your entire organization
- Create the focus on customer culture
- Provide a common language for change
- Make customer culture real and actionable
- Drive change in your organization
- Measure and benchmark your progress
- Leave a legacy of an enduring business

Our aim is to make customer culture tangible, measurable, and memorable so that it is easy to communicate and demonstrate. We will also show how a strong customer culture supports and links to business strategy and which elements drive particular business performance improvements.

You will read stories of some of the world's most customer-centric companies and how they have been able to defy the short-term obsession that Wall Street brings to bear on companies to produce ever-improving quarterly financial results. For so many businesses the goals of Wall Street, steeped in short-term trading, drive the behavior of senior executives and boards to an excessive preoccupation with shareholder value at the expense of customer value. We contend, supported by extensive research, that it is customer value that creates shareholder value—not the other way around. In today's "age of the customer," it is the customer culture imperative that creates customer value; that, in turn, delivers shareholder returns.

Jeff Bezos's Amazon.com has held firm on its vision of being the world's most customer-centric company, against periodic criticism, to deliver exceptional growth and innovation. Costco's founder, Jim Sinegal, has brushed aside the financial critics who want the company to charge more, to stay true to the company's promise to its customers and trade short-term profit for long-term growth and profitability. Howard Schultz, the founder of Starbucks, has retained an obsession with outstanding customer experience with the culture to support it—with an impressive long-term growth record. David Thodey, CEO of Australia's largest telecommunications company, has withstood pressure for "quick fixes" to hold firm to his vision of transforming Telstra into a customer-centric organization, which will result in superior financial returns. Richard Branson, head and founder of the Virgin Group, is unfettered by the stock market and operates in a variety of businesses as "the customers' champion." The Virgin businesses—airlines, banking, mobile phones, and many others—all share the Virgin values of caring for customers, fun, innovation, and value. These stories and others show what it takes to build enduring customer-centric companies with long-term benefits for customers, employees, shareholders, and the wider community. These people are leaving a legacy with the people they employ, the community they serve, and the sustainability of a culture that delivers long-term prosperity to investors.

The following chapters will show you what is involved, what to do, and the benefits that will flow to you, your team, and your company.

Chapter 1

What's Best for the Customer Is Best for the Business

There is only one boss: the customer. And he can fire everybody in the company, from the chairman down, simply by spending his money somewhere else.

—Sam Walton (1918–1992)

Customer focus is a term both overused and underdone. It sounds good in a mission or vision statement, but many leaders don't really know how to achieve a customer-focused culture, nor are they doing anything specific about improving it in a sustainable way. Many other leaders may know how to do it but feel it may not be worth the effort and time required to achieve it.

There are many reasons the leadership of companies talk about customer focus. They believe their customers and employees want to hear the "customer first" story. It sends the right message. Most leaders believe, at some level, focus on the customer is an important part of running a successful business. They understand that without customers there is no business.

So why do leaders of companies talk the talk but do not walk (or run) the walk?

The reality of being truly customer focused—that is, fostering a customer culture—is difficult. The task is challenging, particularly when companies have developed habits and structures that work against it. Internal focus on operations, processes, and working in silos creates habits that can be hard to change.

As companies grow they become more complex: communication becomes difficult and frequently confusing, and processes are set up to maintain quality and improve efficiency; often these get in the way of doing the right thing for customers. Silos develop, and internal politics result in people acting in their own best interests above that of the customer and the business. We have all experienced being sent from one department to another by customer service representatives who are not empowered to take ownership of our problem.

Sometimes people are compensated in ways that work against the best interests of customers. There is no better example of this than the 2008–2011 mortgage crisis in the United States and elsewhere, where mortgage salespeople were incented to sell mortgages to people who could not afford them. Obstacle after obstacle arose to make doing the right thing for customers less and less achievable.

Another reason for the lack of customer culture is the short-term behavior driven by an investor focus and reporting of quarterly results. An underlying customer culture that provides a sustainable business focus will lead to more integrated thinking and reporting based on medium-term performance trends.

Many of today's professionals are specialists with highly developed technical skills in their areas of expertise. This can and does lead to a narrow focus without a broader understanding of how they affect the value received by customers.

In larger organizations it can be easier not to put the customer first, particularly when the customer problems may involve difficult longer-term issues that need to be resolved. Some professionals even view customers as inhibitors to getting their jobs done—an annoyance to minimize. For example, the university academic may lament the fact that he has to teach students rather than focus 100 percent on research, or a surgeon may dislike having to communicate in person with her patients. Others focus on profit to the exclusion of customer interests. When this attitude takes hold in organizations it becomes a significant roadblock to a customer culture, regardless of what the mission states.

Against this backdrop, developing a customer culture is a challenging transformation for most organizations, but the rewards for getting it right are massive. It is an imperative of leadership to lead a customer culture change. Active senior leadership is critical to its success. The role of senior leadership in customer culture change is laid out in Chapter 9.

The Drive toward the Ultimate Customer Experience

The rapid globalization and digitization of industries have resulted in exponential increases in the competitive intensity and market shifts for many business sectors. That has resulted in rapid commoditization and cannibalization of core products and services and the creation of new markets. The result is falling margins, stagnating growth, and large numbers of layoffs. The quest for differentiation and value creation has never been greater.

We are now seeing the emergence of a new cross-functional endeavor known as customer experience and the hiring of chief customer officers to implement it in many of the Global Top 1000 firms. This function is designed to look at the entire customer interaction cycle that occurs with a company. Every touchpoint is evaluated with the goal of improving the customer's experience and creating loyalty, customer advocates, and repeat business.

This shift from a one-off product sales to ongoing engagement with customers is a significant challenge for new leaders taking on these new roles. In response, the Chief Customer Officer (CCO) Council was established in 2008 by Curtis Bingham to help new leaders collaborate and share techniques designed to transform their customers' experiences.

In order for customer experience initiatives to be successful, however, every employee must buy in to the concept of customer culture and his or her role in contributing toward the customer experience. Leaders of the company need to develop and believe in a culture that behaves in a customer-focused manner rather than just saying it.

A perception is created by every interaction with a company over time. One way of thinking about it is to use the banking analogy developed by Stephen Covey in *The 7 Habits of Highly Successful People*. Every interaction results in either an emotional deposit (a good experience) or an emotional withdrawal (a bad experience).[1] So a customer will probably feel differently at one point in time than at another about a company depending on the latest experience, which is usually the most top of mind.

This can result in a "death by a thousand cuts" for companies that consistently provide bad experiences. As competition increases and alternatives emerge, customers shift their business to others that provide better value and better customer experiences.

The importance of customer experience varies across industries, but as products and services appear more and more similar, customers will increasingly distinguish companies based on more than just their core offering. The prerequisite for consistently good customer experiences is a strong customer culture.

Figure 1.1 shows customer culture as the foundation that creates customer experience that in turn provides customer satisfaction and advocacy. When customer advocacy is created, you have consumers or business customers who are trusted, influential, and talking about your business in a positive way. You can think of advertising as the

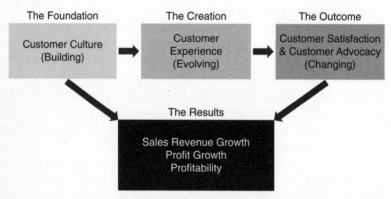

Figure 1.1 Customer culture driving customer experience and profitable growth

cost of not having advocates. So these customer attributes and actions impact business performance positively in terms of revenue, profit, and profitability. A strong customer culture will create a positive customer experience, customer advocates, and superior business results.

Customer culture is both an attitude and a skill set that translate into how people think, what people do, and how they behave. People are the critical ingredient. For customer culture to take hold in an organization it must form an integral part of the corporate culture.

It is because of these changes in the business environment that we see customer culture as imperative to driving future market leadership and sustainable business performance improvement, which results in enduring organizations.

Customer Culture: "Are We There Yet?"

On August 6, 2006, at the Spanish Bay golf clubhouse at Pebble Beach, California, we were listening to our friend and business colleague John Stanhope vent his frustrations about his inability to create a strong customer culture in his company—a large, long-established telecommunications business. Recently he had asked himself the question, "Are we there yet?" His answer was a resounding "No!" He was lamenting this fact and asking us what needed to be done and how does one know when one gets there.

What was inspiring was that John was the chief financial officer of his company. We collaborated with John over the following three years on a customer culture journey with his finance group of more than 2,500 staff members across a wide range of financial and administrative functions. The results were outstanding—a clear vision and mission of how to create more value for customers and the business, a common language around a "value service culture," and enhanced collaboration toward a common customer value creation goal. We saw substantially increased staff engagement and a real buzz in the offices, great stories about customer service, and staff members rewarded for customer-centric behavior. By 2010 the group had become one of the most customer-centric finance functions we had seen.

John was so passionate about this that it inspired us along the way to look more deeply at what is involved in actually developing a strong customer culture, how to measure it, and what must be done to get there.

What Is the Evidence?

Thus began a three-year research project. We started by pouring over more than 200 separate in-depth academic research studies covering primarily the marketing, management, and social sciences disciplines. We interviewed scores of business leaders on the subject of customer-focused culture and reviewed countless business articles on the subject. There is a large body of academic work that has concretely and empirically established the link between business performance and alignment with customers and markets.

These studies highlight the importance of a business being aligned to customer needs with respect to competitors' offers. The studies also highlight the importance of changes in the wider environment that impact customer needs and the cultural capability of a firm to deliver superior value to customers that creates sustainable profitability. Many of these studies recognize the central role of culture—of behavioral habits that create alignment with customers and competitors and drive business performance.

From a distillation of this research we identified several categories of behavior that studies showed to be drivers of superior business performance and sustainable growth.

We then conducted a large-scale empirical foundation study to measure the validity of customer culture, reflected in people's behaviors, and its link to business performance as measured by profitability, profit growth, sales revenue growth, innovation, new-product success, and customer satisfaction. This study is described in Appendix 1.

The overall correlation we found between customer culture and business performance is high at 0.57, as shown in Figure 1.2. We compare this correlation with other commonly known correlations and see this is almost as strong as 'temperature and nearness to the equator' - indicating the further you are from the equator the colder it is. In contrast, the correlation between SAT score and college grade point average is 0.35.

Through our own experience and research we have discovered that strong customer-focused behaviors of an organization reflect a

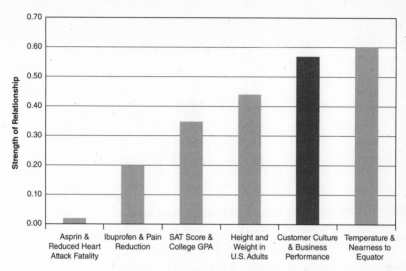

Figure 1.2 Customer culture and business performance are highly correlated

culture that is embraced by every individual, team, and business unit. It is embedded in people through orientation, leadership, processes, rewards, key performance measures, a common language, and an expected way of doing things. Individual and team decisions are based on the belief that "what's best for the customer is best for the business."

We found that customer culture is the foundation for driving future business results such as sales growth and profit. A firm's current level of customer culture is an important predictor of future results. It is an early-warning indicator of both the risks and opportunities related to retaining customers and the capability of acquiring new ones.

What Are the Customer Culture Factors that Drive Performance?

Our study found seven critical cultural traits of customer culture. These determine if a business can create customer advocates and win in the marketplace. They expose the risks that a company's capabilities will not support its strategy. The names we have given these seven traits and their associated behavior summaries are given in Figure 1.3.

Traits	Behavior Summary	
Customer Insight	The extent to which employees monitor, understand, and act on current customer needs and satisfaction	
Customer Foresight	The extent to which employees monitor, understand, and act on potential customer needs and opportunities	
Competitor Insight	The extent to which employees monitor, understand, and respond to current competitor strengths and weaknesses	
Competitor Foresight	The extent to which employees monitor, understand, and respond to new market entrants and potential competitors	
Peripheral Vision	The extent to which employees monitor, understand, and respond to trends in the larger environment (Political, Economic, Social, and Technical)	*"Peripheral Vision": Our thanks to Prof. George S. Day at The Wharton School of the University of Pennsylvania, and coauthor of a book of the same name, who suggested that the term "peripheral vision" aptly describes our factor that represents a wider vision of the strategic trends that must be monitored in a firm's external environment.*
Cross-Functional Collaboration	The extent to which employees interact, share information, work with, and assist colleagues from other work groups	
Strategic Alignment	The extent to which employees understand, and enact the vision, mission, objectives, and strategic direction of the company	

Figure 1.3 The seven customer culture traits

Factors	Customer Satisfaction	Innovation	New-Product Success	Profit Growth	Profitability	Sales Revenue Growth
Customer Insight	✓	✓	✓			✓
Customer Foresight		✓				
Competitor Insight				✓	✓	✓
Competitor Foresight		✓	✓		-	
Peripheral Vision		✓				
Cross-Functional Collaboration	✓	✓	✓	✓	✓	✓
Strategic Alignment	✓	✓	✓	✓	✓	✓

Figure 1.4 Customer culture drivers of business outcomes

These traits also have a decisive impact on sales growth, profit growth, profitability, customer satisfaction, new-product success, and innovation. In Figure 1.4 they show each trait as a driver of particular business performance outcomes. These customer culture traits predict better, sustainable business results. Each trait drives predictable and measurable improvements in sales, profitability, and new-product or new-service success.

We have come to realize that customer culture is a discipline— a set of behaviors and skills that can be developed, refined, and practiced to become habits that lead to better personal and business results. We now describe each of the seven disciplines that reflect a strong customer culture.

1. The Customer Insight Discipline

There are *two customer traits* reflected in workforce behaviors and prevalent activities that give a company a deep and dynamic understanding of current and prospective customers. Without these strong drivers, the company cannot stay in touch with its market and is at high risk of losing customers, market share, and profitability. The first of these is related to satisfying the needs of current customers; the second discipline relates to a company's ability to obtain new customers profitably and anticipate future needs. We have called this first discipline *customer insight* behaviors.

> **Customer insight:** *Does the company understand its current customers' needs? Does it know how satisfied or dissatisfied they are with its products or services? Does it act on this knowledge? Does it communicate to customers its actions resulting from their feedback?*

> **Link to strategy:** Strength in this discipline is particularly relevant to a strategy designed to focus on existing customers in order to retain them, create customer advocates, and increase the average revenue per customer.

> **Driver of business performance:** This measures a business's ability to improve customer satisfaction and retention and impacts customer advocacy and sales revenue growth, innovation, and new-product success.

For most companies this is at the heart of their strategies. Think about the many ways customers interact with your business every day. Every one of those interactions presents an opportunity for your staff members to demonstrate their understanding of the customer's environment. Whether it is as simple as respecting a retail customer's time by offering a callback option to resolve a problem or as complex as managing the expectations of enterprise customers by implementing leading-edge technology. All staff behavior is driven by your culture and the expectations placed on everyone to know his or her customers and treat them in a certain way.

Zappos, the online footwear retailer, requires all new employees, regardless of their role, to work in the customer-service call center as part of their training program. At Le Touessrok Hotel, on the island of Mauritius, the executive chef requires his staff to learn each guest's special diet requirements. At Telstra, Australia's largest telecommunications company, senior executives receive daily updates of the company's customer advocacy score based on feedback from 40,000 customer interactions from the previous day. Verbatim summaries of these interactions are sent to the source of the customer interaction within Telstra in close to "real" time. On the company's intranet the prime space shows the daily advocacy score as the focal point above the space that shows the company's stock price.

2. The Customer Foresight Discipline

This second customer discipline relates to a company's ability to obtain new customers profitably and anticipate future needs. This discipline is related to *customer foresight* behaviors.

> **Customer foresight:** *Does the company gather information on potential customers? Does it target them based on its opportunity for competitive advantage? Does it understand and invest in meeting future needs of prospective customers? Does it understand and act on unarticulated needs?*

> **Link to strategy:** Strength in this discipline is particularly relevant to a strategy designed to obtain new customers in order to increase the customer base and grow the size of the business.

> **Driver of business performance:** This measures a business's ability to acquire new customers and meet future customer needs and specifically impacts innovation. It will drive future sales revenue growth

Your company's ability to attract new customers is based on its willingness to embrace new ways of providing service. Will it lead the market by launching new services before customers recognize their own changing needs?

Intuit, the financial software company, makes sure that 80 percent of the participants in its usability studies are noncustomers; the company wants to know what these people think. Allen Medical Systems, a maker of medical equipment, puts its people in hospital operating rooms to learn what equipment is needed for a particular kind of surgery as part of a product development project. While in the operating rooms, they routinely ask what might be needed for related surgeries. A continuous stream of new products is the result.

3. The Competitor Insight Discipline

There are *two competitive traits* reflected in workforce behaviors and prevalent activities that give the company a deep and dynamic understanding of its competition. Without these strong drivers, the company cannot stay in touch with its competitors' strategies and is in danger of losing market share and profitability. The first of these is related to understanding and acting on the strategies of current competitors; the second relates to a company's ability to foresee new competitors that could impact its markets in the future. We have called this first competitor discipline *competitor insight*.

> **Competitor insight:** *Does the company monitor, understand, and respond to its competitors' strengths and weaknesses? Does it factor competitors' current strategies into its own strategies? Do staff members understand how they contribute to the firm's current value proposition and competitive advantage, and do they act to support it?*

> **Link to strategy:** Strength in this discipline is particularly relevant to a strategy designed to defend and take market share from competitors, strengthen short-term competitive advantage, and consolidate current competitive position in the marketplace.

> **Driver of business performance:** This measures a business's ability to implement differentiated value propositions, improve profit margins, and achieve ongoing revenue growth, profit growth, and profitability.

Your company's understanding of its customers' alternatives is crucial to its ability to compete. Which service offerings are competitive, and which are not? How do customers perceive your offers: are they simple and transparent and clearly better than the alternatives? Are staff members in all functions factoring into their work the value propositions of current competitors to produce additional value for the business and its customers?

Speedo, a maker of both recreational and competitive swimsuits, gathers information from channel customers, past employees, public and industry reports and forums, consumer research, and discussions with retired industry "old-timers" to develop an in-depth understanding of key competitors' strategies. This includes their value propositions, capabilities, cost structures, profit drivers, the strengths and weaknesses of their competitive positions, and the cultural drivers of "how they compete and react." Speedo has found that its strong product and brand quality are becoming less important advantages than customer service, product availability, and product styling—aspects in which their competitors have been beating them. These findings have been widely discussed within the company, resulting in a new strategy focused on customer service, new designs, point-of-sale merchandising, more efficient warehousing and distribution, and a new product-returns policy. Speedo has regained its competitive advantage and increased its market share and profitability growth.

4. The Competitor Foresight Discipline

This second competitive trait relates to a company's ability to foresee new competitors that could impact its markets in the future. New innovative competitors have an impact on uncovering latent needs of customers and influencing their perception of their future needs. We have called this discipline *competitor foresight.*

> **Competitor foresight:** *Does the company consider potential competitors when making decisions about customers? Does it identify market shifts in order to foresee potential competitors? Do staff members contribute to competitive intelligence relating to potential new competitors, and how they might affect future customer needs?*

> **Link to strategy:** Strength in this discipline is particularly relevant to two types of competitive strategies:
> a) One designed to defend competitive position and preempt new competitors in the medium to longer term in industries experiencing market shifts
> b) One to increase market share by creating a new competitive advantage in a new emerging market.

Driver of business performance: This measures a business's ability to account for future competitors and their strategies and create new products and value propositions. This behavioral trait impacts innovation and new-product success.

How does your company stay ahead of potential competitors? Which businesses should your company cannibalize before your future competitors do it for you? How does your company address the threat of future competition? Are staff members actively aware of and signaling new competitive threats and their likely impact on your customers and businesses?

Orica, a global specialty chemical company, foresaw the emergence of Indonesian and Chinese competitors. Armed with this foresight, it moved to protect its current market and expand into new markets. Known for its technical expertise and product safety record, Orica introduced new services to augment its core chemical products, a move that reduced costs for its customers and repelled new foreign competitors. With support from well-selected alliance partners, it launched ChemNet, an online chemical trading business, to expand its product and service reach in the wider Asia-Pacific market.

5. The Peripheral Vision Discipline

This trait reflected in workforce behaviors and prevalent activities gives the company a deep and dynamic understanding of its broader external environment. Without these strong drivers, the company will miss opportunities and risk the loss of customers due to market and industry shifts. Changes in technology, economic conditions, government policies, and society all impact current and future customer needs. We have called this trait *peripheral vision.*

Peripheral vision[2]: *Does the company monitor, understand, and respond to the political, economic, social, technological, and natural environment trends emerging on the periphery that could affect its customers and its business? Are all staff members encouraged to scan their respective fields of expertise for new ideas relevant to the changing external environment? Does the company act on this flow of new ideas?*

Link to strategy: Strength in this discipline is particularly relevant to an innovation strategy reflected in two types of strategies:

a) One based on new products and services as the means for growth and profitability
b) One requiring a new business model to cope with disruptive technological changes

Driver of business performance: This measures a business's ability to scan for, be aware of, and act on threats and opportunities emerging in its external environment. It impacts innovation. Those companies that have it show capabilities of effective innovation that drive future sales and profit growth from new market opportunities.

Experience shows us that new ideas and resulting innovation can come from internal and external sources—staff in all departments, suppliers, contractors, customers, and competitors. Are your staff members actively encouraged to signal threats and opportunities observed in the external environment? Is there a mechanism for logging these and taking action on those that have merit? Are your people rewarded for communicating ideas related to the changing external environment that are acted on by the company?

Ericsson, the Sweden-based global provider of telecommunication and data-communication systems, has used scenario planning as a means of clarifying its corporate vision for many years. This involves painting several different pictures of possible futures using different assumptions about regulation, globalization, technological change, market uptake of new types of telecommunication products and services, the convergence of industries and regions, and the emergence of national markets such as China and India. As a result, Ericsson has been much quicker to move resources into China and other Asian growth markets than have its traditional Western competitors, such as Motorola. Ericsson has also been in a strong position to compete with rapidly emerging Chinese competitors. The firm's scenario planning continues. Ericsson is already planning for what life and business might be like in 2020.

These five externally oriented disciplines—customer insight and foresight, competitor insight and foresight, and peripheral vision—are focused into action for the entire company, business units, and teams through two enabling disciplines: *collaboration* and *alignment*.

6. The Collaboration Discipline

Collaboration is another category of workforce behavior that enables a strong customer culture and makes it possible for the company to transform the information generated by the externally oriented traits into value for customers and shareholders. Without strong collaboration within a business, valuable information is squandered and business opportunities are lost. Also, the impact of value delivered to customers is weakened. We have called this discipline *cross-functional collaboration*.

> **Cross-functional collaboration:** *Do colleagues from different work groups share information and work together? Are "silos" tolerated or even encouraged? Are your people working cross-functionally to solve customer problems and deliver better service to customers? Are mechanisms in place to encourage cross-fertilization of ideas, practices, and value creation? Do staff members receive individual recognition for initiating end-to-end solutions for the customer? Is internal competition managed in a way that it creates better customer solutions rather than destructive silos?*
>
> **Link to strategy:** Strength in this discipline is relevant to all business strategies by enhancing innovation and delivery of value to customers and strengthening competitive advantage.
>
> **Driver of business performance:** This measures a business's ability to leverage its resources and advantages across its organization to deliver differentiated value. This impacts customer satisfaction, innovation, new-product success, sales growth, profit growth, and profitability.

Virgin Radio has 19 radio stations in several countries. Each station operates autonomously and has 30 to 50 staff members covering all functions of the business. These businesses are close-knit teams of people who know one another's roles and how they complement one another to produce a number-one-rated radio station. This is done through careful orientation and training and weekly cross-functional review meetings to create improvements in line with weekly customer feedback and ratings results. People in each function know how they affect consumer experience and advertiser customer value. If customer feedback requires a substantial change to a station's program format, as happened with the launch of Virgin Hitz in Dubai, it is able to make a complete change of format in less than 24 hours.[3]

That level of adaptability can only be implemented if there is strong cross-functional collaboration.

7. The Alignment Discipline

The final category of workforce behavior that enables a strong customer culture and makes it possible for the company to create and deliver value for customers and shareholders is its level of internal alignment. Without strong alignment within a business, there are inefficiencies that affect customers and lack of employee engagement that affects business performance and customer satisfaction. We have called this discipline *strategic alignment.*

> **Strategic alignment:** *Is the firm's strategic direction discussed regularly with all employees? How quickly are work group priorities changed when the firm's strategic plans change? Do staff members fully understand and buy in to the company's vision and values and see how it relates to them personally and how they work? Can all people in the business tell you how they are working differently to implement a customer-focused strategy? Are people adapting their behavior in line with their business unit's strategy?*

> **Link to strategy:** Strength in this discipline is relevant to all business strategies by enhancing delivery of value to customers and strengthening competitive advantage.

Driver of business performance: This measures a business's ability to align its people to its vision, mission, values, and strategy. It impacts customer satisfaction, sales growth, profit growth, and profitability.

Jason Kreiser, Allen Medical's general manager, drives strategic alignment at every opportunity. "We have a very simple mission statement that everyone knows," he explains. "Our mission is to be the global leader in innovative patient-positioning accessories for the operating room." All quarterly reviews and town hall meetings with employees begin with the mission statement; all acquisition, licensing, and capital investment decisions are tested against it. The mission to be innovative "drives everything we do," says Kreiser. "If it's not innovative, we don't do it. We're not into me-too products. About 18 months after we introduced this mission and worked to get the organization aligned with it, we went from growing at the market rate of 2 percent or 3 percent per year to growing four or five times the market, year in and year out."[4]

How Can We Measure Our Level of Customer Culture?

As Peter Drucker once said, "What's measured improves." Another related view is "you can't manage what you don't measure." If you want to lose weight, you should first get on the scale to see where you are. The same applies to customer culture. No matter where you stand on the customer culture spectrum, start by benchmarking where you are now.

By definition, a company's competitive strengths and weaknesses exist only in comparison to those of its competitors. From our research we developed a measurement tool to benchmark a company's customer culture relative to a database of more than 100 companies and several hundred business units. This measures a business's customer cultural strengths on the seven disciplines, provides a risk assessment in relation to its strategy, and gives guidelines for action to strengthen the business's customer culture.

The *Market Responsiveness Index (MRI)* tool provides benchmarks as percentiles (similar to reported SAT results used by universities for student assessments) rather than raw scores on each of the seven cultural traits. The MRI measurement tool uses a survey completed by all relevant staff in a company or in one or more business units. The result is a snapshot of where the overall company and each business unit stand compared with a large number of similar businesses. It measures the behavioral heartbeat of the organization and the degree to which it has a customer culture and can respond to its markets and proactively engage market shifts.

The database includes businesses that range from low to high customer culture on these seven traits. The MRI may tell you, for example, that your company's ability to monitor, understand, and respond to its competitors' strengths and weaknesses is in the 82nd percentile (better than four-fifths) of all companies in the benchmark database. This may be considered a relative strength, whereas customer insight at the 60th percentile could be improved significantly by introducing behaviors and processes designed to improve current customers' experiences with the business.

Figure 1.5 shows the customer culture model in which the seven cultural traits are measured. It depicts a hypothetical business with the highest level of customer culture in which all traits are measured at 100 percent. This means it has scored higher than all businesses in the database on all customer culture disciplines.

In practice we have not seen one company with a profile like this, but some that are described in the chapters that follow have come close. Even in companies that have very strong customer cultures there is always room for improvement in one or more disciplines. Also, a company's profile is a moving target as businesses continue to improve and strengthen their customer culture.

What Do High Performers and Low Performers Look Like?

Figure 1.6 shows an example of the Market Responsiveness Index results of two real companies—one for a high-performing business, and the other for a low performer. The more shading reflects a stronger customer culture that drives better business performance. The *low-performing business* (depicted on the right side of Figure 1.6) shows low benchmarked scores on customer disciplines

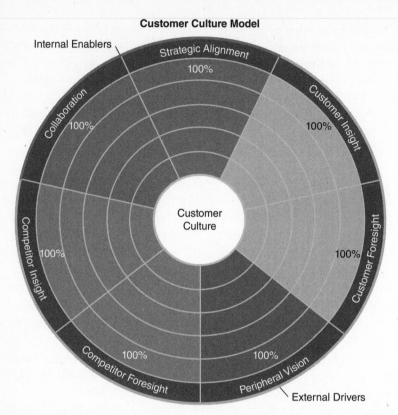

Figure 1.5 Measuring customer culture using the Market Responsiveness Index

being the 34th percentile on customer insight and 4th percentile on customer foresight, which indicates significant risk on those factors. Collaboration is above average at the 60th percentile, but very low scores on the competitor disciplines, peripheral vision, and strategic alignment indicate a business that is predominantly internally focused. It would have many more customer detractors than advocates. It would have no competitive resilience and would experience declining profit margins and profitability if left unchanged.

Since a core part of this business's strategy is to provide enhanced value for existing customers and create new value for new customers, it is at high risk of losing customers and not having the capability of acquiring new ones profitably. Its cultural capability is completely unaligned with its strategy for growing its business through new customers, and its likelihood of achieving its objectives is very low. Low scores on customer insight and foresight suggest it has "weak" behavioral disciplines around understanding the needs of current and prospective customers.

The high-performer business is a manufacturer of medical devices and is the undisputed leader in its market. Prior to benchmarking it reported higher than average performance than its competitors in terms of sales, profit growth, and profitability. It had achieved its revenue and profit goals for 21 straight quarters. In the Figure 1.6 image on the left it shows this firm is relatively strong on all elements of customer culture, which links to a sustainable competitive advantage. This business is highly likely to outperform its competitors for the foreseeable future if it maintains or adds to its customer culture strengths. Its one area of vulnerability may be customer insight that indicates a lesser emphasis on the needs and servicing of its current customers. This may open the way for an existing or new competitor to chip away at its customer base.

Amazon.com and Jeff Bezos, its CEO, are the best examples of a leader and a company that act in the best interests of customers as the

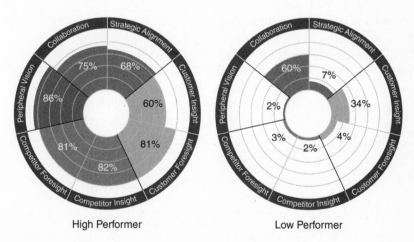

High Performer   Low Performer

Figure 1.6 MRI profiles of two businesses: High performer (left) and low performer (right)

means of creating long-term shareholder value. Since Amazon.com's launch in 1995, Bezos has developed a strong customer culture there based on the belief that in the long term the interests of customers and shareholders converge. Amazon.com excels in all seven disciplines of customer culture. Growth and investment have taken priority over net earnings, but stock prices have shown substantial and progressive growth since its 1997 initial public offering at $16 per share; as of September 25, 2013, its price is $314. This 18-year-old company has built a long-term foundation for a sustainable future based on a customer culture as core to its DNA.

We have presented the evidence supporting the importance of customer culture to business performance and shown the links to business strategy. We understand how to measure it. We know what the seven disciplines are to strengthen it. But, what does it look like? How does it feel?

What Does Customer Culture Look Like?

Some of the world's luckiest business professionals commute to work by ferry across Sydney's spectacular harbor from Manly to Circular Quay. If you are fortunate enough to take this trip one day you might be surprised to learn that your ferry captain, Richard Overton, is one of the world's most customer-focused entrepreneurs. His story of the start of his company, Overseas Shipping Services (OSS), illustrates what customer culture looks like. It is a story of consistent growth and profitability over many years. It highlights the essential elements of what a business with a strong customer culture looks like.

The Birth of Overseas Shipping Services (OSS)

While working for a freight forwarding company, Richard Overton was visiting Sydney's wharves and noticed a long queue of trucks waiting to be unloaded. Being a curious character he asked the foreman some questions and found out that all of these trucks had personal and household items to be shipped to Greece. Further enquiries revealed that Greek families who had immigrated to Australia in the 1950s were now retired and were going back home permanently.

A little more research revealed that at the time there were more Greeks in Melbourne than in Athens; a very large community also lived in Sydney.

He visited the main Greek social club in Sydney and learned that Greeks going back home were nervous and unhappy about trusting their most valuable belongings to professional movers. As Richard talked with different members of the Greek community he started to understand their concerns. When planning to return home they were asked by a moving company to hand over their most treasured possessions. What's more, this company and their people who were unknown to them would pack up all their possessions and put them in large boxes and containers in some remote warehouse before loading them on to a ship. Would they ever see them again? How secure were they? Could these people be trusted? The people moving back to Greece felt powerless. These personal and household possessions were the fruits of their labor in Australia and symbolized their success in their adopted country.

Richard realized that this was a very emotional decision that required more control in the hands of the customer and above all trust in the moving company. He investigated further, looking for identities of people within the Greek community who were asked advice when it came to moving. He found them—Greek travel agents. Most of their business was done at the social club. Greek people sought the agents' advice on real estate, taxes, even marriage counseling; of course, they also sought advice about travel. Richard found that, for the travel agents, giving advice on the best moving company to use was becoming a problem, and they were receiving complaints.

Understanding what the relocating Greek community needed and who they sought advice from to help make a decision formed the basis of the launch of Overseas Shipping Services (OSS). From his previous employment in the shipping industry, Richard knew how the competitors approached this market, how they priced their services, and what they offered in terms of a complete, professionally packed end-to-end delivery and shipping service. Also he was aware of changes taking place in the airline industry that were increasing capacity, dropping prices, and making overseas travel more affordable to the average Australian. There was an observable increase in the number of migrants flying back home and needing a moving service to transport their belongings by sea.

Richard "saw" the opportunity, developed an understanding of the customer, could see the changes in the market environment affecting demand, and knew how the incumbent competitors operated. He created an offer and launched the business all in the space of three months.

OSS launched with one product: UPAK, meaning "you, the customer, can pack your own possessions" using standard sizes of cartons and boxes supplied with a pricing formula per cubic foot that enables customers to estimate the costs of their shipments. Customers could also deliver their packed items to the OSS depot if they wished. This was a complete "do-it-yourself" service: you pack it, you price it, and you deliver it. It gave the customers more control, a greater feeling of security, more convenience, and at a price seen as value for their money. This was launched through the Greek travel agents, paying them a sales commission for converted referrals.

The result was spectacular. Within three months of launch, OSS had taken all of the Greek market for overseas relocations. As time went on OSS set up in Melbourne and captured many of the other ethnic markets for long-term relocations such as the Italian, former Yugoslav, and Turkish communities.

Is Richard of Greek ancestry? You might ask this question because he seemed to understand the Greeks so well. No. He was raised by English parents in Tasmania. Was he trained in marketing, selling, or customer service? No, but he seemed to understand the powerful affect of customers on the success of a business, particularly the benefit of being able to think like a customer and keep an open mind on different solutions to meeting their needs. Through observation and discussion with his business colleagues he developed a customer mindset—a view that's what's best for the customer is best for the business—and used a customer perspective as the frame of reference for all his decisions.

Richard sold his business to long-standing employees who have the same customer culture. OSS is now more than 40 years old.

The success of OSS needed more than a leader who practiced the customer culture disciplines. A customer culture has to be adopted by everyone in the company. It requires all people in the business to have the customer mindset and the skills to deliver the value that customers need and value. Richard set about continually enthusing his staff on the benefits to them of excellent customer service—praise from satisfied customers, getting it right so that there are few complaints or no need to "do it again," working in close communication and collaboration across functions to ensure the customers' needs are met. This was a business in which almost everyone had contact with the customer—drivers, warehouse staff, salespeople, accounts staff, shipping clerks, and so on. They all regarded themselves as in "customer service." The aim was for the end customer and the travel agent to feel that it was easy to do business with OSS and there was a personal connection. Processes were set up that made it easy for customers to complete necessary documentation for shipping and insurance and for employees to track customer jobs and keep customers informed. So what are the essential customer culture traits of Richard and his business?

Developing a Customer Mindset

Richard and his staff developed a mindset where the customer formed the frame of reference for decisions. Questions were raised such as "How does the customer see this? How will this affect the customer? Will this interaction solve the customer's problem? Will this change in process or service increase perceived value for the customer?"

Part of this customer mindset is developing a habit to put yourself in the customers' shoes—feel it from their point of view. Having traveled to other countries, Richard could understand why Greeks were unhappy with the existing movers' services and could empathize with them from a human perspective.

Actioning a Customer Culture in the Business

You will note from this story that Richard and his staff spent a lot of time talking with prospective customers and those who understand them (in this case, the Greek travel agents) to understand their needs and concerns. This is seen as an essential way to do business, not an extra duty on top of the job. This also assists the aim of connecting at a personal level with customers and engendering a sense of trust and care. Richard would have weekly meetings involving all staff members dedicated to the topic of customers—experiences, suggestions for improvements, and problems that require better solutions.

Insights from consumer interactions must be used to work out how to do things differently from the status quo. At OSS, this provided much more value and ability not to be constrained by what currently exists. The OSS story is an example of where you can take away services from customers (such as packing) that results in *increasing* their perceived value. In fact, enabling customers to pack it themselves had a huge positive emotional value. When members of a Greek family were preparing to go back home they had a "going home packing" party. This involved all the extended family and friends coming together to help pack all the household items that were to be shipped.

Questioning must always be done. Everyone in a business can ask this question: "Does our offer deliver perceived value that meets the customer's real needs?" The aim is to explore what the business can do to improve every customer's experience. This was done in OSS in the weekly meetings dedicated to talking about customers.

Developing staff with the same customer mindset and customer interaction skills is vital to providing a consistent service that meets customers' changing needs. This was done in OSS by careful recruitment of people who already understood the importance of customers, irrespective of function, and by ongoing training of staff members to strengthen and refresh their human interaction and collaborative skills.

Empowerment of staff members to solve a customer's problem, take ownership, and fulfill their promises to a customer must be embedded. OSS supported this approach with processes designed to log problems and record follow-up actions, time frames, and outcomes for the customer. This log was reviewed daily.

Incentives and rewards for staff should be designed in relation to delivery of outstanding service and customer value. OSS celebrated this recognition with rewards such as travel and entertainment, including spouses and partners of employees.

Contrast Richard Overton's story with everybody's everyday experiences. We all experience frustrations with our phone or Internet service, our bank, our retail experiences, relocation services, and providers of services to our home or office.

Sometimes we see artificial attempts to improve our experience as customers. The importance of making customer focus a culture in the organization is highlighted by the following story. A few years ago one of the major U.S. retail chains realized that customers like to receive a smile from staff members who are engaged with them. It initiated a "smile" campaign in which for a given month the retailer promised customers that when they paid for their goods if the staff member did not say "have a nice day" with a smile they would get their money back. A few weeks later a customer, after paying for her items, told the salesperson that she wanted her money back because the employee did not smile. The employee, with a smug smile on her face said, "No, it doesn't apply because that campaign was last month." Superficial attempts like this that do not involve a cultural change to create real customer focus at best fall flat and at worst are detrimental to customer relationships.

Bad experiences are common. Look online to see customer complaints in almost every industry. We have conducted hundreds of seminars and workshops where we have asked participants to tell their stories of good and bad customer experiences. Nine out of ten are bad experiences, not only because they are ones we can easily remember but also because there are so many of them that occur in daily life.

These examples and the ones we have heard show that most companies do not have a true customer culture. While a product may be good, service is poor. Or perhaps there is resistance to correcting a product defect. Or the customer may be treated as a statistic, not a person. The breakdown can occur at any point in the process, from buying a product or service right through to handling complaints. These examples reflect businesses that have a weak customer culture.

How to Keep a Customer Culture: The Need for Vigilance

Just because you have a customer culture does not mean you will stay that way. Jim Collins, in his book *How the Mighty Fall*,[5] chronicles how once successful companies turn inward as a result of arrogance and an undisciplined pursuit of more. It can happen to any successful company. Note the following:

Share Price Decline from $304.79 to a Low of $62.37 within
   One Year
Loss of 800,000 Customers in a Quarter
First Net Loss Since 2005

These were some of the headlines surrounding one of the most
customer-focused business success stories in recent years. How could
it be?

Reed Hastings revolutionized the movie business when he began
his U.S.-based mail-order movie rental business Netflix in 1997. After
receiving a $40 late fee for renting the movie *Apollo 13* he decided
there was a better way to offer rentals to customers. In 1999 he hit
upon the unique subscription value proposition that would launch
Netflix to great success. For a low monthly fee, customers could get
DVDs by overnight mail and enjoy them with no late fees. Within
a short period of time this forced Blockbuster, the market leader, to
substantially diminish its business, as it was slow to respond and then
unable to provide a compelling alternative.

Netflix has since transitioned to the online world, offering instant
streaming of movies to TVs and computers. It has been held up as an
example of a customer-focused business that has been flexible and
adaptable to changing customer needs.

Even the best can stumble, however, and in 2011 it alienated a
large number of customers. In July of that year, Netflix shocked its
industry-low-cost-leader video customer base with an abrupt out-
of-nowhere 60 percent price increase without any clear increase in
value.

Then in August, Netflix required its customers to do the grunt
work of separating Netflix into streaming and DVD businesses by
requiring customers to sign up and maintain *two* separate Netflix
accounts—not one. Netflix mercifully recanted that inexplicably bur-
densome customer directive later that year. The result was a loss of
800,000 customers in a single quarter!

Reed Hastings, in a letter to shareholders, wrote: "We com-
pounded the problem with our lack of explanation about the rising
cost of the expansion of streaming content. . . . [So] many perceived
us as greedy. . . . There is a difference between moving quickly—

which Netflix has done very well for years—and moving too fast, which is what we did in this case."[6]

Even companies with strong customer culture disciplines can be tripped up by a lapse. Eternal vigilance and constant monitoring and listening to customers are the price companies must pay to stay ahead. Customer culture is the only constant in a business while everything else is changing. It is the only sustainable advantage that you can have and keep. It is *the* imperative in today's unpredictable, changing, and often chaotic business environment.

What Results Can the *Business* Expect from Enhanced Customer Culture?

It was 10 p.m. and Susan had just celebrated her husband's birthday with friends at a local restaurant in Branford, a small town in Connecticut in the United States. She had been excited all day thinking about the surprise she was going to spring on her husband. As the group strolled back to their car Susan suggested they cross the road. There was something she wanted to see in the window of the store on the other side. Susan was imagining the window display: balloons, ribbons, and a shiny red 10-speed bike in the window with the words "Happy Birthday Mike! From your number one cycling fan. Love, Susan." Susan had been in the bike store earlier that week; it was one of those stores customers raved about. Zanes Cycles was so customer focused it was legendary. Chris Zane, the CEO, had grown the business every year for the past 20 years based on his passion for customers. It was now the number one dealer for Trek and Specialized bikes, the two largest bike manufacturers in the world. Tom, the store manager, had helped her select the right bike based on a description of Susan's husband's riding interests and color preferences and had promised to display the bike in the window later that week on the night of her husband's birthday.

As the group approached the window, Susan immediately sensed something was wrong. Instead of the bike display there was a large poster of the latest cycling hero. The special bike was nowhere to be seen. Embarrassed, Susan quickly diverted the attention of the group and went home a very unhappy customer.

The next day she got straight on the phone to Tom, the store manager. Clearly upset, she complained about how disappointing and embarrassing it was for her. Tom and Chris quickly convened and brainstormed some ideas for how they could make things up to Susan for their mistake. Eventually Tom decided it would be best if they forgave the 50 percent still owing on the bike, provide a dinner certificate for her and her husband to go out and celebrate, and provide some lunch for the coworkers and friends who were trying to work out what went wrong that night. The result? Later that day Chris Zane received a call from Tom, "How did it go?" asked Chris, "Dude, she kissed me!!"

What is even more impressive about this story is the young employee who had been responsible for putting the bike in the window was so concerned that he mailed a check to Chris Zane the next day for $400. This was the money that Zane's had invested in recovering the situation. Chris Zane had created a culture at Zane's where everyone was invested in customer satisfaction. The check was never cashed but was framed and still sits in Chris's office to this day as a reminder of its commitment to customer satisfaction.[7]

Ultimately, creating a customer culture is about one thing: improving business performance. Customer culture is a means to an end; it allows a company to maximize its operating performance in an ever-changing business environment and reduce the risk that it will be caught unawares by customers, competitors, or market shifts.

A key tool used by many successful businesses that have strong customer cultures is placing a financial value on customers and viewing them as assets just like plant and machinery. This does two things. Firstly it recognizes in financial terms just how valuable customers are and secondly it creates a focal point for employees to rally around customer-focused initiatives. In the story from Zane's Cycles, Chris Zane determined early on that customers were worth $12,500 over their lifetime of purchases. He uses the metric, lifetime value of customers, as a long-term customer-centered view of his business. What is the value, in revenue and profit terms, of an average customer over the potential life of the business relationship? This is not a static number but an active one that can be used to value his business and identify opportunities to grow that number. By using this knowledge, everyone in the business is focused on increasing that lifetime value by providing high-quality service. Each person is empowered to do what is necessary to retain customers.

Its real power is in galvanizing everyone in the company around the importance and value of customer relationships. It proves the tangible logic for why every interaction matters and connects everyone with the ultimate customer. It embeds a mindset that focuses on the ongoing relationship with each customer over time and helps staff members make decisions at the point of interaction with customers to ensure that customers are completely satisfied. This sometimes means forgoing short-term revenue for long-term satisfaction—for example, by providing replacement parts for a bike service free of charge.

When we interviewed Chris, we asked what he does to really get to know his customers. Chris said that he takes the time to watch how customers spend time in his store, where do they go, what they look at, and what questions they ask his staff. Spending time observing customers allows him to make better decisions about where to place his displays in store and what information to provide on displays to help customers self-select the right product.

What Results Can *You* Expect from Enhanced Customer Culture?

It was 9 p.m. and Gary was packing up after a long day in the office. As an accountant for a large utility company he was used to working long hours at the end of the month. As he walked down the corridor toward the exit he noticed John, one of his internal customers in asset management, still working away. John seemed to live at the office. In fact, Gary could not recall the last time he went past John's empty desk. Gary decided to drop by to see what John was working on. John explained that he had to complete a weekly reconciliation of the assets he was responsible for as a new requirement of the government regulator. The task took him about 15 hours to complete each week on top of his normal workload.

Gary asked John to stop by for coffee the following day to see if it was something he and his team could help speed up. After reviewing the material and John's process for developing the spreadsheet, Gary knew immediately he could create an automated process that would cut the task down to an hour each week. Judging from John's reaction you would have thought he had just won the lottery![8]

Being focused on your customer is about being proactive, noticing things that others do not, being curious about why things are the way they are, and taking action to improve how work gets done inside the company as well as with external customers.

It's a simple example, but when you think of the volume of work and interactions that take place daily in the world's large corporations, if this type of initiative were taken more often the impact on productivity would be enormous.

Creating a customer culture requires leadership at all levels throughout the organization and effort on the part of all employees. So what is the payoff?

Creating this type of culture in a business will have a large lasting effect—a deep impact. Not only will it have a deep impact on business performance but it will also positively affect employee engagement through customer interactions and feedback. Every employee has a customer; some may have external customers, others have internal customers, and many have both. Part of gaining enjoyment and satisfaction from work involves a feeling of purpose. Providing great customer experiences and seeing customers benefiting from the company's products and services goes a long way toward providing this sense of purpose. It validates the value of our contribution. Positive feedback from customers lifts motivation and energy to excel personally. New skills, purpose, and satisfaction results from appreciative customers.

The Seven Customer Culture Disciplines and a Road Map to Get There

An organization does not develop a customer culture in a linear progression. There are many twists and turns along the way determined by strategy, unforeseen external events, disruptive internal reorganizations, and turnover of senior management. Several things may need to be focused on at the same time. At other times it may only be one thing. However, it can be broken down into focus on building and strengthening the seven key disciplines.

A four-phase road map lays out the pathway our research shows that companies use to successfully make the journey to a strong customer culture. These are shown in Figure 1.7.

The first phase requires engagement of senior leaders and planning the way forward, including an assessment of the current level of customer culture and clarity of vision, values, and strategy. Phase two focuses on the implementation of the culture change or enhancement initiative and needs to ignite all leaders with a customer mindset and toolset to inspire change across the entire organization. Phase three involves embedding customer culture behaviors with supporting processes formalized to help everyone in the business to become customer-centric. This sometimes lengthy phase is followed by initiatives to fortify and maintain a strong customer culture.

The next seven chapters each explore one of these disciplines starting with the customer, then the competitive disciplines, followed by peripheral vision, collaboration, and finally alignment.

Once we have examined these disciplines we will describe in Chapter 9 the four-phase process and specific steps needed for making it happen. This is followed by a chapter exploring why a variety of business leaders decided to build businesses with a strong customer culture and what leadership characteristics are important to achieve it. We examine their real motivations and why their journey was worth the effort. The final chapter suggests the first steps you can take to get started on the journey.

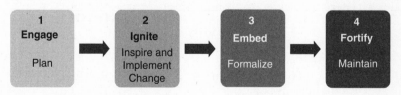

Figure 1.7 Four-phase road map

CHAPTER SUMMARY

Does customer culture matter?
- Yes, building a lasting culture pays more. Countless studies tell us businesses with high levels of customer culture sustain a growth path and are much more profitable.
- It's more satisfying. A pat on the back from a customer makes all the hard work worthwhile.

Why do so many companies espouse it and not deliver?
- It is obvious and expected that companies talk about customers being important, but many do not "get" that customer focus is a culture.
- Customer culture is somewhat abstract, not readily measurable, and not easily understood by business leaders.

What's the evidence?
- Our quantitative study (detailed in Appendix 1) shows:
  - A high correlation between customer culture and business results.
  - Firms with a strong customer culture show significantly higher sales growth and profit growth than those with a weak customer culture.
- Many corporate case studies show that businesses that have adopted a strong customer culture produce superior business results.

What are the customer culture disciplines?
- There are seven disciplines of customer culture:
  - Customer insight
  - Customer foresight
  - Competitor insight
  - Competitor foresight
  - Peripheral vision

- Cross-functional collaboration
- Strategic alignment

How can we measure it?
- Customer culture behaviors can be rated and benchmarked at a work group level and overall for a business unit, function, and company.
- Individual customer culture can be assessed using key performance measures and assessment of behaviors.
- Customers tell us when we have it. Track customer feedback.

How does a customer culture business and team think?
- It has a shared belief that "what's best for the customer is best for the business."
- The customer is at the heart of all decisions. It is enacted by asking, "How will this decision affect the customer? How will it benefit the customer?"

What are the benefits?
- To the organization
  - Higher growth and profitability
  - Higher engagement and retention of staff
  - Increased productivity through focus on delivery of value to customers
- To individuals
  - New skills, purpose, and satisfaction result from a common collaborative focus on value for customers and positive feedback from customers.
  - Higher levels of engagement and enjoyment at work.
  - A sense of pride and camaraderie from membership in a high-performance team with shared vision and satisfaction from success.

(Continued)

What are the phases in the journey?
- The four-phase journey starts with engaging senior leadership, followed by implementing a change initiative that leads to embedding desired customer culture behaviors and processes across the organization. The final phase is designed to reinforce and maintain a strong level of customer culture.
- Each phase has several steps, which are described in Chapter 9.

Chapter 2

Customers' Rules

There is never a good sale for Neiman Marcus unless it's a good buy for the customer.
—Herbert Marcus, advice to his son Stanley Marcus, circa 1926

In 2006 AOL suffered a completely avoidable and costly self-inflicted injury to its reputation. The story of how and why it happened, in full view of the public, serves as a cautionary tale for all business leaders. But the story also highlights the crucial importance of a strategic asset that CEOs must not fail to protect and cultivate—a culture that understands that profitability and competitive advantage depend on having a customer-centered organization.

The AOL misadventure started when a customer, Vincent Ferrari, an active blogger, decided to cancel his AOL account. Having heard rumors about the high-pressure tactics of the company's customer service department, Ferrari decided to record his phone call with AOL. A customer service rep spent five minutes trying to convince Ferrari that it would be a terrible idea to cancel his account. By ignoring Ferrari's many demands to cancel the subscription the rep crossed into dangerous legal territory.

So Ferrari posted the conversation on his blog, and within hours his Internet server crashed as it tried to deal with 300,000 requests for downloads of the audio file. Within four days, copies of the damaging phone call were all over the Internet. The *New York Post* and the *New York Times* covered the story, and six days after he posted the recording Ferrari was interviewed on CNBC, NBC, and the *Today* show.

AOL's customer service failure plagued the company. The least significant cost was the $3 million compensation to customers in 48 states for aggressively resisting closure of their accounts. Much worse, tens of millions of people were exposed to the negative stories about AOL. AOL's subscriber base dropped 32 percent in the United States and 61 percent in Europe between 2004 and 2006. From the evidence, it seems that, rather than focus resources to create superior value for its subscribers, AOL chose to try to hold those subscribers hostage.[1]

Is the AOL story just about poor customer service? No. Customer service in this story was merely a symptom of a pervasive problem within AOL's organizational culture. A company's culture influences every decision it makes. It is the constant expression of what the company is really like, how it operates, what behaviors it rewards, what it focuses on, and how it treats customers.

The AOL case also illustrated how by 2006 power had shifted in the marketplace from sellers to buyers, making it easier for them to fight back against companies that don't deliver the appropriate value. Now that an angry blogger can expose a company's failures overnight, it is no longer feasible to hide adverse customer experiences. Instead, company culture has to be focused on addressing customer problems forthrightly and creating a responsive culture that provides ongoing competitive advantage.

Today it's the customers' rules that determine how a business can operate profitably.

The Business Case

Imagine you are facing this situation:

- A large and increasing number of customer complaints
- Customers leaving and going to competitors
- Declining customer satisfaction trend

- More customers being hostile when communicating with the company
- Sales reps reporting that customers have become "unreasonable"
- Customers saying your products or services are too expensive

Is this happening to your business?

What's Your Response?

Is your reaction to tell customers you really "love" them, give customers more incentives to buy, and promise it won't happen again (wishful thinking)?
Or
Is it to take action to deeply understand *why* customers are complaining, are hostile to your people, and are leaving your business? *Then to act to fix the problems?*

What's the Difference?

A deep customer understanding that creates customer insight results in higher customer retention and more advocates leading to revenue growth and increased profitability.

Link to Business Performance

As a driver of business performance it measures a business's ability to improve customer satisfaction and retention and impacts customer satisfaction, new product success, and sales revenue growth. It drives shorter-term competitive advantage.

Link to Strategy

Strength in this discipline is particularly relevant to a strategy designed to focus on existing customers in order to retain them, create customer advocates, and increase the average revenue per customer.

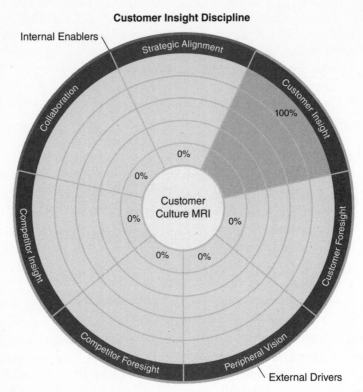

Figure 2.1 Customer insight discipline

Figure 2.1 highlights customer insight as the focus of this chapter. The goal is for companies to improve their absolute and relative strength in this discipline. The score of 100 percent simply means that a company is above all others in our Market Responsiveness Index (MRI) global database in terms of customer insight behaviors.

Customers' Rules

Business success in competitive industries is dependent on having satisfied customers and on the ability to keep them. To do this we need to understand the customers' rules that determine whether we will retain them. These include:

Rule 1: Understand my current needs (listening, sharing, cocreating).
Rule 2: Show me you are authentic in solving my problems.
Rule 3: Give me something of value.
Rule 4: Keep me engaged with new things I value.
Rule 5: Help me solve my problems.
Rule 6: Show me what I will need in the future.

This chapter examines the first customer discipline and what is required to gain *customer insight*. It describes the behavioral habits that must be embedded in an organization's culture to enable it to satisfy the customers' rules. We define what customer insight is, who has it, and how you can get it.

What Is Customer Insight?

Customer insight comes from a deep understanding of customers' needs and drivers of customer behavior at a level well beyond what customers themselves can explain. These needs are understood from what customers tell us, but more deeply from what we observe customers doing and the frustrations they have in using particular products, services, and companies.

In a workshop, a team member from Virgin discussed how Richard Branson tries to identify industries in which to enter a new Virgin service. Branson simply starts by asking the brainstorming question: "What are 10 things that nobody would say about this industry?" He and his team then prioritize those ideas that would create value for customers and profits for Virgin. The next step is decide if a Virgin service can be designed to profitably deliver some of these unspoken values in that industry. It is a great example of outside thinking, starting with the customer's pain points or needs and working backward.

In another workshop we conducted, a member of the Mercedes-Benz team explained to us that people at Mercedes-Benz, rather than asking customers, "What do you think of Mercedes-Benz?" (a standard question that gets the standard answers about high quality, luxury, and so on), they reverse the question, "What do you think Mercedes-Benz thinks of you?"

This unique twist on a common question results in much deeper insights. Many customers responded initially by saying things such as, "You think we are made of money ... that we have all the time in the world."A response such as this leads the company to find ways of making its car servicing much more convenient for customers and to build in servicing costs to the initial purchase or lease arrangement.

In both cases these are questions designed to get customer insight that goes beyond what customers will normally tell us.

Lex Dwyer, a Melbourne, Australia–based fitness instructor, repositioned his services as a result of observing customers for hours at a time. At first he was providing "light relief" at corporate planning workshops by giving executives tips on how to look after their health. He then added to this physical challenges for managers working in teams, to achieve a specific goal such as building a bicycle without assembly instructions. Each team would have an incorrect collection of parts that had to be traded with other teams to complete the task. These "games" added value to the planning sessions by incorporating leadership, collaboration, and teamwork principles. However, as Lex attended his clients' working sessions he was able to design physical challenges as games that reinforced their business goals. He did this by listening to their discussions, observing their frustrations and disagreements, and understanding their business challenges. This insight enabled him to operate with appropriate exercises as a real-time response to their observed needs and tie their thinking together in a more holistic approach. Lex found he had a particular talent for seeing the "big" picture and tying together his games with the client's strategy. As a result he repositioned himself as a provider of leadership services and now works with corporate clients and with business schools' executive education programs. The net result: delighted clients and consumers, higher revenue, and making a difference to people's lives. Lex's personal vision of "making a difference" is a reality.

The customer insight discipline is exemplified by Lex Dwyer's approach. To obtain deep customer insight, you have to ask questions and observe customers in many different ways with disciplined processes. Insight comes from integrating different pieces of information and gaining a multifaceted knowledge of your customers. It is gained from knowledge of how the customers think and act before, during, and after their purchase. It requires knowledge of the whole customer experience.

Why Is Customer Insight a Cultural Discipline?

No one person or department has the monopoly on customer insight. Customers interact with a business every day in different ways across the customer experience spectrum. They even come into contact with employees of a business in a wide range of social settings. Every one of those interactions presents an opportunity for your staff members to demonstrate their understanding of the customers' environments and gain new insight about the customers' needs. By harnessing the inputs of everyone in the organization you can start to complete the jigsaw puzzle of what the customer looks like and how she or he feels and behaves. These inputs provide a down-to-earth view of the customer's reality. When accompanied by formal research that yields its own insights we are seeing the development of a customer insight discipline—a set of behaviors designed to gain and retain customer insight that is essential to respond to customers' rules.

As deep knowledge of customer segments is gained and business strategies are founded on customer insights, it becomes clear what every individual in the business must do to deliver value for customers. A cultural discipline of *customer insight* is one in which all staff share their experiences and knowledge of customers and use that shared knowledge to deliver more value. A shared belief of "what's best for the customer is best for the business" becomes a reality when based on deep customer insight. All staff behavior is driven by this culture, as are the expectations placed on everyone to know his or her customers and treat them in a certain way. Once this mindset and behavior pattern is embedded at the heart of the business, a firm's customer culture has a firm foundation.

Who Has It?

Can you imagine knowing everything about another human being? Her favorite places to hang out, where she goes on holidays, what colors she prefers, what music and movies she likes, who her friends are, where she lives, even what she ate for breakfast this morning?

Welcome to Facebook.com. With more than 1 billion users, nothing comes close to the repository of real-time information on customers and potential customers. The promise of knowing everything you ever would want to know and more about your customers is becoming a reality. Facebook users volunteer information on a scale unseen in human history.

The challenge is what to do with this information. It is a treasure trove of insights into customers' behavior, their likes and dislikes, who is influential, who is an advocate, and who is a detractor.

While marketing professionals have been quick to embrace social media as a way to engage and communicate with customers, it is still early days in terms of extracting the most value from what is available.

Costco

Customers walk in to a huge warehouse to buy six months' worth of toilet paper and walk out with the latest flat-screen TV and a case of champagne. Where else would this type of consumer behavior be possible but at Costco, the most successful warehouse club and retailer in the United States?

Costco has an interesting mix of customers. It attracts more affluent customers in as great a volume as lower-income ones. It is very selective about the products it chooses and is always varying the merchandise on offer. Customers shop there regularly and come back for that intangible feeling that is created by the store's atmosphere. It is always busy; goods are stacked in large warehouse-style pallets; and there is a "racetrack"-style circuit that shoppers are guided through, which means they get to see virtually everything on offer each visit. Even the jumbo-size shopping carts create a mindset and expectation on the part of consumers.

Why Is Costco Successful?

One of the key reasons for Costco's success is its ability to allay all the fears consumers have when making purchase decisions; for example:

1. Will I get the right product for my needs?
2. Will I get the best price available?
3. Will the product be high quality?

Costco takes the risk out of purchasing by having one of the most generous product return policies on the planet. During a store site visit with a Costco executive we saw a woman return a vacuum cleaner that was at least five years old and considerably used. She was refunded—no questions asked. Does this make good business sense? If you look at this one incident in isolation, Costco has lost money on this transaction; if every customer behaved this way, the company would go out of business. Costco, however, has defined a simple policy to be applied across the board. For employees this takes the angst out of having to challenge specific customers and results in a trust-first relationship with customers. Yes, some customers will abuse store policies, but the lesson here is not to treat every customer as though he is trying to take advantage of you. This policy reinforces the company's customer-centric approach and makes it easy for employees to deal with potentially difficult customer situations.

A Powerful Customer Culture

In an April 2012 CNBC documentary on the "Costco Craze," Jim Sinegal, Costco's cofounder and former CEO, described the secret of the company's success as its culture. He said, "Culture is not the most important thing, it's the only thing."

Jim has created a culture where there are no divisions between senior leadership and their staff. *Everyone is on the same page when it comes to understanding Costco's customers* and what makes the company's model work. All employees know their role in creating the right environment for customers to have the "Costco experience." They even refer to their customers as club members. Employees are also paid fair wages (higher than competitors) and receive good health insurance. These employee benefits allow Costco to attract and retain higher-quality staff members that have the capability to deliver a better customer experience. The company treats its customers with respect, limiting markups on the bulk goods the stores sell to the point that it has frustrated investors who felt higher prices could be charged.

As CEO, Sinegal was constantly on the move, visiting Costco's 580 stores across nine countries every year, getting direct feedback from customers and his employees as to what's working and what is not. This is how customer insight is gained and also how it is shared across all people in the business. Remember, this is a $93 billion business, the fifth-largest American retail chain.[2]

How Do You Develop Customer Insight?

Customer insight is the extent to which employees monitor, understand, and act on current customer needs and satisfaction.

Customer insight, at its pinnacle, is an understanding of customers so as to be able to create superior value for them continuously. It is a continuing and painstaking effort to "live" with customers and to translate understanding into satisfaction.

Clif Bar is an example of "living" it. During the early 2000s, Clif Bar saw a new market emerging. Triathlons were becoming increasingly popular with white-collar workers looking for an outlet from their busy and often-stressful office jobs. Clif Bar had been successful targeting outdoor enthusiasts, in particular hikers and runners, with its line of energy bars. The triathlon market, however, was one it was yet to crack. To really gain an understanding of what triathlon was all about, several Clif Bar executives decided to get involved in the sport. One thing that became immediately apparent was that triathlon swims were quite chaotic. Imagine two thousand amped-up and anxious athletes starting a swim all at once.

The company used this insight into what the sport was like to make a clever video making fun of the unique experience. The humorous video became a YouTube sensation; it really got to the heart of what triathletes would experience in a chaotic swim start.

This unique customer insight and communication vehicle told potential Clif Bar customers: "We understand you, we know what it's like to be a triathlete, and we are one of you." The result? An instant connection between triathletes and the Clif Bar brand that has resulted in significant sales growth for the company.[3]

Customer insight can be represented in innumerable employee behaviors. A few examples: visiting customers, communicating with customers, seeking customer feedback, measuring customer satisfaction, and acting on customer issues and feedback.

As Alex Bard, a senior vice president of salesforce.com, described in a recent interview with us: "You need to continually get out of the building. We do a monthly series of company customer tours where we deeply engage with our customers; we create an environment where they can collaborate with one another. We find that where our customers are talking to their customers, that's the most powerful kind of environment that you can be in, and you just step back and you watch magical things happen. We do dinners around those events, where we share ideas and talk about what we're seeing in the world, what are the challenges that they're having, and how we help them address those challenges."

It is important to note that customer insight is not customer following. Input from customers can be superficial or shortsighted. Henry Ford used to joke that if he had listened to his customers he would have built a faster horse. Instead, Ford understood the customer's need for a faster, more reliable form of personal transportation (that is, a car). The key is not just to listen to and follow the customer but to gain a deep-seated understanding of the customer's needs, behaviors, and (dis)satisfaction with current offerings and the current relationships.

Weakness in this area is of major concern, as it is a leading indicator for customer satisfaction, customer retention, new-product success, and sales growth. Companies weak in this area can survive if their customer base regularly turns over; there would be limited need to pay attention to existing customers, as they would be replaced by new customers.

The best starting point for gaining customer insight is interacting with customers—listening to and talking with them. For the non-customer-facing functions this should start with top management—the CEO and all C-level officers. A consistent ongoing program of customer interaction should engage employees in all functions. They should report to customer discussion forums on their experience and the actions they have taken personally to increase the value they are delivering to customers and to the business. One of the best documented examples of this is by Tony Hsieh in his book *Delivering Happiness*, which chronicles his experience in developing a customer service philosophy and culture inside Zappos.[4]

A major customer insight understood by Zappos through talking with customers was the customer perceived risk and hassle around returning shoes that did not fit or look right when purchased online. Zappos's response to this was to reduce the time, risk, and cost to the customer of a return. It did so by providing a prepaid return label that could be placed on the back of the box with the shoes in it; the customer could then call the courier to come and get it. This was consistent with Zappos's customer service philosophy and also its guarantee of customer satisfaction. The process became even easier than purchasing at a store, where the customer would have to make a store visit to return shoes. Zappos also invested in high-quality photography and web content to most accurately describe products and help customers make the best decision upfront.

Another example of "living" with the customer is found at Credit Suisse. Credit Suisse, based in Switzerland, follows a five-step process for immersing executives and senior managers in a customer perspective:

1. Be a customer: the executive goes into a branch, waits in line, and conducts business with a teller.
2. Observe customers: look at what the customer looks at and see how he or she behaves when doing business with the company.
3. Interact with customers: ask questions of customers, and listen to their responses.
4. Experience other channels used by customers such as the website, call center, and the company's publications. Apply for credit, get an answer from a sales rep, and decipher brochures.
5. Report on the experience at a workshop: discuss insights and compare experiences and lessons learned.

Adobe recognized it wasn't always easy to do business with and was not consistently delivering the level of service customers expected. Adobe's Customer Immersion Program provides Adobe's senior leaders with the opportunity to experience firsthand what their customers experience when they engage with Adobe. Like Credit Suisse, executives and senior managers at Adobe have the opportunity to experience what a customer would experience by playing the role of a customer. Also they experience the interaction with customers when they call in with a problem or a need.

Adobe's Customer Listening Post facility brings customer experiences to life—live video and data feeds showing what's happening in real time.

In your business you can leverage readily available technology such as camera phones, digital video cameras, and online diaries to document the customer immersion process. These technologies enable any employee to play back interactions and experiences they have with customers.[5]

What Behaviors Draw Out Customer Insight?

When individuals and teams set their priorities based on a deep understanding of their customers' needs they adopt a customer-centric culture. By discussing customers at most meetings, measuring customer satisfaction regularly, getting to the bottom of customer complaints, acting quickly to address customer feedback, and communicating to customers the actions taken as a result of their feedback, individuals and teams will gain customer insight. By sharing this knowledge across the business, all functions gain an insight into what they need to do to increase customer value.

These are examples of customer insight disciplines:

- Setting priorities based on a deep understanding of customers' needs
- Visiting and interacting with customers
- Seeking customer feedback
- Acting on customer issues and feedback
- Dealing with customer complaints

- Communicating with customers the actions taken to address their feedback
- Measuring customer satisfaction regularly
- Sharing knowledge with team members
- Discussing customers at most meetings

What Are Some of the Best Practices?

Several companies practice customer insight behaviors as a discipline, which makes them very successful in their industries. The following examples illustrate some of the best practices.

Mindset Shift at American Express

For decades, as with many other call centers, American Express provided tight scripts to its call center agents. The prevailing mindset was that customer contact was a cost to the business to be reduced or even eliminated, if possible. The goal was be friendly but get the customer off the call as quickly as possible. Scripts were used as a way to standardize service and resolve customer queries fast. That's great for driving down call length, but what about the customer's experience?

Things started to change in 2006 after Jim Bush, whose early training was as an accounting major, took on the role of executive vice president of world service.

"I was asked to move into this job by Ken Chenault, our chairman," he said. "At the time I was thinking the way most people think—that these are back-office operations. But as I thought about the millions of interactions we have with customers, I said, 'If we can unleash the power of that customer-facing organization, think of the value we can create.' "[6]

Jim believed that by breaking down those scripts to empower his customer care professionals to have meaningful human conversations with customers, American Express would get a big payoff.

This change required a shift in thinking from a transactional focus to a relationship focus. Customer care professionals needed to develop the skills to connect personally with customers, really listen to what they are saying, and to use their own judgment to get them a solution. An example is when a customer has lost a wallet with credit cards. Not only is the Amex card canceled and a new one delivered quickly, but customer service people will connect the cardholder to other card providers to cancel those. Also cash will be arranged, if the cardholder needs that urgently.

A key customer-facing metric was implemented, known as the "net promoter score." This score measures the number of customers who would recommend your company, known as "promoters," versus the number who would not, known as "detractors." It was used to track the performance of customer care professionals and provide an overall score that could be evaluated strategically.

Over the past five years American Express has been able to drive up the number of loyal customers while also reducing costs.

"For a promoter who is positive on American Express," says Jim Bush, "we see a 10% to 15% increase in spending and four to five times increased retention, both of which drive shareholder value. In fact our operating expenses associated with service have gone down because we're more streamlined, and we limit friction points and errors."[7]

What are the lessons for your business? Think about how you view customer service in your company. Is it viewed as a cost to be minimized or as an investment in customer loyalty that will pay back over time?

Customer-centric organizations take a balanced approach to customer service, which ensures that customers are treated with respect and in a way that values them. Product or service failures are dealt with in a way that builds trust with customers. When something goes wrong for your customers, how does your company respond?

Amazon.com: Reminding Customers of Their Best Interests

Amazon.com was the first online seller of books to show negative customer book reviews as well as positive ones. While criticized by other book retailers because of its potential negative impact on the sales of some books, it was done in the best interests of customers to enable them to make more informed decisions. Also if a customer orders a book from Amazon.com that has been ordered previously, the customer is reminded that he has already purchased that book. These practices illustrate that Amazon.com has the best interests of the customer at heart. The online retailer is thinking from the customer's point of view: What are they frustrated by? What are they trying to achieve? By placing yourself in the customers' shoes and experiencing what they experience, a new perspective is developed that allows for new ideas to develop.

Amazon.com's CEO sums it up best in the following quote: "Let's be simpleminded. We know this is a feature that's good for customers. Let's do it."[8]

What are you doing at your company to demonstrate you have your customer's best interests at heart?

Barclaycard US: Bringing the Customers' Voice to the Leadership

Barclaycard US, the United States–based credit card division of the United Kingdom–based Barclays Group, begins each day by listening to its customers. The company recognizes the importance of ensuring the customer's voice is heard regularly by everyone in the organization. As a result the leadership introduced an initiative to deliver a random service call to the company's entire senior team each morning. A recording of a call is sent to senior leaders to keep them connecting with what is actually happening at the front lines of the organization. It helps them maintain empathy for customers by hearing about their experiences, both good and bad, on an ongoing basis.

By exposing people who don't have direct customer-facing jobs to this feedback, this practice has been one of the catalysts for customer-centric culture change across the organization.

The most challenging customer calls are played to the executive committee during a monthly forum; the aim is to institute changes in rules to make things easier for customers. This forum has demonstrated a willingness to place the customer ahead of short-term profit. It sends a clear message to the rest of the organization that customers are really important and aligns all employees with this way of thinking and behaving.

Barclaycard US formed a "Customer Engagement Council," where 75 leaders from all levels and functional areas look at a number of key customer programs—service, incentives, agent support, hiring and training, and customer tools—in order to make rapid improvements. In the first quarter after the initiative was begun, the company implemented 25 key initiatives and plans to execute another 60 by year's end.

These programs have paid off for Barclaycard US, and the company has seen customer complaints drop by 50 percent and has reduced customer attrition by 28 percent. The company estimates that these improvements result in annual benefits up to $10 million.[9]

TELUS Telecommunications: Connecting Leadership with Customer Insights

When the authors met with Carol Borghesi in 2012 at a conference in Miami she described TELUS as "the least bad of the not very good [referring to the whole telecommunications sector]." The telecommunications industry in general is not known for its high levels of customer satisfaction, but this is changing. Carol is the senior vice president of the Customers First Culture at TELUS, one of the largest telecommunications companies in Canada.

As part of the organization's quest to improve customer understanding and loyalty Carol embarked on a program to bring TELUS's top 356 leaders to the front line to have them hear firsthand what challenges were being faced by customers. This program resulted in the identification of 96 burning customer issues that were then categorized into short and longer term and assigned to leaders across different functions. By experiencing firsthand the frustrations customers were having, the leaders bought into solving the problems and took ownership of pushing through changes.

These types of executive customer immersion programs are powerful programs for elevating customer insights and pain points to the leaders who can make things happen quickly in large organizations.

CHAPTER SUMMARY

Are customers' rules important?
Yes; companies that hold customers hostage, provide poor service, do not keep customers engaged with perceived value, and show a lack of care in delivering to customers' needs will lose customers when they are able to switch to alternatives.

What is customer insight?
Customer insight is the extent to which employees monitor, understand, and act on current customer needs and satisfaction. Customer insight, at its pinnacle, is an understanding of customers so as to be able to create superior value for them continuously.

Why is customer insight a cultural discipline?
No one person or department has the monopoly on customer insight. Customers interact with people in the business every day in different ways across the customer experience spectrum. A cultural discipline of *customer insight* is one in which all staff members share their experiences and knowledge of customers and use that shared knowledge to deliver more value.

What behaviors lead to customer insight?
By discussing customers at most meetings, measuring customer satisfaction regularly, getting to the bottom of customer complaints, acting quickly to address customer feedback, and communicating to customers the actions taken resulting from their feedback, individuals and teams will gain customer insight.

Leader's Guide to Customer Insight

Customer Insight discipline: *Does the company understand its current customers' needs? Does it know how satisfied or dissatisfied they are with its products or services? Does it act on this knowledge? Does it communicate its actions to customers resulting from their feedback?*

Rate where *you and your team* stand on customer insight by checking the relevant box in answering each question.

Rating descriptors: 0 = never; 1 = almost never; 2 = rarely; 3 = occasionally; 4 = sometimes; 5 = regularly; 6 = frequently; 7 = often; 8 = very often; 9 = constantly; 10 = all the time.

- [ ] 1. To what extent do you and your team understand the needs of current customers?
- [ ] 2. To what extent do managers and staff that are non-customer-facing interact with customers?
- [ ] 3. To what extent do you obtain systematic measures of customer satisfaction?
- [ ] 4. To what extent do you act on customer problems or complaints?
- [ ] 5. To what extent do you communicate to customers the actions you have taken as a result of their feedback?
- [ ] 6. To what extent do you elicit customer insights from all members of your team?
- [ ] 7. To what extent do you share customer insights with all members of your team?
- [ ] 8. To what extent do you and your team share insights across other functions and teams outside your group?
- [ ] 9. To what extent do you publicly recognize individuals who have acted on deep customer insights?
- [ ] 10. To what extent do you reward individuals who have acted on deep customer insights?

Chapter 3

Customer-Inspired Innovation

Some people say, "Give the customers what they want." But that's not my approach. Our job is to figure out what they're going to want before they do.

— Steve Jobs, cofounder of Apple

The customer foresight discipline is really about customer-inspired innovation. The quote from Steve Jobs gets to the essence of this competency—imagining solutions to problems even customers do not know they are experiencing.

This is a challenging discipline to master because it requires blending a deep understanding of the customer's environment with knowledge of the organization's technical competencies.

Many companies try to innovate by questioning their customers. This often falls short when it comes to real breakthrough innovation. Customers cannot envision the future—you need to show it to them. A recent example comes from Apple. When Apple released its first tablet computer, the iPad, it was described by one well-known blogger as "an utter disappointment and abysmal failure."[1] In fact *BloombergBusinessweek* magazine stated that "consumers seem genuinely baffled by why they might need it."[2] Well, we now know that the iPad has become perhaps the most successful product launch in history.

What Steve Jobs had was an ability to uncover needs that customers themselves could not visualize. For businesses to thrive in the future, this needs to become an organizational capability.

The story of the development of the iPod is one of great customer foresight and cross-functional collaboration. While Steve Jobs is widely known, the head of product engineering responsible for bringing the first iPod to market, Jon Rubinstein, is less so.

In an interview with Ken Aaron of *Cornell Engineering* magazine[3] Jon described how the project came about. The development of the iPod started with the insight back in the mid-1990s that consumers in the future would have a variety of electronic devices that would tie into their home computers.

Rubinstein described the discussions at Apple at the time: "Our strategy here at Apple has been the digital hub. We saw the trends starting to form with digital video cameras, digital still cameras, with Palms [PalmPilot personal digital assistants], with cell phones and all of that. We started developing applications for all of those devices."

To execute on this strategy Apple began developing software for the Mac that helped users edit videos (iMovie), organize photos (iPhoto), and keep track of their music (iTunes).

The challenge with the Mac platform being the digital hub was that even though its hardware and software were widely considered superior to personal computers running Windows, there were still far more Windows PC users than Mac users. The Mac's market share was below 10 percent and falling. Apple had developed some great applications for editing photos and videos, and this attracted some people to the Mac platform, but it was not enough to really have a large impact.

"While iTunes was under development, we looked at the devices that were available on the market," Rubinstein says. Video cameras and still cameras, Rubinstein and his crew found, were pretty well designed.

"When we got to digital music players, what was out there was awful. They were big and they were heavy; the user interfaces were terrible," Rubinstein says.

The problem with existing solutions at the time was a hard drive that made the players too large. Other players that used a smaller flash drive suffered from a lack of capacity, so they could only play a small number of tracks. Also with both of these solutions it took too long to transfer songs from computers to the devices, and navigating through those songs was painful enough to make users long for something else. "So Steve asked me to go do a music player," Rubinstein says.

What then began was an unrelenting focus on designing a product and user experience that was end to end far superior to anything on the market.

Rubenstein described this approach: "The iPod is successful because we work on the whole user experience. It's not impossible, but it's really hard for other companies to duplicate what we've done."

This experience begins with the out-of-the-box experience. The packing is simple and intuitive, and there is no instruction manual, which suggests the product should be intuitive to use from the moment you turn it on. The rest, as they say, is history.

So what does the man who helped reinvent the music business think is the next major trend impacting customers?

"I think the future is mobile,"[4] he says, alluding to Apple crossing the 50 billion mobile app download milestone achieved in May 2013.

The Business Case

Imagine This Situation
Imagine you are facing this existing or potential future:

- Growing at a rate slower than the overall market
- Increasingly high costs of new customer acquisition
- Lack of innovation of existing products and services
- Loss of customers to competitors with more innovative offers

Is this happening to your business?

What's Your Response?
Is it to spend more money on advertising to attract new customers, get more new products to the market, and follow your competitors' innovations?

(Continued)

Or
Do you closely analyze, understand, and act on the unarticulated needs of your customers, your competitors' customers,
and potential future customers through the development of new
products and services?

What's the Difference?

A strong customer discipline that creates customer foresight
results in gaining new customers, revenue growth, and success-
ful new products and services.
This discipline is related to *customer foresight* behaviors.

Link to Business Performance

A deep understanding of future customer needs that creates
customer foresight results in revenue growth and addition of
new customers. As driver of business performance it measures
a business's ability to acquire new customers and meet future
customer needs and specifically impacts innovation and new
product and service success. It drives medium- and longer-term
competitive advantage.

Link to Strategy

Strength in this discipline is particularly relevant to a strategy
designed to obtain new customers in order to increase the
customer base and grow the size of the business.

Figure 3.1 highlights customer foresight as the focus of this
chapter. The goal is for companies to improve their absolute and
relative strength in this discipline. The score of 100 percent means
that a company is above all others in our Market Responsiveness Index (MRI) global database in terms of customer foresight
behaviors.

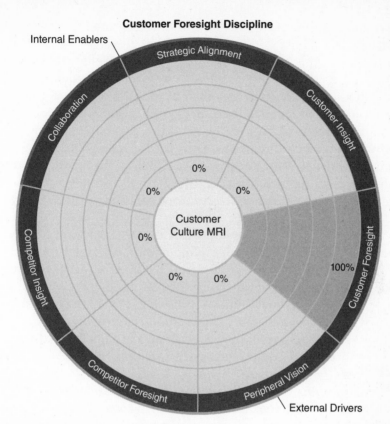

Figure 3.1   Customer foresight discipline

What Is Customer Foresight?

Customer foresight is the extent to which employees anticipate emerging customer needs, recognize unspoken needs, and take action to satisfy them. Foresight focuses on the latent and future needs of both potential customers and future customers.

Customer foresight is an orientation toward two types of customer needs: latent needs and future needs. *Latent needs* are needs and solutions of which the customer is unaware. They exist below the surface, outside the consciousness of the customer. *Future needs* are needs that do not currently exist for the customer but will in the future. Both types of needs are unexpressed by the customer and require a deep understanding of the customer and market. Customer foresight allows a group to lead their customers, proactively, not just respond to their requests. These behaviors include thinking beyond the current needs of customers, thinking beyond current product offerings, predicting future customer needs, and collaborating with customers to innovate and cocreate. This might mean attending customer planning meetings, knowing your customers' plans and strategies, and being aware of future events that will impact your customers' needs.

Foresight is really important for an organization's ability to innovate. Weakness in this discipline points to a lack of vision for the future. Customer foresight creates customer-inspired innovation through the imaginative discovery of new products, services, and business models by matching deep foresight into future customer needs with an organization's capabilities. As a result new needs of customers are discovered, new growth opportunities are identified, new organizational competencies are developed, and new solutions are created.

Organizations that have customer foresight are able to envision a future that is different from today. They engage customers, particularly lead users and opinion leaders, in the journey and inspire staff to think about future needs and propose innovative new ways of meeting those needs.

Why Is Customer Foresight a Cultural Discipline?
Connection with potential future customers and an understanding of future needs and ideas for possible new solutions can come from anyone and everyone inside and outside the company if it is fostered as an expected practice or behavior. This cultural discipline needs to be deliberately developed and nurtured for customer foresight to become an organizational capability. It is not enough to gain the foresight. The organization needs to be able to act on it to design and implement innovative solutions. Virgin deliberately recruits people who have a natural insatiable curiosity. There is a saying used inside

Virgin that "there is always another way." Virgin explicitly places value on ideas and innovation, and staff are encouraged to find ways of doing things better that will uncover latent needs of customers and satisfy future needs.[5]

Those companies that do this, such as salesforce.com, Apple, and Amazon.com, have developed customer foresight as a discipline that enables them to lead their markets with innovative products and services that appeal to new customers by tapping future needs.

Who Has It?

How Amazon.com's Customer-centric Culture Breeds Innovation

Amazon.com has an incredible history of putting the discipline of customer foresight into action. From its early days the company has taken an outside in approach to innovation. In other words it has been obsessed with understanding its customers' environment in order to solve valuable problems for them.

A great example of this is Amazon.com's decision to offer free shipping on all orders of more than $25. Effectively lowering prices like this will undoubtedly hurt business in the short run. But by saving their customers money they increase customer satisfaction and bring the company to the front of mind when they are considering online (and offline) purchases. Customers win with lower prices, and Amazon.com wins with more customers and more business with each of those customers.

Another controversial decision inside Amazon.com was to open up the Amazon.com platform to competitors, allowing them to sell their products on the platform. Again this is a decision driven with a customer mindset. It recognizes that customers want a range of choices and the tools to make the best decisions. Even though competitors may have the same product at a lower price, Amazon.com bets on the fact that by creating more choice for customers it will win over the longer term.[6]

As Jeff Bezos has said: "What we talk about is inventing on behalf of customers. It's not a customer's job to invent for themselves. You need to listen to customers. If you don't listen to customers, you will go astray. But they won't tell you everything so you will need to invent on their behalf."[7]

In 2004 Amazon.com decided to look at how it could create a better reading experience for customers. This meant designing a way for customers to read books on digital devices and give them the ability to store, buy, and read books on the move. It was a radical, ambitious idea to reinvent reading in the way the iPod had reinvented the way consumers listened to music. This was Amazon.com in customer foresight mode, looking to develop a solution that customers themselves could not fully articulate.

Bezos insisted the product needed to be always connected but rejected the use of Wi-Fi due to its lack of simplicity. This meant the product would need to seamlessly connect to the cellular network. It also needed to be as easy to read as a normal paper book, without the glare of a computer screen. These were formidable technical challenges that took until 2007 to resolve with the launch of the original Kindle.

With Kindle customers received a breakthrough innovation and Amazon found a way to extend its reach and connection with customers via a device that would allow them to better use and consume Amazon.com's digital books and content.

The company has continued to innovate in the physical world as well as the online world. One of the problems all online shoppers face is what happens when they get something delivered and they are not home. The result is missed deliveries, frustration, and delay. To address this need, Amazon.com has begun expanding its physical footprint in the United States by providing the Amazon Locker. This push first started with the 24-hour convenience chain, 7-11.[8]

It recently announced a partnership with Staples to extend Amazon.com's Locker footprint to their stores. Customers can opt to have packages sent to their nearest Staples store, at which time they are e-mailed a code and have three days to pick up their packages.[9]

Given Amazon's mission is essentially to save customers money, it is a great strategy designed to expand its options available to customers without increasing its costs substantially. It is an interesting win-win partnership with Staples, which competes with Amazon .com in the online environment. With this arrangement, Staples gets a fee and more foot traffic and Amazon.com gains a physical footprint to provide more convenience for customers.

How Do You Develop Customer Foresight?

Deep inside a mountain in a remote part of west Texas, a chime rings out from a clock that is more than a hundred feet tall.[10] The clock is unusual not only for its size and remote location but also for its timekeeping. This is a 10,000-year clock. What is traditionally its second hand only ticks once a year, with the century hand shifting once every 100 years and the cuckoo coming out once a millennium.

Jeff Bezos has invested more than $40 million in the clock project, which sits on his land in a remote part of Texas. When asked why he took an interest in such a project he said "The clock is a symbol for long-term thinking. . . . I think symbols can be very powerful."[11]

In many ways customer foresight is about having a vision of the future, a vision of how things really should be—this requires long-term thinking. A future orientation requires patience, persistence, and a willingness to accept failures along the way.

Bezos explains his thinking this way: "Any company that wants to put customers first, that wants to invent on behalf of customers—has to be willing to think long-term. And it's actually much rarer than you might think. I find that most of the initiatives that we undertake may take five to seven years before they pay any dividends for the company. They may start paying dividends for customers right away, but they often take a long time to pan out for shareholders and the company."[12]

When asked by *Harvard Business Review* editor Adi Ignatius about how to institutionalize this way of thinking, Bezos responded with two points, one related to the use of stories and the other on hiring the right type of people. In Bezos's words: "We have a lot of internal stories that we tell ourselves about persistence and patience, long-term thinking, staying heads down, focused on the customer even while being criticized."

Bezos also described the type of people they select to work at Amazon: "When they wake up and are thinking in the shower in the morning, they're thinking about customers, and thinking about how to invent on behalf of customers, and they find that fun."

What Behaviors Draw Out Customer Foresight?

When individuals and teams discuss the benefits and shortcomings of their products and services for potential customers they start to act on customer foresight. By gathering market intelligence to identify potential customers and actively discussing how to attract potential customers and then targeting new customers, individuals, and teams, they will gain customer foresight. By sharing this knowledge and activities across the business, all functions gain foresight into what they need to plan and do to create customer value for the future.

Examples of customer foresight behaviors include:

- Discussing the benefits and shortcomings of current products and services for potential customers
- Thinking and discussing beyond the current needs of customers
- Thinking and discussing beyond current product offerings
- Predicting future customer needs
- Collaborating with customers to innovate and cocreate
- Attending customer planning meetings
- Knowing and discussing your customers' plans and strategies
- Identifying future events that will impact your customers' needs
- Gathering market intelligence to identify potential customers
- Actively discussing how to attract potential customers

Sharing this knowledge and activities within the team enables all members to gain foresight into what they need to plan and do to create customer value for the future.

What Are Some of the Best Practices?

Many companies practice customer foresight behaviors as a discipline, which makes them very successful in leading their markets and industries. The following examples show how customer foresight strengthens customer culture through customer-inspired innovation.

Markit: Customers Are Owners

"You need your customers close to you. The closer you are to your customers the better opportunity you have to innovate—and to innovate correctly," says Lance Uggla of London-based Markit. Lance is the CEO and cofounder of a business that provides services to the financial markets.

In 2001 Lance and his team recognized the need for reliable, independent valuation data for credit default swaps (CDS), at the time a new and fast-growing market. To address this need, they founded Markit in 2003 to create CDS pricing, thereby increasing transparency in the market and helping their customers manage risk. They have been innovating ever since with the launch of more than 40 successful products over the past 10 years. Lance and his team of 3,000 people spread around the globe have known nothing but change in building this company from scratch to almost $1 billion in revenue in 2013.[13]

Lance recognized the importance of being close to customers from the beginning, and to cement this he sold them equity in the business. Along the way he has used several models of partnering with customers, from revenue sharing to equity ownership. This arrangement has ensured the close collaboration and cocreation of new products with customers. The use of customer user group forums and customer advisory boards has ensured that innovation is customer inspired and product design has been customer-centric.

Starbucks: Innovating Means Pushing the Boundaries

"Success means never standing still"[14] says Howard Schultz of Starbucks. The company has been innovating from its early days. In the 1990s Starbucks demonstrated customer foresight with its recognition that Americans would appreciate better-tasting European-style coffee with a store experience that creates the "third" place, a place to meet between home and work.

But innovation does not always mean success, and to be innovative means having not only a tolerance for failure but embracing the lessons learned. In Schultz's book, *Pour Your Heart into It*, he describes how Starbucks early in its retail development partnered with PepsiCo to develop a carbonated coffee beverage with the

Starbucks brand called Mazagran. The product was tested with customers in California, and the results were polarizing: some people loved it, and others hated it. Shultz came to the realization that Starbucks had a niche product that might go mainstream after a long ramp-up period.[15]

After persisting with the product for some time, the executive team was forced to rethink their approach. The product was just not made to go mainstream. "No one in America wanted to drink it," recounts Schultz. "We have tons of it still laying around."

This is just one of many Starbucks failures that we hear little about, from entering the movie business by backing the movie *Arctic Tale* to the magazine business with *Joe* magazine or the CD burning service HearMusic.[16] However these brand-stretching ideas have helped Starbucks remain focused back on its core. If you don't test the boundaries, you don't know where those boundaries exist.

It is this type of relentless innovation and willingness to fail that keeps Starbucks ahead of its competitors. After some recent success launching cold drinks in select stores, Schultz suggested they try bottling the new Frappuccino product. It became a massive success.[17]

So what is Starbucks doing to improve its innovation capability right now?

In a recent interview[18] Mary Wagner, senior vice president of Global R&D at Starbucks, described two areas the company is working on specifically: "We set out on a journey to closely examine the 'pockets of innovation excellence' occurring throughout Starbucks in order to learn and understand why we were enjoying success in specific areas. We sought answers to questions like, 'What leadership characteristics do our most successful innovators have? Why are they so successful?' and, 'What do their teams do differently?' My goal is to help Starbucks transform its innovation capability to move beyond 'pockets of success' occurring periodically—to a global organization delivering consistent, predictable innovation success."

Starbucks's second initiative comes from its success at drawing in countless ideas from customers, partners, and suppliers. As Mary describes it, "Our ability to generate so many good ideas has created a need for us to be even better at something else—prioritization! So, the second initiative is establishing a way to prioritize and select projects that will contribute most to our business strategies. Making tough go/kill decisions is very difficult to do. And, given the importance of preserving Starbucks's entrepreneurial culture, we worked together to customize gate scorecards, prioritization criteria, and portfolio charts so they worked well for our needs."

Where is Starbucks taking its customers next?

In a recent interview with the authors, Arthur Rubinfeld, the chief creative officer and president of global innovation at Starbucks, described how the company innovates. He says, "We focus on creating the highest quality products and enhancing the customer's Starbucks Experience..............................trending" enhancing the customer experience. By making it easy for customers to share ideas about what's important to them through their "My Starbucks Idea" online forum, Starbucks can get ahead of where customers are trending. Arthur describes two major trends related to health and sustainability as being areas around which Starbucks can innovate.

A proof point of this is the Evolution Fresh business at Starbucks. Evolution Fresh is fresh-squeezed fruits and vegetables, cold bottled, and processed under high pressure to bring maximum flavor and nutrients direct to customers. Most Evolution Fresh products are not pasteurized. Pasteurization is a process used for food safety purposes that diminishes the nutritional qualities of the product. Evolution Fresh uses a process called High-Pressure (HP) Processing to give it the safety factor without sacrificing efficacy and taste.

Starbucks, in its store environments, is the leading international retailer designing and constructing sustainable Leadership in Energy and Design (LEED) certified stores.

HP: "Next Bench" Customer Foresight

In recent months we have met several ex-HP employees who told us about the great times they had at HP when the culture embedded by Bill Hewlett and Dave Packard prevailed—a culture of innovation, customer focus, and respect for individuals as flesh-and-blood people.

One, Jerry Gleason, who worked 18 years in HP's corporate labs, told us of his early days as an engineer working in one of the R&D labs in the Test and Measurement Division at Palo Alto, California. While working on a project at his bench he was expected to watch his colleague working on the next bench and through observation and discussion see what the colleague was struggling with—then to see if he could solve the problem. If he could, there just might be a lot of other engineers in the marketplace who are struggling with the same problem—and this solution might create a new market.

This practice, or cultural discipline, heightened the awareness of engineers at HP to be looking for problems that their engineering colleagues had that created a sensitivity to the potential future needs of their "engineer" customers. In effect, it made the R&D employees at HP customer focused and looking for customer-inspired innovation.

Imagine if accountants in certified public accounting firms or financial services firms adopted the "next bench" practice—or IT technologists in IT service firms practiced it, or HR professionals in large corporations did it. We would see stronger customer cultures emerging organically.

Westpac: Banking on Customer-Inspired Innovation

Jason Yetton, group executive in retail and business banking, initiated an innovation system, called Mr. Easy, in 2003 within a division of Westpac Banking to easily enable staff members to feed in well-thought-out ideas for continuous improvement. The Australian bank started its transformation toward a customer culture in 2008, and this system was extended across the entire bank in 2009 to enable staff members in Westpac to provide ideas for change and improvement. Ideas that benefit the customer and the business are structured, costed, and proposed, and a senior management panel evaluates, prioritizes, and approves. There was an immediate upsurge in customer-inspired ideas across the business, and as one of the panel Jason had to sort the best ideas from what were all good ideas. He said, "Almost all the ideas are right, so we had to select 'right from right' based on the ones that were most relevant to the future direction of Westpac." Some of the best innovations are short term and easy to implement while others are longer term and require substantial investment but are aligned with the bank's strategy. This has become a powerful engine for customer innovation, cross-functional collaboration, and transparency for all staff members to see which ideas are prioritized and implemented. Many of these ideas now relate to online banking services that enable customers to easily see, manage, and transact across their whole financial spectrum from normal bill paying to savings and investments.

An example is Westpac's innovation in retirement fund services. In Australia, the superannuation market for workforce retirees is large and growing rapidly due to legislative requirements for all firms to pay an additional 10 percent of employee wages into investment funds for their retirement. It is a type of compulsory 401(k) fund. But Australians have not been very interested in this until they get close to retirement. Westpac wanted to create interest, relevance, and involvement in this area so it could become involved in the management of retirees' retirement funds as well as their other financial needs. It introduced an online product called BT Super for Life for Westpac customers in 2007 and was the first bank in Australia to add it to customers' online banking capability; they could then view all of their financial affairs on one page. This helped to make it relevant by enabling customers to view their overall wealth easily. What was unique about this was the customer-centric design process that involved customer inputs, which required many iterations before it was launched. Initially it took about 10 minutes for a customer to set up. By 2013 it took 60 seconds and three clicks. Westpac dominates this market in the banking sector as a result of following through the customer foresight in recognizing the unmet need that would become increasingly relevant to Australia's aging population.

Another example of customer foresight was the early recognition in Westpac of the trend toward mobile banking. Westpac was the first Australian bank to provide an app for mobile users that resulted in rapid take-up of its services and attraction of new customers.[19]

CHAPTER SUMMARY

Why is customer-inspired innovation important?
The future is rushing toward us at an ever-increasing rate. Innovating using foresight obtained from observation of, inputs from, and cocreation with customers enables us to meet and exceed their future expectations—with customer-inspired new products and services. This helps ensure the future of the business.

(Continued)

What is customer foresight?
Customer foresight is the extent to which employees anticipate emerging customer needs, recognize unspoken needs, and take action to satisfy them.

Why is customer foresight a cultural discipline?
Connection with potential future customers, an understanding of future needs, and ideas for possible new solutions can come from anyone and everyone inside and outside the company if it is fostered as an expected practice or behavior.

What behaviors lead to customer foresight?
By gathering market intelligence to identify potential customers and actively discussing how to attract potential customers and then targeting new customers, individuals and teams will gain customer foresight. By sharing this knowledge and activities across the business, all functions gain foresight into what they need to plan and do to create customer value for the future.

Leader's Guide to Customer Foresight

Customer Foresight: *Does the company gather information on potential customers? Does it target them based on its opportunity for competitive advantage? Does it understand and invest in meeting future needs of prospective customers? Does it understand and act on unarticulated needs?*

Rate where *you and your team* stand on customer foresight by checking the relevant box in answering each question.

Rating descriptors: 0 = never; 1 = almost never; 2 = rarely; 3 = occasionally; 4 = sometimes; 5 = regularly; 6 = frequently; 7 = often; 8 = very often; 9 = constantly; 10 = all the time.

☐   1. To what extent do you discuss the benefits and shortcomings of current products and services for potential customers?

☐ 2. To what extent do you think and discuss beyond the current needs of customers?

☐ 3. To what extent do you predict future customer needs?

☐ 4. To what extent do you collaborate with customers to innovate and cocreate?

☐ 5. To what extent do you gather intelligence to identify potential customers and future needs?

☐ 6. To what extent do you know your customers' plans and strategies?

☐ 7. To what extent are you aware of future events that will impact your customers' needs?

☐ 8. To what extent do you understand the future needs of current and new customers?

☐ 9. To what extent do you act on customer foresight?

☐ 10. To what extent do you share foresight across other functions and teams outside your group?

Chapter 4

Relentless Positioning

Only the paranoid survive.
> —Andy Grove, former CEO, Intel

Ben Wignall, former owner of the Tasmanian firm Blue Banner Pickles, used to get a lot of customer complaints. Each time Ben's response would be the same—he raised his prices.

The complaints were from supermarkets that were not able to get enough stock of the famous (in Tasmania) pickled onion brand. Ben figured that if he raised the price, it would dampen down demand and the complaints would disappear. He was right—and the results were profitable. Blue Banner had 90 percent of the Tasmanian market for pickled onions—a virtual monopoly—and, like other monopolies, it could dictate the terms and not be too concerned about focusing on customers.

Ben was in for a shock when he expanded into other geographic markets in Australia where there was strong competition and his Tasmanian strategy would not work. He hadn't realized that the island state of Tasmania acted as a market fortress where he could act as a monopolist—but not elsewhere. If you have a monopoly you can probably succeed without focusing on customers, but in today's world how long will that last?

At Telstra, Australia's largest telecommunications company, the CEO, David Thodey, has instituted a much higher level of respect for competitors as part of Telstra's culture. He recognizes that they include very capable people and that to know and understand your competitors reduces any surprises in the marketplace. This has required a cultural change. It's harder today to know if companies are customers or competitors. Telstra does business with Apple and Google while at the same time these companies use competing networks that bypass Telstra's service. The CEO welcomes so called over-the-top competitors like Skype and Viber because they open up new opportunities and drive new demand. This means Telstra needs to review its value proposition to make sure it delivers the value that customers want. David says, "It is up to us to make sure customers are getting value. We have to educate customers more about the value they are receiving and make the plans we offer more understandable."[1]

In fact, where everyone in an industry provides a poor customer experience it is still possible to be profitable. Forrester's Customer Experience Index[2] shows this to be the case in the wireless services industry in the United States in which all competitors show similarly low scores. Customer experience is not a differentiator, and other factors such as market footprint and price dictate results in this growth industry. As a colleague, Malcolm McDonald, emeritus professor of marketing, Cranfield Management School, used to say, "Even Donald Duck could run a company profitably in a rapid growth market!" He maintains, as do we, that the real test is to achieve sustained profitability under all types of changing market and competitive conditions.

Dominant market leaders can survive offering poor customer experience for a time due to better distribution or a broad product range. Inertia carries these companies through. But a time comes when these factors are not enough to retain leadership. We have seen this with the successful emergence of online (only) banks and online retailers that have decimated competitors in those industries that could not provide a consistent high-level valuable customer experience.

These are some of the reasons why companies can be successful while offering poor customer experiences. But it is important to know why you are winning in the marketplace. If it is not based on a good customer experience, it is likely you are living on borrowed time. For

Ben Wignall and Blue Banner, competitors became an important element in his future business success. Also for Telstra, it has required a cultural change for leadership and staff to consider their competitors as an important part of the customer's world.

The key point we want to make in this chapter is that competitors are part of the customer's world. Understanding the competitive environment is integral to understanding the alternatives customers have in the marketplace.

If leaders and their teams do not understand the alternative ways customers can solve their problems, they are very likely to get blindsided with little or no time to respond. But what's needed is more than understanding; it is *competitor insight*.

The Business Case

Imagine This Situation

Imagine you are facing these existing or potential threats:

- Declining market share
- Resistance from customers to your value proposition
- Competitive price cuts
- Shrinking profit margins

Is this happening to your business? If it isn't, it probably will be soon.

What's Your Response?

Is it to match your competition with price cuts, give more incentives to the sales force to sell more, implement massive cost cuts, or just blindly panic?

Or

Do you closely analyze and understand your competitors' strategies, review their current value propositions and your own as seen by customers, and take account of these to forge your strategies?

(Continued)

What's the Difference?
A strong competitive discipline that creates competitor insight results in higher margins, profit growth, and increased profitability.

Link to Business Performance
A deep competitor understanding that creates competitor insight results in superior revenue growth, profit growth, and profitability. As a driver of business performance it measures a business's ability to implement differentiated value propositions, improve profit margins, and achieve ongoing profitable growth.

Link to Strategy
Strength in this discipline is particularly relevant to a strategy designed to defend and take market share from competitors, strengthen short-term competitive advantage, and consolidate current competitive position in the marketplace.

Figure 4.1 highlights competitor insight as the focus of this chapter. The goal is for companies to improve their absolute and relative strength in this discipline. The score of 100 percent means that a company is above all others in our MRI global database in terms of competitor insight practices.

What Is Competitor Insight?

Competitor insight comes from a deep understanding of the current competitive landscape and of the goals, strategies, and mode of implementation of those specific competitors that have the greatest impact on your business. It includes a clear understanding of their strengths and weaknesses and their likely response to your market initiatives and those of other competitors. Its foundation is a mentality that references the value you offer in relation to the alternatives available to customers.

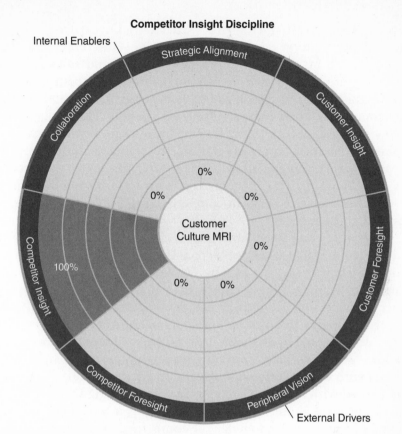

Figure 4.1 Competitor insight discipline

Your company's understanding of its customers' alternatives is crucial to its ability to compete. Which service offerings are competitive, and which are not? How do customers perceive your offers? Are they simple and transparent and clearly better than the alternatives? Are staff members in all functions factoring into their work the value propositions of current competitors to produce additional value for the business and its customers?

Competitor insight relates to a company's understanding of how to take action in a competitive environment where the task of positioning and repositioning the value offered is relentless.

Why Is Competitor Insight a Cultural Discipline?

An in-depth view of competitors is crucial. Our research shows high correlations between *competitor insight* and sales revenue growth, profit growth, and overall profitability. Competitor insight is a capability that enables a company to really understand its current competitors and position itself for success. The implications of low performance on this discipline have a significant impact on businesses, as they simply are not able to compete effectively. The only companies that can afford to be weak in this area are monopolies or dominant firms in industries with high barriers to entry. Other firms that are weak in competitor insight can face extreme business consequences.

It became clear to us how important competitor insight is as a cultural discipline when we were asked by a senior management team to help them with a pricing decision. This company was the market leader in a highly competitive mature market supplying paper products to businesses. Its major competitor had substantially reduced its prices to all of its high-volume customers. The market leader was tempted to do the same or go one better and reduce them further. When we met the senior leadership team we were confronted with widely different opinions on what to do. Each opinion was backed with high levels of emotion surrounding why his or her individual view should be adopted. There was very little market intelligence upon which to judge the competitor's response to different pricing moves. There appeared to be little understanding of the competitor's strategy and pricing intent and the profit implications of such a move.

In discussions there was no reference to the value propositions of both companies. Here was a company that was about to destroy its own profitability and that of the industry with the ultimate impact on product quality, service, and customer experience. In that meeting there was no reference to customers and what they really valued. The leaders were getting conflicting advice from their colleagues in sales, marketing, customer service, finance, delivery, and operations. There was no clear framework or intelligence for making the best decision for customers and for the business. We set about working with them to focus first on competitor insights, clarifying their own competitive advantage and that of the competitor and what different segments of customers most valued.

Given the high levels of anxiety in the leadership team, there was pressure to act quickly. We were able to do a quick assessment of the competitive landscape and talk with some of the paper company's customers. We discovered that many of the unsupported assumptions made by the leadership did not reflect reality from the customers' points of view. We made the recommendation that the company should hold prices but add a new service element that customers had told us they valued—and we held our breath.

Soon after this move the competitor raised its prices back to original levels, and an industry price war was averted.

Oftentimes emotions blind leaders when competitors act aggressively in the market, and the result can be negative for everyone involved. Customers may win in the short term, but longer term the industry's product and service standards decline as there is not enough profit to provide real value and invest in meeting customers' future needs.

Everyone in the business needs to know what its value proposition is and how each contributes to it. The value proposition includes how you are different from competitive alternatives and why customers should buy from you instead of your competitors. When competitor insight is shared across an organization, all individuals and teams have an opportunity to evaluate the value they are providing for customers within a competitive lens. They can then act to strengthen a company's delivery of its value proposition through their own contribution. It may be related to relative speed of new products to market, relative service satisfaction, relative product quality, or relative ease of access to the company's products and services. Ultimately, competitive advantage is affected by all individuals and teams doing their part to deliver value that is superior to their competitors. When a business has a competitor insight discipline it is able to make decisions more quickly and with more confidence. It can also implement relevant changes where all parts of the business know the role they are playing to deliver superior value to customers.

Who Has It?

The Mars Corporation, like many food-manufacturing companies producing brands sold in supermarkets, has a long history of fighting for market share in mature, slow-growth markets in developed economies. This has created a competitive mentality in which the understanding of existing competitors, their strategies, capabilities, and leaders has developed into an art form as a means of gaining one market share point. Sometimes this combative competitive culture has inhibited innovation by competitors who focus too much on each other and not enough on customer needs. However, the story that follows illustrates how a customer culture that incorporates both an understanding of changing customer needs and a deep knowledge of competitors and their strategies yields a competitive advantage and increased sales and profitability.

Taking Candy from a Kid

The product manager at Mars Corporation did not like what she saw. The sales of Milky Way bars were trending down without any obvious reason. There had been no changes to the product or its price in recent months, and there had been no changes to competitors' products. In fact, the whole category seemed to be in decline. Competitors were starting to discount their prices, and she knew this was one of the few actions they could take to try to influence their sales. Before taking action she decided to talk to parents within the business who had children aged between 8 and 10, the primary consumers of Milky Way. They told her that their kids wanted candy snacks at about four o'clock in the afternoon after school, but as responsible parents they were resisting buying Milky Way because it filled the children up and they would not eat their evening meal. The product manager checked this by interviewing afternoon shoppers with their kids and found this resistance to be real. Mars was one of the few competitors that could change its candy bar production molds quickly and at reasonable cost. While other competitors were reducing prices, she ordered a change in production of bars at two-thirds their original size, left the price unchanged, repositioned Milky Way as "a snack that won't fill you up" by saying, "So light it won't ruin your appetite"—and sold an additional 70 million bars.

Mars was able to understand what was driving customer decisions in relation to the competing choices available and the strategies of current competitors. It was able to act quickly to harness all functional resources to change the offer, its positioning, and its appeal to customers—resulting in sales and share increases, margin improvements, and increased profitability.

A strong competitor insight discipline enables the business to respond rapidly to competitive threats or act quickly to preempt competitive moves before they occur. Access across the business to competitive intelligence is a prerequisite for effective positioning and delivery of the company's value proposition.

How Do You Develop Competitor Insight?

As with all customer culture disciplines, the role of senior leaders is decisive. Larry Ellison, CEO of Oracle, is known to be the fiercest competitor in Silicon Valley, a place famous for its cutthroat competition. At a staff conference several years ago, Ellison showed a photo of a competing company's headquarters and said, "We're going to run them out of business and buy that building, which we're going to bulldoze."[3] Ellison has been heavily influenced by his experience working in Japan, where the competitive mentality of relentless pursuit of market share has been embedded by the quote from Genghis Khan: "It's not sufficient that I succeed. Everyone else must fail."

Ellison seems also to be influenced by his involvement in America's Cup yacht racing, where there is a winner and a loser. This extreme attitude to competition will succeed long term only if the interests of customers are paramount in competitive strategy. Ellison has shown that he and his company are attuned to customer needs by being early investors in "cloud" computing software. Also they have managed the transition from software licensing to cloud services well by recognizing the reluctance of many large companies to change.

Oracle has continued to offer new multiyear software licenses while allowing those who want to move to the cloud a year to upgrade to the latest software. Most cloud software companies run the latest version of their software in their own data centers and upgrade their customers en masse every time a new version of the software is ready.[4]

This is an example of a skillful blend of understanding customer needs, your own competitive advantage, and competitor insight.

Most of us develop a competitive instinct and insight from the sports we love—as a player or spectator. We learn the rules, study the game, practice and play, compete, and learn how to win.

John Walker, the New Zealand 1500-meter runner at the Montreal Olympics, had a clear competitive plan when preparing for the most important race of his career. His goal was clear: win the gold medal. So he trained with that in mind. He knew his competitors and exactly how he would run the race. He would pull to the front with 300 meters to the finish. He would "kick" and never look back until after crossing the line. Nobody would get in his way. So he trained that way on the track. He even trained in his car by moving his car into the fast lane with 300 meters to the turnoff from the freeway to his Auckland suburb. For a year before the Olympics he did this *every time* on the track and in his car. What happened? He ran the race as planned, "kicked" at the 300-meter mark, didn't look back, and led the whole field by one yard to the finish and the gold medal.[5] Walker knew his competitive advantage, how to compete to win, and exactly how he would run the race. The same applies in business where the focus is on how to win with the customer.

In business, the competitive mentality is clearly evident in sales, marketing, and customer service. In sales you win or lose customers, in marketing you gain or lose market share, and in customer service you gain or lose a customer. In business, as in sports, we all love to be part of a winning team. Everyone in the organization contributes to that winning feeling and being competitive in the marketplace.

Leading the customer experience race starts with one person— someone who has "winning" with the customer as a clear goal, who makes a habit of understanding customers and the alternative choices they have, and who creates a discipline of doing what's right for the customer *every time*. If this is done with perseverance, growing skill and enthusiasm, it becomes infectious and others will follow. No matter where in the organization this person sits, he or she can be a leader in the customer experience race against competitors. When everyone in your organization thinks and acts like this, you have a strong competitor insight discipline.

Which Behaviors Draw Out Competitor Insight?

Each person in the organization should understand how the work he or she does contributes to its competitive advantage. It is when individuals and teams regularly discuss their competitors' strengths and weaknesses and make decisions with current competitors in mind that competitor insight creates value for customers and for the business. This involves monitoring the current strategies of competitors and evaluating where competitors have succeeded and failed. A shared knowledge of this intelligence throughout the organization enables employees to use competitor insight to create value for customers.

How can we ensure that everyone in the organization has an understanding of competitors' strategies? The following examples illustrate how competitor insight behaviors can occur across the organization:

- Discussing customers' alternatives to understand the ability of one's own company to compete
- Discussing and clarifying how customers perceive offers by the company: are they simple and transparent and clearly better than the alternatives?
- Determining which service offerings are competitive and which are not
- Regularly discussing and understanding competitors' strengths and weaknesses
- Monitoring the current strategies of competitors and evaluating where competitors have succeeded and failed
- Discussing and understanding the value proposition of one's own company and those of current competitors
- Making decisions with current competitors in mind that creates value for customers and for the business
- Sharing knowledge of this intelligence throughout the team to enable employees to use competitor insight to create value for customers

A great story about how the disciplines of deep competitor insight combined with customer insight shared across the business resulted in profit and revenue growth comes from Overseas Shipping Services (OSS).

OSS World Wide Movers[6]

Many years after the birth of OSS (recounted in Chapter 1), the company had entered all main segments of the international movers market remaining specialized in shipping personal and household belongings overseas by sea and air. The company had entered the main English-speaking markets of the United Kingdom, the United States, and Canada through advertising in the yellow pages, the newspapers, and the relevant newsletters of associations such as the American Australian Association.

This story comes from a time when a large part of OSS's market still preferred to find information on moving services in newspapers.

For years OSS had run a small ad in the Saturday paper's "Travel" section, while its competitors were advertising in the "Moving" section. This was based on a unique insight that people who were relocating first organized their travel before considering a moving service. The ad brought in many enquiries, most of which were converted by OSS into business.

One day the team discovered to their horror a much larger ad from a competitor right next to the OSS ad.

They had to consider how to respond, so they reached out to some people in their network. One of the team members had a friend in an advertising business, and she asked him for some ideas. He suggested simply to increase the size of the ad to match the competitor's. He said, "You are in with the big boys now; you need to start spending more on advertising." An advertising man suggesting OSS spend more on advertising—what a surprise!

Recognizing there probably was not a quick and easy answer, the team decided to step back and ask themselves the following questions: What do we know about our competitors? How do they compete? What is our competitive advantage? Are we facing a tactical decision or is this strategic? How do our customers buy? How would they view two alternatives presented side by side in the newspaper?

The advertising team set up a cross-functional meeting attended by the chief financial officer, sales, operations, pricing, advertising, and the call center to get everyone to weigh in on these issues. Here is what they came up with:

1. **How to compete:** OSS couldn't compete with its competitor's budget. Just to match the competition would require five times its current budget, and this would then raise its cost structure for this market segment. What's more, it might force the company to reconsider its pricing. Knowledge of its competitor's resources told team members that the company could spend much more on advertising and still hold its prices where they were.
2. **Competitor's advantage:** If OSS were to match its competitor's ad size, the competitor would then double the size of its ad and would keep doing so if OSS kept matching the size. This strategy is based on a traditional dominant competitive position: dominant companies compete by outspending the competition and relying on their brand names to get business.
3. **Customer behavior insight:** OSS already knew more about customers than its competitors did. Another unique insight it had was that customers nearly always get at least two quotes.
4. **What to communicate:** Now that OSS was in a directly competitive media situation, it would need to change its message to "get your second quote from OSS."
5. **How much to spend:** Since its competitor would now be doing the advertising for this market segment, OSS could reduce the size of its ad just a little and save money.

OSS team members were tuned into competitors and customers. They could all agree on the previous assessment because of strong customer and competitor disciplines embedded in the OSS culture. They all had a clear understanding of the customer's buying behavior as well as their competitors' current strategies and how to effectively compete with much larger organizations. They were basing a decision on clear customer and competitor insights.

The decision was made quickly, and the call center and field sales team developed a process to obtain ongoing customer and competitive intelligence relevant to this market segment to monitor the effect of this decision. The results were outstanding. OSS received more enquiries from this advertising than before and converted about 80 percent of them into new clients with a positive trend in sales growth and profit margins.

This example shows how a relatively small tactical decision can have a big impact on the profit and growth of a business. But also it shows how a team that is tuned into customers and competitors as the way in which they make decisions can find a solution quickly.

What Are Some of the Best Practices?

Those companies that have competitor insight behaviors as a discipline are very successful at gaining competitive advantage. The following examples show how competitor insight strengthens customer culture.

Konica Minolta: Competing as the Underdog

David Cooke, managing director of Konica Minolta in Australia, the Japanese technology company, believes a clear understanding of competitive differences are a key to success in delivering superior value to customers. He tells the following story about when he was executive general manager and he and his then managing director, Hiro Kaji, made a sales call to the Finance Department of the Australian government.

"The federal government in Australia had not had a procurement contract for imaging equipment multifunction devices—printers, scanners, copiers, faxes, and so on—for about 10 years," he says. "A department could buy from whomever they chose, and they decided that it was far more sensible to leverage their massive power. They're the largest customer in Australia, and so they would go to contract and they would have a limited number of people on a panel. So out of 12 possible providers, they might have four or something like that, and we were invited to go to Canberra and meet with the team that had been set up to make that decision, and there were about eight people all sitting in a row. It was very daunting. It was a bit like a big senate enquiry—and the very first question that we were hit with, and they directed it at me—there were three of us—was, 'You're not as big as some of your competitors. Why would we give you a spot on our panel?'

"And my response to that question was, firstly, to acknowledge that I was very glad that they had asked it, but then to say, 'I think the answer to your question is actually inherent in the question itself, and you are dead right. We are not as big as Xerox, Canon or HP, but that's the reason why you should put us under contract,' because they had associated big with better. And what I went on to explain is that I think big is not necessarily better, and I talked about the fact that, as a midsized manufacturer and supplier, we actually have a flatter management structure, and I had our Japanese managing director with us, and I said, 'May I ask if any of the other companies had their managing director come and speak to you today?' And they said no. And I said, 'There's a very concrete example of the difference between us and some larger companies.'

"In our midsized culture that we've developed, we do take the time at the most senior management levels to come and meet with prospective customers, to regularly visit our existing customer base. I said, 'We don't always get it right. When we do drop the ball, if you ever felt the need to escalate something above the local management here, then you can ring me at any stage as the executive general manager. You can ring our managing director at anytime, and he will take your phone call, and you've met him. You've both met each other already.'

"So I think that resonated with them that our approach would be more flexible, more approachable. Keeping the lines of communication more open was a massive advantage, and they scribbled lots of notes and put us under contract."[7]

David Cooke reinforces the competitive positioning of his company with everyone in the business by telling this story. The sales and marketing people continually gather competitive intelligence from customers, competitors' marketing campaigns, and competitors' ex-staff members to help them understand current competitors, their strategies, and their intent. Competitor insights are disseminated throughout the organization to enable all staff members to live up to their company's promise: "more flexible and approachable."

James Hardie: Sharing Competitive Intelligence Globally to Preempt Competitors' Strategies

James Hardie is the global leader in fiber cement technology, providing siding, external cladding, walls, fencing, and roofing and accessory building product solutions to architects, builders, and homeowners for over 100 years. The company's largest business unit, fiber cement in the United States, has made substantial inroads into the U.S. market for external walls of buildings for decoration and weatherproofing, where it is now one of the largest manufacturers.

Its competitive intelligence practices involve detailed tracking of new competitive products as they are rolled out across the globe. This includes direct market intelligence in specific countries, news clippings, social media, and customer feedback. This information is packaged in a way that is usable, highlighting only the most crucial competitor insights and sharing them with leaders globally.

By tracking the patterns of competitive new-product rollouts James Hardie has been able to preempt these new-product entries into its own markets by introducing new and enhanced products earlier. Sharing of competitive intelligence between regional divisions has sharpened urgency throughout the business and increased the speed of new-product introductions.

Netflix: Learning from Competitive Battles to Keep Focused on Customers

Netflix holds a position as dominant leader in the online video streaming industry. This is due in part to being the first large-scale operation of its kind, a huge amount of content, and the ability to meet increased demand. In 2013 the service has been feeling the heat from a few smaller but growing services, many of which are starting to mimic the larger company's moves and, in some cases, improve upon them. Amazon Prime, HBO GO, and VUDU are three that are making an impact.[8]

Netflix has been able to compete aggressively since its founding in 1997. A four-year war with Blockbuster started in 2004 when the latter tried and failed to crush its upstart DVD-by-mail competitor. CEO Reed Hastings believes "the reason we won is because we improved our everyday service of shipping and delivering. That experience grounded us. Executing better on the core mission is the way to win. I was confident that our best odds were to be very steady and focus on improving the service".[9]

In addition to its excellent service Netflix understood where the market was heading and how it would outmaneuver Blockbuster with a more efficient and compelling value proposition. Blockbuster charged per movie and was notorious for charging late fees while Netflix charged a flat monthly subscription with no late fees. With the trend toward online services increasing and the high cost of retail, Netflix made the strategic decision to move into online video.

In 2011, Hastings noted that his greatest fear was not being able to make the leap from success in DVDs to success in streaming. By early 2013, Netflix had added 3 million new customers in its past 12 months and was winning with its video streaming consumer value proposition—on-demand: what you want, when you want it, how you want it, and at your pace.

Netflix has gone from being the challenger in the market to the leader and that requires new thinking about the competition. No longer are the traditional retailers in the picture, and its new competitors are very capable and technology-centric. Netflix has been able to outcompete them by providing the most desirable content on a service that is the easiest to use and available across the most devices. It has been ahead of customers by providing easy access across the most popular devices such as the iPad, Sony PlayStation, Xbox, and TiVo.

Its customer-first mentality has led to the dual competitive advantage of consumer loyalty via subscription and scale. While being intensely competitive, Netflix has always viewed competition through the lens of the customer.

Virgin Radio: Master of Competitor Insight

Ian Grace and the team at Virgin Radio are masters of competitor insight. They have been able to launch successful number-one-ranked music stations in a number of cities around the world. Virgin Radio's first success was in Bangkok against entrenched competitors. There are 41 FM radio stations in Bangkok, many of which had been operating for 15 years prior to the Virgin launch. At the time the leading top 40/adult contemporary music stations were extremely cluttered with 30 minutes of music, 15 minutes of commercials, and 15 minutes of talk. Virgin Radio conducted extensive market research and found that listeners just wanted the music and no "clutter." VirginHitZ and Virgin Soft were launched respectively in 2002 and in 2004 with clean music-dominated formats playing less commercials and with less talk. Within six months the stations were numbers one and two in the overall market rankings. The stations were broadcasting in the Thai language and playing Thai music with limited commercials per hour and more focused talk and information. A third Virgin station was subsequently launched in Thailand and it became the number-four ranked station in the market. Incumbent competitors were unable to react quickly because of their advertiser commitments and their legacy of the way it had always been done. Ian Grace said "Our format appeared to be very simple, however we very carefully provided consumers with exactly what they wanted, and advertisers followed."[10]

Stations in Delhi, Dubai, Canada, and Italy have all followed with similar success.

In each case people at Virgin Radio developed insight about the entrenched competitors by understanding their product, the people who led them, and their competitive constraints. Through ongoing research they learned what consumers wanted and monitored their perceptions. Most importantly, competitor insight was embedded in each radio station team as a cultural discipline so that all team members could assess their customer performance in relation to competition and contribute to the value delivered to both consumers and advertisers.

Warning: Don't Forget the Customer!

Competitive intelligence is clearly necessary, but you must be sure not to become myopic. This is one of the reasons that many customer-focused leaders tend to downplay the importance of competitors.

A great example of this myopia is the Duncan Hines product launch into Japan. As a major producer of cake mix in the United States, the company discovered that Asia was an untapped market.

Market researchers investigated the Japanese per-capita income, grocery spending, and even consumer tastes to determine the right level of sweetness in the consumers' baked goods. A check of potential competition showed that there were virtually no competitors in this space—an incredible opportunity was just waiting!

The product launch was a failure. It turns out the Japanese generally do not have *ovens* in their apartments. The question the marketers failed to ask was, "Why are there no competitors in this market?"

Other examples point to the damage caused by an excessive focus on competitors that leads to damaging price wars. The "last-person-standing" mentality destroys profitability, wipes out the capability to fund innovation, and ultimately reduces value for customers. Periodic price wars in the U.S. airline industry have driven major airlines into bankruptcy and reduced customer service in the United States to a level that results in poor customer experiences compared to airline services in other countries. Virgin Atlantic, Southwest Airlines, and Emirates airlines are good examples of airlines that know how to compete.

Another form of the last-person-standing mentality is the two-company competitive wars that can shift a business away from focusing on changing customer needs. The cola wars by Coke and Pepsi became so intense with Pepsi's mantra "Beat Coke" that Coca-Cola completely misread the market with the debacle of its "New Coke" in response to the "Pepsi Challenge" in the 1970s and 1980s.[11] Both companies missed the emerging growing market for mineral waters and were subsequently driven to acquire companies that became established in that market.

The current intense "smartphone wars" between Apple and Samsung, with Google trying to become a force in the smartphone hardware business, can easily muddy the waters when it comes to staying focused on customer value. Both competitor insight and customer foresight are vital disciplines for these companies in such a competitive and fast-changing environment.[12]

CHAPTER SUMMARY

Why are competitors important to customer-centricity?
Customers face a range of choices that can fill any one particular need. So competitors' offers are part of the customer's world. To be truly customer-centric all leaders and staff need to understand from the customer's perspective what these choices are, who is offering them, and how your company's value proposition is superior to those from competitors. Leaders and staff need to be able to be responsive to changes in competitors' offers and continually act to increase customer value relative to alternatives.

What is competitor insight?
Competitor insight is a capability that enables a company to really understand its current competitors and position itself for ongoing success. Competitor insight comes from a deep understanding of the current competitive landscape and of the goals, strategies, and mode of implementation of those specific competitors that have the greatest impact on your business.

Why is competitor insight a cultural discipline?
Everyone in the business needs to know what its value proposition is and how each contributes to it. The value proposition includes how you are different from competitive alternatives and why customers should buy from you instead of your competitors. When competitor insight is shared across an organization, all individuals and teams have an opportunity to evaluate the value they are providing for customers within a competitive lens.

What behaviors lead to competitor insight?
This involves monitoring the current strategies of competitors and evaluating where competitors have succeeded and failed. A shared knowledge of this intelligence throughout the organization enables employees to use competitor insight to create value for customers. It is when individuals and teams regularly discuss

their competitors' strengths and weaknesses and make decisions with current competitors in mind that competitor insight creates value for customers and for the business.

Leader's Guide to Competitor Insight

Competitor Insight: *Does the company monitor, understand, and respond to its competitors' strengths and weaknesses? Does it factor competitors' current strategies into its own strategies? Do staff members understand how they contribute to the firm's current value proposition and competitive advantage and act to support it?*

Rate where *you and your team* stand on competitor insight by checking the relevant box in answering each question.

Rating descriptors: 0 = never; 1 = almost never; 2 = rarely; 3 = occasionally; 4 = sometimes; 5 = regularly; 6 = frequently; 7 = often; 8 = very often; 9 = constantly; 10 = all the time.

☐ 1. To what extent do you discuss customers' alternatives to understand your ability to compete?

☐ 2. To what extent do you discuss and clarify how customers perceive your offers compared with alternatives?

☐ 3. To what extent do you evaluate from a customer perspective which service offerings are competitive and which are not?

☐ 4. To what extent do you regularly discuss competitors' strengths and weaknesses?

☐ 5. To what extent do you monitor the current strategies of competitors and evaluate where competitors have succeeded and failed?

☐ 6. To what extent do you discuss your value proposition and those of current competitors?

☐ 7. To what extent do you use what you have learned from competitors' successes to improve your own value for customers?

(Continued)

☐ 8. To what extent do you make decisions with current competitors in mind that create value for customers and for the business?

☐ 9. To what extent do you evaluate how your work contributes to the firm's competitive advantage?

☐ 10. To what extent do you share competitor insights with teams across functions and outside your group to enable employees to create more value for customers?

Chapter 5

Competing for the Future

Winning in business today is not about being number one—it's about who gets to the future *first.*
                                        —Gary Hamel and C. K. Prahalad[1]

A 2012 Harvard Business School survey on U.S. business competitiveness confirms what we already know—U.S. businesses have been losing the ability to compete internationally.[2] As well as a relatively unfavorable U.S. business environment that needs to be addressed by government, the fundamental problem lies within business practice itself. In this study the authors conclude that much of the problem results from an obsessive focus by senior management of publicly listed companies on short-term profits, meeting the quarterly numbers expected by analysts, and the stock price. They go on to suggest that the core of this short-term mentality is learned by business leaders in American MBA schools.[3]

Our experience of short-term focus supports this thought. We have seen many situations working in U.S. companies where short-term tactical moves to achieve immediate sales improvement or profit increase to achieve quarterly targets have resulted in undermining longer-term competitive advantage. Sometimes this has delayed or even stopped the introduction of new products or services while resources have been diverted to short-term marketing campaigns.

Other times, innovative projects designed to improve the customer experience to preempt new competitors have been shelved in favor of short-term incentives to placate dissatisfied customers. Also initiatives designed to build customer culture have been diluted midstream with a change of senior leadership or a short-term crisis with the sales numbers. These experiences are all too common, not only in the United States but also in other western countries.

But it doesn't have to be that way. A key competitive advantage is a customer culture that incorporates *competitor foresight*—a shared set of behaviors across the organization, led from the top, that fosters activities taken in the present to identify and act on potential future competitors. These behaviors spur the entrepreneurial and innovative spirit in leaders and their teams to take actions that will enable the business to compete for its future. They go hand in hand with customer foresight—a future-oriented view of changing customer needs. Strong competitor foresight will also provide clues as to the form future competitors will take and who some of the most likely candidates will be. It is more than likely that many of your new competitors don't yet exist, but when they do, they will enter your market with a different business model. This is a time of unprecedented change and low barriers to competitive entry in a large number of industries that provide an ever-increasing spectrum of choices for customers to fill the same need. So competitor foresight provides a key advantage for corporate sustainability.

It is not enough that just the senior executives engage in future thinking and competitor foresight. It requires creativity and innovation to form competitor foresight and act on a strategy for the future. Research has shown it is not the problem *solvers* who are needed to chart the future. It is the problem *finders*—those people who can sort through vast amounts of information, often from multiple disciplines, and creatively experiment with a variety of different approaches to identify the competitive problems of the future.[4] These people may sit anywhere in the organization. Once the key future competitive problems are found, they need to be acted on, not by just a few, but by the entire organization.

Figure 2.1 highlights competitor foresight as the focus of this chapter. The goal is for companies to improve their absolute and relative strength in this discipline. The score of 100 percent means that

The Business Case

Imagine This Situation

Imagine these potential future competitive threats:

- Your industry converging with another industry, creating new competitors
- Overall sales volume in your market becoming static or declining
- Innovators carving out new adjacent markets
- Substitution of the value you offer occurring with new and different value propositions of emerging competitors

Is this happening in your industry? If it isn't, it probably will be . . . sooner than you think.

What's Your Response?

Is it to hunker down, focus on protecting your existing products and markets, and ignore the possible impacts of new competitors?
Or
Take action to preempt new competitors by cannibalizing your own products and services through new product and services innovation?

What's the Difference?

Strong competitor foresight discipline identifies opportunities and fuels innovation, which results in revenue growth and successful new products and services that preempt the impacts of new competitors.

Link to Business Performance

This measures a business's ability to account for future competitors and their strategies and create new products and value propositions. This behavioral trait impacts innovation and new-product success and drives longer-term competitive advantage.

(Continued)

Link to Strategy:

Strength in this discipline is particularly relevant to two types of competitive strategies, both of which require a longer-term commitment:

a) One designed to defend competitive position against new competitors in the medium to longer term in industries experiencing market shifts

b) One to increase market share by creating a new competitive advantage in a new emerging market

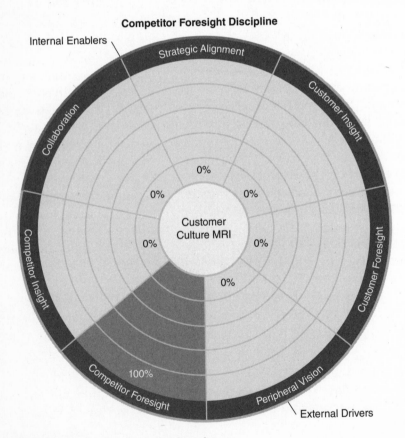

Figure 5.1 Competitor foresight discipline

a company is above all others in our MRI global database in terms of competitor foresight behaviors.

What Is Competitor Foresight?

Does the company consider potential competitors when making decisions? Does it identify market shifts in order to identify potential competitors? Does staff feed in competitive intelligence relating to potential new competitors and how they might affect future customer needs?

Answers to these questions will provide an indication as to what extent your business has competitor foresight.

A strong competitor foresight discipline identifies opportunities and fuels innovation that results in revenue growth and successful new products and services that preempt the impacts of new competitors. It is a future-oriented discipline. An in-depth view of emerging competitors is central to understanding future competitive threats. Competitor foresight is a capability that enables a company to really understand what impact emerging competitors are likely to have and position itself for success. The implications of low performance on this measure have a significant impact on businesses, as they simply are not able to compete effectively in the future.

How does your company stay ahead of potential competitors? Which businesses should it cannibalize before its competitors do it for them? How does your company address the threat of future competition? Are staff members actively aware of and signaling new competitive threats and their likely impact on your customers and businesses?

Leaders and all other employees in the business need to know how emerging competitors are likely to impact the value they are delivering and what changes they can make to preempt the impact of future competitors' offers. With this foresight, every leader, team, and individual can evaluate the value they are providing for customers within a future-oriented competitive lens.

Why Is Competitor Foresight a Cultural Discipline?

It is one thing to gain insight on current competitors. It is quite another to gain competitive intelligence and a pervasive discipline throughout the company relating to possible future competitors.

There are many examples of companies that have identified future competitive threats but have been unable to take action to preempt those threats or become part of the new competitive paradigm until they lost their leadership position. One of the most famous is Kodak. The company invented the digital (filmless) camera, but it was unable to make the full transition to the digital world until it was too late.

In a world of rapid change in which new competitors emerge and can grow rapidly without warning, it is not possible to preempt or counteract their impact on your future unless competitor foresight is built in as a cultural discipline across the business. What this does is to spur innovation for the future that can act as a competitive shield. It also creates vigilance across the entire organization to identify early warning signs of innovation by existing or new competitors that could impact future markets and customer value. It also creates a preparedness by staff members in all functions of a business to act quickly if there is a need to do so. There are many examples of companies that have waited too long or were not quick enough to act. Most of the incumbent telecommunications companies that controlled printed yellow pages advertising did not see or act on the revolutionary impact of Google on the advertising industry soon enough to be among the first to surf the new wave.

Until 2008, Starbucks had experienced 25 years of continuous growth and profitability. It dominated the premium coffee market in the United States and had been successful in a number of other countries as well. In the two years before the global financial crisis it lowered its standards to accommodate massive growth and lost sight of what it was that helped Starbucks succeed—unmatched customer experience and emotional connection with loyal customers. They also had rising competition in the coffee sector. What hit Starbucks out of the blue came from a completely unexpected quarter. Even though, since 1993, McDonald's had operated a chain of premium coffee shops under the name McCafé in many countries outside the United States, it was not considered an important competitor. McDonald's had opened its first McCafé premium coffee store in the United States in 2001 but closed it within a year. However, in 2007 it expanded its specialty espresso coffee section in U.S. McDonald's stores. This was a long overdue move by McDonald's. Research showed that there was demand for less-expensive relative quality coffee to Starbucks. This loss of competitor foresight as a cultural discipline along with the negative impact on customer experience of changes in stores meant that Starbucks was ill-prepared. It required the return of Howard Schultz, the founder, to lead a transformation of the Starbucks business. The story of this transformation is told in Chapter 9.[5]

Who Has It?

In 1993 Samsung embarked on a program to transform into a global powerhouse with a relentless investment both in resources and culture to compete for the future. Its so-called New Management initiative used competitor foresight to fuel innovation. Twenty years after its inception the spirit of competition has borne fruit. Samsung is adaptive, innovative, and customer-focused, borne out by its global leadership in core businesses of smartphones, semiconductors, and TV sets and its spectacular growth in revenue and profitability in recent years.[6] Samsung Electronics Co., Ltd. is now the world's largest technology company in terms of revenues. In 2011, Samsung ranked second on the list of U.S. top patent assignees. More patents strengthen Samsung's position among its competitors but also illustrate its innovativeness and competitiveness for the future.[7] Samsung's restructuring in 2012 has three goals: first, to fill the entire product lineup with world-best products; second, to improve relations with its global partners, including Sony and Apple; and, third, to shift its paradigm to a "Software Driven Company."[8]

Samsung's history and plans for the future show it to be a company with competitor foresight as a discipline and a key part of its customer culture. It also shows that it can take many years to build a really strong competitor foresight culture that translates into innovation and market leadership. Combined with customer foresight this discipline is a decisive means of creating and retaining long-term competitive advantage.

The Virgin Group, a central support function for the Virgin businesses, conducts wide-ranging studies across many industries to identify future gaps. Its core businesses are in travel and transportation, media and telephony, health and wellness, leisure and entertainment, and financial services. Its customer culture includes strong competitor foresight. It is known to be seeking industries in which there is a history of poor customer experience such as airlines and banking and where innovation and a sense of fun are lacking. It aims to compete for the future in those industries using a customer-centric approach. Virgin Galactic is pioneering the future of space travel as a result of seeing that NASA was not going to provide this service for a consumer market.

The business philosophy is to enter industries where consumers are getting a bad deal and to innovate in those industries in a way that will also provide sustainable financial returns. The idea of radical innovation and sustainable financial returns are thought of internally as the "Virgin paradox." It requires a forward-looking competitive mentality that sees longer-term competitive advantage and profitability. A cultural capability to identify industries that could benefit from the Virgin approach requires an ability to envision what the future industry and the competitive landscape might look like. While not successful every time, Virgin has been able to choose industries in which it can get and sustain a competitive advantage. Virgin Radio is an example of a business that has been developed with competitor foresight. Careful analysis of current and expected future competitors along with customer insight has resulted in the successful establishment of radio stations in Thailand, Canada, India, the Emirates, Italy, France, Turkey, and more recently Lebanon. CEO Ian Grace says: "We focus on the consumer and the market dynamics first and foremost and create radio stations designed to fulfill the listener expectation in that particular market. The product or offering is not generic. It is based on cultural and listener expectations in each respective territory."[9]

How Do You Develop Competitor Foresight?

Competitor foresight starts with the individual. It is a view held from a young age when you decide to invest in your own future. You borrow to go to college to get an education and knowledge that will make you competitive in the jobs marketplace. As time goes on and circumstances change, you invest (time and money) in further education, experience, and new skills to remain competitive. These investments and the accompanying longer-term view enable you to become more flexible, adaptable, and employable and to compete for your future. For entrepreneurs, it is to invest in an idea that becomes a new product or service. In both cases it requires a vision of a future that you want to create and be a part of.

When we consider this as a shared discipline in a company, we find that this is much more difficult to create in large established businesses, but is often part of the culture that is retained in start-ups. Even in successful start-ups, as they become larger, more established, and more complex through added products and services, it takes a deliberate focus on the part of the leaders to maintain competitor foresight. It can become even more difficult with mergers and acquisitions, when companies that were once competitors become one business. Another factor, particularly with technology companies, is the maverick inventor who is so far ahead of his time that he is not able to inspire his vision in others or it is just seen to be too focused on the long term. A friend and colleague, Len Hughes, who worked most of his life in Silicon Valley technology businesses after his first job in the computer industry with Digital Equipment Corporation, told us that almost all tech companies have a visionary maverick who is well ahead of his time and finds it hard to connect with the rest of the organization.[10]

Martin Cooper of Motorola is considered to be the inventor of the first practical mobile phone. On April 3, 1973, he called a rival at AT&T's Bell Labs on the first Motorola prototype. He envisioned a world where people would walk around with devices planted in their bodies. He had the idea that the phone number would be a part of you and that if you just thought about calling a friend the phone would automatically call the number.[11] This was too visionary for Motorola, which left other companies to lead the way.

A Kodak engineer credited with inventing the digital camera has revealed how his fellow executives couldn't see why anyone would ever want to look at images on a TV screen when he first proposed the idea of a "filmless camera" to them in 1975. The first prototype was developed by Steve Sasson and his team from the Kodak Apparatus Division Research Laboratory. When company executives asked Sasson how long it would be before his invention had consumer potential, the inventor said 15 to 20 years.[12] This was too long for Kodak, and even though it was an early entrant with digital cameras in the early 1990s, it was not committed to that technology's future, and other companies led the way.

A new future was born when Robert Noyce, the visionary, and Gordon Moore, the researcher, broke away from Fairchild Semiconductor with six colleagues in 1968 to form Intel; later they appointed Andy Grove (who was there from the start) as CEO. For them it was all about challenge and discovery, and as a team they created the future that was to become Silicon Valley. The long lead times and large investments needed to build chip-manufacturing capacity has helped continue the future competitive orientation that has enabled Intel to maintain its global lead as a chip manufacturer to the present day.[13] Its preference for insiders to be appointed CEO and hold tenure for several years has reinforced this culture. The latest appointee in May 2013, Brian Krzanich, has had 30 years with the company.

It seems that this discipline of competitor foresight is created by a curiosity for new things, a vision of what could be, and a preparedness to invest in one's own vision and continually take on new challenges. Lance Uggla, CEO of Markit, a global financial services firm, has maintained this discipline over the 10 years since start-up. Richard Branson has nurtured a curiosity for "what could be" in the Virgin Group as a way of developing a competitor foresight discipline through leaders in the Virgin businesses.

To take hold in a company it requires visionary leadership that permeates throughout the company as a part of its culture. Both Uggla and Branson are visionaries.

What Behaviors Draw Out Competitor Foresight?

How can we ensure that everyone in the organization has an understanding of potential new competitors? When leaders and their teams take time to discuss what gaps might occur in their future markets, what will be required to fill them, and who their competitors are likely to be, they are developing competitor foresight. By gathering competitive intelligence and actively discussing how the industry structure might change with emerging new competitors, individuals and teams will gain competitor foresight. Examples of competitor foresight behaviors include the following activities:

- Monitoring potential future competitors
- Tracking global trends in industry competitive changes
- Making decisions with future competitors in mind
- Discussing and clarifying how future competitors' offers can impact the value of one's own products and services
- Identifying areas where potential competitors could succeed
- Monitoring changes to barriers to entry and future industry structure's impact on potential new competitive entries
- Mapping the convergence of one's industry with adjacent industries
- Sharing competitor foresight across functions and teams

By sharing this knowledge throughout the company and individual teams employees are able to use competitor foresight to contribute to innovations that will create future value for customers. The company will also be able to compete in the future against existing competitors and new ones that may emerge.

What Are Some of the Best Practices?

Having competitor foresight behaviors as a discipline makes companies very successful in competing for the future, as it creates new markets. The following examples of best practices illustrate the importance of competitor foresight to a company's customer culture and sustaining its competitive advantage.

Google: Using Competitor Foresight to Strengthen Competitive Advantage

Google is a company with deep competitor foresight. It has along history of outmaneuvering both its current and future competitors. As a future-orientated innovator Google is always looking around the corner for what's next for its users, whether it is a new way to access the world of information via Google Glass (a futuristic-looking pair of Internet-enabled glasses)[14] or a novel means of accessing the web via weather balloon, as is the case in a remote part of New Zealand.[15]

The company has managed to keep one step ahead of potential competitors through a combination of long-range internally generated innovations and smart acquisitions designed to plug holes in its user offering. Google has purchased more than 100 companies in the past 10 years with the goal of ensuring it continues to be the preferred search company. When it saw competitors such as Jumptap growing rapidly in the mobile advertising space, it purchased AdMob, a platform for mobile advertising. As customer usage has shifted from computers to mobile devices, Google has moved quickly to position itself in emerging search and advertising markets. It has developed the Android mobile operating system and purchased Motorola Mobility. When Google saw competitors moving into the local search markets, it purchased Zagat to bring more value to users by providing restaurant reviews as part of its local search results.

Google is constantly monitoring the technology environment, looking for opportunities to add capability to its current offerings and keep ahead of future competition. Its latest acquisition of a free Global Positioning System (GPS) application called Waze was a move designed to keep its lead as the preferred mapping and mobile device navigation provider after Apple launched Apple Maps in 2012. Waze differs from traditional GPS navigation software, as it is a community-driven application that learns from users' driving times to provide routing and real-time traffic updates. Additionally, people can report accidents, traffic jams, speed cameras or traps, and any number of things others would find useful. Google outbid competitors Microsoft and Yahoo! to purchase YouTube, which now generates more than \$4 billion in revenue, according to Morgan Stanley estimates.[16] This move also made it difficult for future competitors to enter the video space.

Google could see the future of the web evolving to increasingly include more and more video. So far it has been proven right. As of 2013 more than 100 hours of video are uploaded every minute.[17]

Google also saw Apple as a future competitor with its domination of the early smartphone market. As a result of this shift to mobile devices Google developed the Android operating system, and as of July 2013 it is the leading mobile platform in terms of users worldwide.

Google's culture of innovation and willingness to both develop and purchase new innovations has kept it ahead of potential competitors.

This is a capability built into the Google culture. People in that organization are curious, always on the lookout for what is next. They are creating new services internally and always looking externally at what other companies are doing that will fit with the company's portfolio.

Verizon and Telstra: Going Head to Head for a Future Market

America's largest telecommunications company (telco), Verizon, is driving hard for corporate customers with its secure Internet and cloud computing products in the Asia-Pacific region. The move into the region puts Verizon in direct competition with Telstra, the large Australian telco that wants its international arm to sell more global data and telecommunications services to companies with offices around Asia.

Verizon also wants more business with Australian corporations. It already provides telecommunications for some Australian government departments and for companies in the financial services, mining, and manufacturing industries. It is also aiming to provide cloud-computing services to medium-sized companies that have only Australian operations.[18]

But how well prepared are these companies for the battle ahead? For Telstra, this type of heavyweight competition is relatively new, and collaboration with new partners in Asia will be important. Telstra's Asian success has been mixed in the past. For Verizon, the Asian markets will pose a new challenge. It will be aiming to sell new disruptive solutions to new customers. This is much harder and riskier to do than selling products that everyone understands to customers you already know.

Which company is best positioned to win this battle? Will it be Verizon, with its larger infrastructure and resources, or Telstra, with its traditionally stronger links in Australian and Asian markets? The answer will ultimately turn on the relative strengths of their customer cultures—their understanding of current and future customer needs and future competitive threats and the ability of their entire organizations to deliver superior value for corporate customers. Their cultures will need to be resilient enough to understand, adapt to, and act on their current and future competitors' strategies and create opportunities that will require product and service innovations.

How Prepared Is Telstra?

Telstra conducts future competitor analysis by assessing market opportunities and threats created by Skype, Viber, Google, and other players that impact the value received by Telstra's customers. Telstra leaders also look for early warning signals provided by staff and shared through the social media network Yammer, used internally by Telstra. There is complete transparency in Yammer for all to see.

The Telstra Strategy Group decides what areas and which competitors to monitor, and the Research Insights Analytics (RIA) group disseminates this information throughout the business and provides special reports to parts of the business that face imminent competitive risks.

The RIA group provides ongoing consolidation of competitive information that continually builds on foresight about future competition. Just how important this is as a mobilizer for action is highlighted in the looming competitive battle with Verizon in the Asia-Pacific marketplace.

PerkinElmer: Making Science Mobile

The world of science continues to rapidly evolve as discoveries unlock new possibilities for the future of humanity. Ray Kurzweil has popularized the convergence of man and machine in his book *The Singularity Is Near*—a world where human intelligence will be supercharged by technology. Stem cell research that allows scientists to combine DNA in a manner that reduces the possibilities of human disease was recently highlighted in the TV series *Through the Wormhole.*

Within this context, the leadership of PerkinElmer is looking to get ahead of their future competition. Robin Smith is a visionary entrepreneur and currently the vice president of R&D for Informatics. He joined the company when his company was acquired in 2011. He along with Mike Stapleton, the division's CEO, and Clive Higgins, the vice president of marketing, have seen the future for the scientific laboratory. They believe that the future will be heavily influenced by mobile technologies such as smartphones and tablets that will enable scientists to continue to push the limits of science in an ever-more-productive fashion.

PerkinElmer is a global scientific instruments and technology corporation, focused in the business areas of human and environmental health. Among other things, it produces highly sophisticated analytical instruments that enable farmers to test soil quality and governments to test air quality. It also makes medical imaging equipment that allows prenatal screening. The Informatics division provides a software suite equivalent to a scientific version of Microsoft Office.

The consumer mobile revolution has been underway for a number of years already, but in the business-to-business environment the penetration of mobile applications has been much slower.

The Informatics division has a history of driving new innovations into the science lab. As a major player in the electronic laboratory notebook business, PerkinElmer has provided the tools to transition scientists from pen and paper to more productive and collaborative technology-based systems.

With market disruption occurring at an increasingly faster pace in the technology world, many business models are being upended, and PerkinElmer has not been immune to this potential.

Hans Keil, the business line leader for desktop mobile apps, along with Robin Smith act as the internal evangelists for this coming wave of change. In their presentations on where science is heading they cite many examples of new mobile applications that leverage the power and mobility of smartphones and tablets to create powerful new tools.

Consumers are being empowered to easily track and share physical information such as bike rides on sites like Strava.com and runs on the Nike+ website. This is now extending into monitoring sleep, health, vital signs, and so on. With the unique properties of devices like the iPhone, with its accelerometer and gyroscope (used to track the device's physical movement) and the application software platform, the possibilities are endless.

With low-cost, easy-to-use accessories to the iPhone, consumers can now test whether their food is organic or not, what allergens may be contained in the food, its levels of fructose, and so on. What are the implications for PerkinElmer's traditional instrument business? Will these new consumer-orientated technologies move up in sophistication and capability? How will a $100,000 analytic instrument compete with a $500 mobile app accessory that in the future will do essentially the same thing?

The answer in the short term is for PerkinElmer to get into the mobile app business. In June 2013 it launched its first iPad applications designed for chemists. It was a smart choice. The team leveraged an existing popular desktop application called ChemDraw to produce a complementary iPad application. The application extends the value of the desktop application by taking advantage of the unique collaboration and portability capabilities of the iPad platform.

With Hans Keil conducting extensive customer usability testing and gathering insights from customers, the chances of a successful launch were high.

Mary-Ann Moore, the executive director of marketing communications, and her team were able to go to market with an exciting new product that was well received by customers, with an average 4.5-star rating. The application has quickly entered the top 10 apps (from more than 20,000) in the education and learning segment of the Apple iTunes Store.

With leaders like these willing to push the boundaries, Perkin Elmer is well positioned to compete for the future.

This major trend toward mobile computing is a trend impacting all businesses. How are you responding to this shift? Are your future competitors already leveraging these technologies to disrupt your future business?

CHAPTER SUMMARY

Why is competing for the future important?

Strong competitor foresight discipline identifies opportunities and fuels innovation that results in revenue growth and successful new products and services that preempt the impacts of new competitors. Without it, companies will be swept away by those innovative companies that implement new business models that create more value for customers.

What is competitor foresight?

An in-depth view of emerging and potential new competitors is central to understanding future competitive threats and opportunities. Competitor foresight is a capability that enables a company to really understand who those competitors might be, what impact they are likely to have, and what action to take to position itself for future success against those competitors.

Why is competitor foresight a cultural discipline?

There are many examples of companies that have identified future competitive threats but have been unable to take action to preempt those threats or become part of the new competitive paradigm until they have lost their leadership position. For companies to be adaptive and in a position to act quickly, they need shared values, mindset, and behaviors around investing for the future with a longer-term competitor perspective.

What behaviors lead to competitor foresight?

By tracking and reporting on industry competitive changes, identifying areas of competitive convergence (such as the printer and photocopy industries), and actively discussing how to plan and invest for future competitive threats and opportunities, individuals and teams will gain competitor foresight. By sharing this knowledge and activities across the business, all functions gain foresight into what they need to plan and do to compete for the future.

(Continued)

Leader's Guide to Competitor Foresight

Competitor Foresight: *Does the company consider potential competitors when making decisions? Does it identify market shifts in order to identify potential competitors? Do staff members feed in competitive intelligence relating to potential new competitors and how they might affect future customer needs?*

Rating descriptors: 0 = never; 1 = almost never; 2 = rarely; 3 = occasionally; 4 = sometimes; 5 = regularly; 6 = frequently; 7 = often; 8 = very often; 9 = constantly; 10 = all the time.

Rate where *you and your team* stand on competitor foresight by checking the relevant box in answering each question.

☐ 1. To what extent do you and your team monitor potential future competitors?

☐ 2. To what extent do you track global trends in industry competitive changes?

☐ 3. To what extent do you make decisions with future competitors in mind?

☐ 4. To what extent do you discuss and clarify how future competitors' offers can impact the value of your own products and services?

☐ 5. To what extent do you identify areas where potential competitors could succeed?

☐ 6. To what extent do you monitor changes to barriers to entry and future industry structure's impact on potential new competitive entries?

☐ 7. To what extent do you map the convergence of your industry with adjacent industries?

☐ 8. To what extent do you share foresight from this intelligence throughout the team to enable employees to use competitor foresight to create future value for customers?

☐ 9. To what extent do you create opportunities for people from different functions to discuss ideas about potential future competitive impacts on your business?

☐ 10. To what extent do you form teams to simulate future competitor entry strategies and how your company will plan for them?

Chapter 6

Tectonic Shifts

Seeing what is happening and responding effectively is a key capability. Arrive too early for the party and there are no guests, arrive too late and you are cleaning up the trash.

—George Day[1]

Several years ago when the Google Books project, which aims to digitize all of the world's printed books, was getting started, the librarian from one of the universities that had signed up for the plan met with Google's two cofounders. When the two asked the librarian if he had any concerns he said, "I'm wondering what happens to all this stuff when Google no longer exists." Later, after that encounter, he said, "I've never seen two young people looking so stunned. The idea that Google might not exist one day never crossed their minds."[2]

Under Andy Grove's leadership and subsequent CEOs, Intel has become the world's largest chip maker and one of the most admired companies in the world. In *Only the Paranoid Survive*[3] Grove reveals his strategy of focusing on a new way of measuring the nightmare moment every leader dreads—when massive change occurs and a company must, virtually overnight, adapt or fall by the wayside.

Grove calls such a moment a strategic inflection point, which can be set off by almost anything: megacompetition, a change in regulations, shifts in consumer behavior, or disruptive technology. When a strategic inflection point hits, the ordinary rules of business go out the window. Yet, managed right, a strategic inflection point can be an opportunity to win in the marketplace and emerge stronger than ever. But there are two things needed to profit from a strategic inflection point—first, to see it coming, and, second, to have the mindset and the cultural and strategic capability to make the change—rapidly, if necessary.

The Business Case

Imagine This Situation
Imagine you are facing this situation:

- A massive shift from your physical products to online delivery (as in book publishing, news, education, retail, advertising)
- A huge disruptive technology substituting your current business model and value for customers (as in the shift from personal computers to mobile devices affecting the computer industry; as in the shift toward different energy sources and generation options affecting the energy industry)
- A shift in regulation compliance (as in the finance industry)
- A shift in demographics and social communication (affecting all consumer markets and many business-to-business markets)

What's Your Response?

Is it to try to protect what you have by becoming more efficient and focused to serve your customers better using your current business model?
Or
To recognize and act on these fundamental shifts to reinvent your business and how it delivers value to its marketplace?

What's the Difference?

An ability to recognize these shifts and act on them requires a cultural discipline reflected in workforce behaviors and prevalent activities that give the company a deep understanding of its broader external environment. This fuels innovation without which the company risks substantial, sometimes catastrophic, loss from market shifts. Changes in technology, economic conditions, government policies, and society all impact current and future customer needs.

We have called this discipline *peripheral vision.*

Link to Business Performance

This measures a business's ability to scan, sense, and act on threats and opportunities emerging in its external environment and impacts innovation. Those companies that have it show capabilities of effective innovation that drive future sales and profit growth from new market opportunities. It builds longer-term competitive advantage.

Link to Strategy

Strength in this discipline is particularly relevant to an innovation strategy reflected in two types of strategies:

a) One based on new products and services as the means for growth and profitability

b) One requiring a new business model to cope with disruptive technological changes

Experience shows us that new ideas and resulting innovation can come from internal and external sources—staff members from all departments, suppliers, contractors, customers, and competitors. Are your staff members actively encouraged to signal threats and opportunities observed in the external environment? Is there a mechanism for logging these and taking action on those that have merit? Are your people rewarded for communicating ideas related to the changing external environment that are acted on by the company?

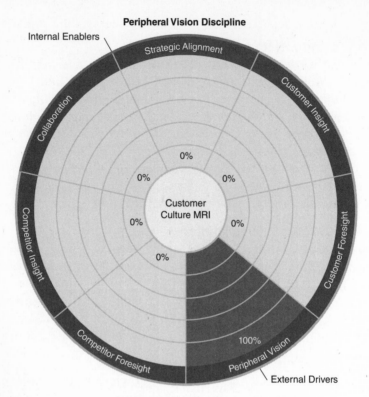

Figure 6.1 Peripheral vision discipline

Figure 6.1 highlights peripheral vision as the focus of this chapter. The goal is for companies to improve their absolute and relative strength in this discipline. The score of 100 percent means that a company is above all others in our MRI global database in terms of peripheral vision practices.

Tectonic Shifts

In the words of one CEO who is a keen surfer: "I don't know if my people have their surfboards out ready to plunge into the ocean, let alone being ready to surf the next wave." He as well as many others are aware that tectonic shifts are with us or imminent, but they are also concerned that their organizations are not prepared for them or capable of adapting to them.

A tectonic shift is defined as having a strong and widespread impact requiring a paradigm shift in the way in which business is done. Tectonic shifts fundamentally change a firm's market environment and require specific behaviors across the business that detect the potential impact and create a shared understanding and capability to respond.

Customer culture requires the consideration of all external forces and trends that affect the creation of value for customers. What is valuable and appropriate for customers is continually being shaped by external factors in the market environment (political, economic, social, environmental, and technological). Leaders and their teams must consider these forces if they are to fully understand their markets and customers now and in the future. Strong *peripheral vision* enables a business to effectively innovate to develop and deliver new products and services with value relevant to shifts in its markets and the emergence of entirely new markets.

In this chapter the discipline of *peripheral vision* to enhance a customer culture is discussed and examples are used to illustrate how these behaviors are developed and strengthened.[4] Richard Branson is an example of an individual leader with peripheral vision. His moves lead us to think about the tectonic shifts taking place in so many industries such as media advertising, education, news media, retail, publishing, and energy.

As a director of AGL, Australia's oldest energy company, John Stanhope says, "At AGL we need peripheral vision—the mindset and capability to understand and respond to our customers' needs and be proactive with the disruptive technologies that will undermine our current business."[5] He says peripheral vision is alerting directors and senior management to the threats and opportunities coming from battery and other disruptive technologies that will eventually transform the energy business.

The story of what has happened to bookshops illustrates the force of tectonic shifts. Megabookshop chains Borders and Barnes & Noble dominated the sale of books in the United States for decades until around the year 2000 when the force of Amazon.com, launched in 1995, started to be felt. Borders was unable to survive it. The company expanded its physical presence but failed to embrace the digital revolution spurred on by Amazon.com. Borders shops closed, and its online store bought by Pearson has been rebranded as Bookworld.[6] An American icon had disappeared into history.

Amazon.com has fueled online purchasing and growth of books, digital devices like Kindle, and e-books. But embracing the digital world does not mean you can necessarily make the transition. Barnes & Noble, the largest bricks-and-mortar bookstore retailer in the United States, has invested heavily in online book sales. Its tablet device, the Nook, competes with Kindle and new devices from companies such as Samsung and Apple. As of early 2013, Nook was still losing money and was declining in sales along with a decline in all e-reader sales, and Barnes & Noble's digital content sales such as e-books were declining against the previous year while the market for digital content grew.[7]

What seems to have happened in just two or three years is that while rationalizing their number of retail outlets and investing heavily online, Barnes & Noble has lost its fundamental competitive advantage—superior customer experience. In 2010, it was the *highest-rated retailer* when it comes to "customer experience," according to Forrester's 2010 Customer Experience Index. In 2012, the company had become one of the *fastest falling retailers on the list.*[8] In 2011, *Amazon.com was number one among all retailers*—physical and online—in customer service according to the Temkin Experience Ratings. In 2012 it was *number two.*[9]

This reflects a weakening of Barnes & Noble's customer culture in making the transition into the digital world against a digital specialist—Amazon.com. These examples illustrate that while companies may have the vision to identify the market shifts, they do not always have a customer culture that gives them the capability to transform effectively.

Disruptive Technology and Digitization

Disruption of traditional ways of doing business is occurring through new technologies and digitization. Both affect the viability of the business models of industry incumbents. The energy industry is an example where new technologies will have a big impact.

Traditional electric utilities are on the verge of facing massive competition. The barriers to entry have fallen, and a large number of new and old companies have entered the power generation business. Numerous and diverse competitors—nonutilities—have already entered the electricity business. Wind farms are expanding. More than a hundred Silicon Valley start-ups are developing new power technologies. Many of these have venture capital funding. Several like the Bloom Box fuel cell, have the potential to transform the industry by bringing power generation to the home. Real estate companies and builders are supplying rooftop solar panels on new homes. Schools, government buildings, and businesses are deploying their own solar panels.

Tie these disruptive technologies to consumer and business resistance to higher energy prices and an increasing drive to seek out lower-cost alternatives and we will soon see the competitive floodgates open. That will put at risk the traditional players with large traditional infrastructure investments.

It is not clear where all of this is going to go. Everything is in the mix—technology, the economy, politics, globalization, and societal trends toward "green and clean." The government plays a big part with its energy policy along with regulation, subsidies, and incentives for various parts of the industry.

The one factor that is common to the longer-term success of each player in this industry is the *adaptability* of its corporate culture that comes from having peripheral vision as a discipline.

The digital revolution is also playing a part in disrupting industries. For example, FitNow, launched in 2008, produces Lose It!, the top application in the iPhone's health and fitness category. FitNow is based on the premise that your phone is always with you and is the perfect platform for tracking your calories. It has more than 10 million customers. This business with less than 10 employees is extremely focused on assessing digital customer feedback, revising the app regularly, and adding new benefits like social connections among users. It is continually looking at ways to add benefits without increasing costs.

There are a growing band of companies like this—digital disruptors using platforms such as iPhone and iPad apps and Facebook to reach millions of people. These new companies have just a few people and move almost at lightning speed. They ignore competitors and traditional channels to market and go directly to end customers. Their costs are low, so their margin per customer is high enough to generate profit through volume.[10]

The traditional publishing and media industries are undergoing a tectonic shift. Book publishing is changing at each point in the value chain—from authoring, "print-on-demand" publishing technology, to digitization and distribution. Traditional newspaper companies are facing the economic challenges of reduced circulation eroded by other media and the need to operate both online and physical product businesses.

We are all now in a faster-moving, more competitive digital environment, no matter what we make and sell. So consider this: if there are low barriers to entry in your business and competitors are able to compete with you easily off a low-cost base and from all directions, what will you need to do differently?

Probably a lot of things. This type of disruption usually requires a transformative change to the way you do things. A good start is to quickly review those things that drive competitiveness, growth, and profitability in your business. You will find that there will be a need to change peoples' habits around speed of innovation and new products and services to market. There will be a need to gain greater insight into customers and how their needs are changing. You will need to look for some benchmarks from these disruptive competitors. But most of all, you will need to embark on a journey to strengthen your customer culture, particularly peripheral vision.

What Is Peripheral Vision?

This discipline, reflected in workforce behaviors and prevalent activities, gives the leader and team a deep and dynamic understanding of their broader external environment. Without these strong drivers, they will miss opportunities and risk loss of customers due to market and industry shifts. Strength in this discipline gives the ability to act to shift emphasis and discard legacy products and technologies. Changes in technology, economic conditions, government policies, and society all impact current and future customer needs.

Peripheral vision is the extent to which employees monitor, predict, and make decisions in consideration of emerging trends in the business environment that have the potential to impact customer needs and the value being offered by the organization. *Customer-centricity requires the consideration of all external forces and trends that affect the creation and delivery of value for customers.* The business environment consists of the following five elements:

- **Political factors:** changes or events related to politics or legislation, such as new laws and regulations, political party dominance, or political stability
- **Economic factors:** changes or trends related to economics, such as labor, interest rates, or economic cycles
- **Societal factors:** changes or trends involving demographics, such as age, nationality, and consumer preferences
- **Environmental factors:** changes or trends in the natural environment, such as climate change, that create threats or opportunities
- **Technology factors:** changes or trends in technology and innovation, such as new business processes or disruptive technologies

What is valuable and appropriate for customers is continually being shaped by these five factors of peripheral vision. Teams must consider these forces if they are to fully understand their markets and customers now and in the future. For a company to have strong peripheral vision, it needs the capability and behaviors to identify these tectonic shifts, the insights to understand the change in value taking place, and the ability to create excellent customer experience in the new environment as well as retaining it in its traditional marketplace.

Why Is Peripheral Vision a Cultural Discipline?

This capability goes beyond just recognizing the shifts that will occur. It needs leaders who can mobilize the business to effectively respond at the appropriate time. It means building in a discipline that creates a shared vision of what is unfolding in the marketplace of the future and an adaptability by leaders and teams to shift from what they are doing to focus on changed priorities.

Kodak, Motorola, and Nortel: Failing to Make the Tectonic Shift?

Kodak cofounder George Eastman had a vision: "One day the camera would be small enough so everyone would carry one in a shirt pocket."' Motorola had an equally exciting vision: "One day we would all be connected without wires." Nortel's view was also visionary—that voice, data, and images would extend to every person and device in the world.[11] All three visions were correct in their direction and predictive of the market shifts that would occur. However, these incumbents did not see it through. It was entirely new firms that made this happen. It was not a case of these firms being blindsided, because they saw it coming and tried to react. They were well-known brands and technology leaders with a global customer base. What was the common missing piece?

They did not embed peripheral vision across the business—the shared early warning system, the willingness and capability to act and change the business model in line with changes in customer behavior. In each case, the discipline of peripheral vision behavior was not part of their cultural DNA.

Intel: Slow to Move on the Tectonic Shift to Mobility

Intel is one of the most successful and enduring companies in Silicon Valley. It has a 45-year history of success. It has managed to successfully surf tectonic shifts like getting out of the memory business in 1985 to focus on microprocessors and more recently retain a leading position in the move from desktop processors to laptops. But its move to bridge the shift to mobiles has been slow. Paul Otellini, who retired as CEO from Intel in May 2013, has peripheral vision. Back in 2005 when he took over as CEO, he could see all the structural changes taking place in many industries and sensed that the world was going "mobile." He saw that Intel had to make low-priced chips for low-cost consumer devices, and he exhorted his top team to move on this. It wasn't until around 2010 that Intel as an organization started to aggressively act on this tectonic shift away from PCs to mobile devices of all kinds. Otellini wasn't able to get the Intel wheels turning fast enough or early enough. It took five years before Intel acted on the explosion of mobile devices.[12]

In June 2013, Intel launched the Haswell chip, known as the fourth-generation core, that is its first-ever high-performance chip built from the ground up for mobile computing. It will be joined later in 2013 by another family of chips known as Bay Trail for the smartphone and tablet markets. Tom Kilroy, executive vice president of the sales and marketing group, says: "This is our largest generation leap ever."[13]

Even though it has been slow to orient the entire organization to this market shift, Intel is now making the move. Time will tell what this lack of faster market adaptability has cost the company. But given its history of successfully making strategic shifts and its culture that is not tied to the cult of its CEO, you would bet in its favor.

These observations point to the challenges large companies have in transitioning tectonic shifts like this shift to mobility. It requires:

1. A balancing of the focus on important current competitors and future changes in market conditions and knowing when to shift emphasis as an organization—balancing the longer term risks and opportunities with short term to medium term competitive pressures
2. An understanding of how customer and market trends are shifting in response to external changes such as disruptive technology, work and lifestyle changes, economic impacts, and political and legislative influences—having peripheral vision of the future
3. The capability of the organization to shift its emphasis from current markets to future markets—having peripheral vision as a cultural discipline

Westpac Bank: Developing Peripheral Vision as a Discipline

Jason Yetton, head of Australian Financial Services, explains how peripheral vision as a discipline is being strengthened at Westpac Bank.

He says Westpac's 2017 strategic plan builds in flexibility for shifts in market priorities in terms of timing, resources, and people. He and other executives in the company are monitoring regulatory trends and make frequent trips to Silicon Valley and the banking centers of the United States, Europe, and Asia to understand what is around the corner.

Jason says that Westpac has an explicit Risk Appetite Statement for the business that is approved by the board and governs limits around risk across credit, operational, reputational, financial, and regulatory risks. He says, "As part of the Board approval process for annual and long-term strategic plans, we conduct scenario planning against which we test the sustainability of our strategy in best, worst and expected case scenarios."[14]

Jason identifies five transformational trends that are part of this assessment and are regarded as directional certainties. These are digitization, Australian population aging, economic transformation of Australia, banking industry regulation, and Asian growth.

These external environmental trends are explicitly considered when the strategic business plan is being developed. By doing that, Westpac is ensuring that it manages its business today while also transforming to take advantage of expected new environmental conditions. At each board meeting, the chief risk officer updates key factors on all strategic risks, their implications, and any actions as required.

Westpac is undertaking some additional capability building to help strengthen its peripheral vision. It is engaged in a new phase of customer culture strengthening in 2013 to enhance people's capability to lead, innovate, and take risks. It has introduced a new corporate value in response to its view of the future—*courage*. It is building an innovative capability with its customer design center to enable it to respond to new opportunities and market shifts. It has introduced a Digital Ambassadors Program to train the best leaders in Westpac.

This is a company that is building its peripheral vision capability as a discipline to scan, sense, adapt, and act on market shifts that pose both opportunities and threats.

Who Has It?

Markit: Born with Peripheral Vision

Vancouver-born Lance Uggla is widely credited with transforming the credit default swap market. A *credit default swap* (*CDS*) is a financial swap agreement where the seller of the CDS will compensate the buyer in the event of a loan default or other credit event. In 2003, using cutting-edge technology, Lance and his starting team of five launched a new pricing service, Markit; it was later built to be a multimillion-dollar business.[15] The first five years were buoyed by strong financial markets, increasing demand for information, and growing credit markets. Through organic growth and acquisitions the business grew rapidly.

But the global financial crisis and its aftermath of government regulatory reform in 2009 threatened a significant portion of Markit's revenue. New regulation, outlined under the Dodd-Frank Wall Street Reform and Consumer Protection Act in the United States and the European Market Infrastructure Regulation (EMIR) in Europe, has forced a substantial portion of derivatives business through clearing houses, eliminating the need for some posttrade services provided by Markit with MarkitSERV. In response the company considered moving into the clearing house business by buying LCHClearnet, but was outbid by the London Stock Exchange.

In the meantime, Lance Uggla put to work 200 people and invested many millions of dollars to repurpose MarkitSERV as a leading provider of connectivity between financial institutions and the new pieces of market infrastructure promoted by the reform agenda.

Lance said: "It was a worrying time, but when the dust began to settle we soon realised that the connectivity we had in place to several thousand derivative market participants around the world could in fact be retooled to support global regulatory reporting requirements. The number of participants that need to be connected to one another is going to increase, and it's going to get extremely complicated and expensive for firms."[16]

How was Markit able to make this transformation? Success was due to its team-based culture, information sharing, and peripheral vision of disruptive technologies, regulatory changes, communication changes, and economic impacts affecting the financial sector. Not only do people across the business have this broader vision of significant changes in the external environment, but also their culture of adaptive change and closeness to customers, modeled by CEO, Lance Uggla, enables them to innovate successfully and act to transform their business. This requires courage and confidence across the business as a transformational shift cannibalizes what are still profitable lines of business and markets.

The company had grown to almost $1 billion revenue by 2013. Lance said, "I'm more enthusiastic and ambitious today than I was when I first started the company." He added, "The global financial crisis definitely put the wind in our sails: the industry needs independent data, connectivity and processing more than ever and this is what we do best."

Starbucks: Tapping Its Peripheral Vision to Remain Relevant

"Peripheral vision to us is really all about how do we stay relevant to our customers by constantly refining and elevating the 'Starbucks Experience'. Our thinking is framed by building on our heritage and striving to improve and innovate new products. This was the way Arthur Rubinfeld described Starbucks's approach to staying in tune with the broad macro trends that may impact its business.

Arthur mentioned three major trends Starbucks has been incorporating into its business strategy to maintain relevance.

The first major trend is social media. Starbucks was early to recognize the value of creating engaging relevant conversations online with its customers. As one of the global leaders with more than 50 million followers on Facebook and 3.5 million on Twitter in October 2013, it is clearly staying relevant and engaging customers in the online world as well as the offline one.

The second is in relation to technology. Starbucks was early to align itself with a new payment system based on an iPhone app called Square. Square is an in-store payment solution that allows customers to simply enter the store with their smartphone Square app active and tell the barista their name and order for the payment to be processed and a receipt to be e-mailed.

The third major trend is locally relevant sustainable environmental design. Arthur described how they set out to design the future Starbucks stores back in 2008 in a way that drew inspiration from these principles. "We incorporate a modern organic design aesthetic to all physical design incorporating metal, woods, stone, recyclables, and organic materials," he said. "We have store designers located in 18 major cities around the world designing interiors incorporating inspirational furniture, fixtures, and lighting to create a comfortable locally relevant unique store experience." The stores are designed for customers to experience the unique environmental principles coming to life through the interior imagery, color choices, and seating.

Companies that are really in tune with the marketplace are curious. They are interested in trends beyond their specific markets. They are looking at broad global trends that impact customers in order to maintain high levels of relevancy.

Starbucks leadership operates with a sense of curiosity and urgency. There are many hallway conversations, and the senior leadership team interacts with all levels on a timely basis. The company has a flat leadership structure, so decisions and new ideas can be socialized across the team quickly.

This openness to new ideas and curiosity about the world beyond coffee has kept Starbucks ahead of the curve on major trends.

Nike: Reshaping the Running World

With the launch of the iPod in 2001, Apple revolutionized the music industry. One company that was paying attention at the time was Nike. With a history of innovation all of its own, it was watching with interest as Apple reshaped the music industry.

Nike from its early days was happy to push the envelope, and it saw an opportunity like no other to reshape the running world through technology. One challenge it faced at the time was that it only came into the consciousness of its customers and potential customers once every 6 to 12 months when people were in the market for running shoes or athletic gear. Nike wanted a way to maintain a consistent relationship with it customers over time.

Nike was also being challenged by Asics in the running segment. Asics was becoming the preferred brand for serious runners, a segment that influenced the broader market. So Nike needed a new catalyst to cement its place as the number-one running brand.

After a number of years of collaboration and experimentation and a partnership between Apple and Nike, Nike+ was born. Originally it was a device that was inserted into specific models of Nike running shoes and would sync with the Apple iPod to provide speed and distance measurements. As technology has changed it has developed into an iPhone app and various other wrist-based devices made by Nike.

The premise was that runners would like to track their workouts and listen to music while they run. This has since developed into sharing workouts online, and Nike even runs global running challenges to get customers motivated.

The Nike+ solution has become a spectacular success. In a June 2013 call with analysts a Nike executive said it has more than 18 million users of the service.[17]

The Nike+ platform has allowed it to be top of mind on an ongoing basis. In 2008 Nike organized a global 10-kilometer run it called the Human Race with 25 cities involved as well as individuals from around the world encouraged to go out and run 10 kilometers on August 31. Almost eight hundred thousand people participated that day, a powerful way to engage customers—impossible to do before Nike+.

An important side benefit of this new technology platform is the customer insights Nike has uncovered. Did you know the average runner in North America runs for 35 minutes? Most runners run on a Sunday and prefer running in the evenings rather than the mornings. The most popular power song artist (the song that comes on when you need that extra motivation to push harder up a hill or to the end of a long run) is from the Black Eyed Peas.[18]

How Do You Develop Peripheral Vision?

There are many ways in which peripheral vision as a discipline can be developed as a cultural capability. The following examples describe different approaches to developing a mindset and capability that enables people to see what might be coming and have the flexibility to act on it. The first is the more commonly used approach.

Telstra: Investing in Capability for the Future
The Telstra 2020 plan addresses how the core business will transform and what are the best bets for the business to extend its core. Actions from this future-oriented work inside Telstra are reflected in investments made from its Venture Capital Fund in new technologies being developed by new companies in Silicon Valley, Europe, and Australia that create an understanding of the disruptive technologies that are likely to impact Telstra's business in the future. CEO David Thodey maintains its biggest impact is its effect on people's thinking inside Telstra and the creation of a mental preparedness and capability for action in response to market shifts. He says it is getting people to think about what might be the shape of future value for customers and the changes that will be necessary to create it.

Virgin Unite: Being a Force for Good Enhances Peripheral Vision
Another reflection of peripheral vision is to be found in the Virgin Group. Richard Branson, as its head, has demonstrated peripheral vision in the extension of the Virgin brand from records to money to rail transport and air travel. He also has found a way to spur and sponsor peripheral vision as a discipline for people in the Virgin businesses.

Branson's broad-based vision has resulted in a nonprofit foundation, Virgin Unite, named by staff and aimed to involve as many people as possible to mix genuine good with a true sense of employee engagement in outside activities. He saw demand from Virgin people to be in a business that is good and makes a profit but also does something for the planet and humanity. It uses the entrepreneurial energy and resources of Virgin people to create change by driving business as a force for good.

The people at Virgin Unite act as a catalyst for leveraging peripheral vision across the Virgin group. They are actively involved with Virgin businesses in helping them rethink their business models, engage in business innovation and transformation, and connect with wider communities. Virgin leaders at all levels are connected with others who have created new models for business and experienced the benefits of connecting people, planet, and profit.

These activities infuse in Virgin businesses a sense of peripheral vision by encouraging employees to look outside their business to broader opportunities and problems in communities and to become more future-focused. They have experienced the impacts of political, economic, social, and technology changes that bring about market shifts.

When it comes to the challenges to Virgin businesses of market shifts and a need to change, many Virgin employees have the mindset and flexibility needed because of their participation in Virgin Unite programs. Their empathy for people translates to a means for the Virgin business to create more value for its customers in the light of change.

Executive Next Practices Institute (ENPI): Learning More about What Comes Next[19]

After speaking at a large leadership conference in Atlanta, Scott Hamilton had a strange feeling of déjà vu. "It feels like this has happened before," he said to himself. Yes, he had presented at the conference in the past. In fact he did so every year for the previous five years, but this time it didn't feel any different than before; it felt exactly the same.

Scott had come to recognize this feeling as one denoting a lack of progress of new ideas. The conference he had spoken at and attended seemed myopic, focused on a single functional discipline or industry. The topics tended to be more about best practices and case studies and less about new ideas and what was coming next.

This spawned the idea for what is now the Executive Next Practices Institute (ENPI). The central idea was to bring cross-discipline senior leaders in large corporations together to listen to and discuss "next practices." Next practices are the emerging ideas impacting businesses across industry boundaries. They are not necessarily fully formed and implemented, but they are worth exploring by leaders wanting to gain an advantage in their careers and marketplaces.

The ENPI has run programs on topics like neuroleadership, an emerging field of research that explores the science of culture change and how employees respond to different types of communication. It is based on actual scans of people's brains as they respond to different types of management communication. The ENPI's research has highlighted very significant implications of poor communication techniques on employee motivation levels and work outputs.

These types of executive networking forums are very useful ways leaders can build their own peripheral vision. They provide the opportunity to be up to date on what's coming next across a wide variety of fields and connect with thought leaders directly.

What Behaviors Draw Out Peripheral Vision?

Strength in this customer culture discipline involves employees that are informed of peripheral trends, consider their implications, evaluate their impact on products and services, determine the risks they pose, leverage them in decision making, and consider them in how future markets and customer needs will be shaped. For instance, this might include proactively meeting with customers to discuss possible major impacts of political and legislative changes and technological changes that will impact the way they receive value from your business.

Examples of peripheral vision behaviors include:

- Proactively meeting with customers to discuss possible major impacts of political, legislative, and technological changes that will impact the way they receive value from your team
- Attending and reporting on relevant conferences on trends affecting customers and future customer value

- Discussing, understanding, and acting on the changes in the external environment that have implications for the company's delivery of customer value
- Discussing and acting on the risks to the company's customers and to the business of current and expected future external changes
- Factoring external changes that affect the value of the company's products and services into the team's decision making
- Factoring external changes that affect the value of the company's products and services into individual work priorities
- Sharing knowledge of external changes and their implications with all members of the team and across silos
- Searching out and reporting on new technologies that could disrupt the entire value chain

What Are Some of the Best Practices?

The following examples of best practices and challenges in bridging tectonic shifts show how peripheral vision strengthens customer culture so long as its focus is vested in creating and maintaining a superior customer experience.

Salesforce.com: Using Social Networks to Share Ideas and Gain Peripheral Vision

The birth of salesforce.com and its subsequent use of disruptive technology illustrates what is required to benefit from these tectonic shifts. Marc Benioff, founder, chairman, and CEO of salesforce.com, had a vision of software as a service that was born from his recognition of the changing technology landscape. Up until that point the customer relationship management industry was dominated by a high-cost software licensing model that generated huge revenues for software companies with often questionable value for customers. He could envisage a day when software could be provided more like a utility, where customers could use what they needed and when they needed it and could then turn it off at anytime. His peripheral vision allowed him to pick up on trends in other businesses and apply them in a way that would ultimately create a new industry.

"We achieved our market position by being born cloud," Marc writes in his book *Behind the Cloud*, "but we are being 'reborn' social. . . . We need to transform the business conversation the same way Facebook and other social sites like Twitter have changed the consumer conversation and created incredible loyalty—and love."[20] Benioff was again in front of this second major shift in technology and societal behavior. Before others in his industry he was able to see the power of social media technologies and how people were sharing information.

Benioff, long seen as the top evangelist for cloud computing, believes it's time to move beyond the cloud to "the social enterprise," where companies rely on public and private social networks and social applications to run their businesses. He argues that customers and employees are increasingly using social networks such as Facebook and Twitter for business tasks rather than corporate websites, corporate e-mail systems, and private cloud networks. "We want to welcome you to the social revolution," Benioff said. "Because this is where people are increasingly spending their time today. Our employees are social and our customers are social."

"It's a new concept for us as a company. It's a new concept for us as an industry," he said. "This is the defining concept for our industry over the next few years."[21]

Social media enables companies to better understand the broad market environment. Smart companies are engaging directly with customers online and analyzing which topics appear to be most important to customers by leveraging trending data available from all of the social media platforms.

In fact in 2011, salesforce.com purchased Assistly precisely because of Marc's peripheral vision. Marc could see that social media was creating challenges for companies when it came to effectively handling customer service. Alex Bard was the entrepreneur that founded Assistly in 2009 with some friends. Alex, like Marc, saw the social media trend and the challenge it was creating for businesses of all sizes.

In our interview with Alex[22] he described the origins of the business and how the founders' peripheral vision had enabled them to develop the original concept.

"The original idea behind the company," he said, "was based on the fact that if you make a customer unhappy in the physical world, they'll tell six people; if you make a customer unhappy on the Internet, they'll tell 6,000. This was a quote that actually came from Jeff Bezos at Amazon at the time. That customer voice was hugely amplified by the Internet.

"The reason that we used Jeff's quote when we were raising money was because it wasn't just about the Internet. It was about a broader trend in the market—social media—and in 2009 social media was exploding and really kind of amplifying the consumer voice. For the first time there was a shift of control from a company to a customer.

"If you mentally rewind back to the evolution of customer service, it started with the innovation in the '70s of the call center, and that came out of consumer packaged goods companies that put an 800 number on the side of toothpaste or a bag of chips because they wanted to connect with their customers. But the company controlled the how (the phone) and the when (Monday through Friday, 9:00 to 5:00).

"And then that evolved in the '90s into [the] contact center, because then you had the Internet and you had chat and self-service and e-mail. But still the company primarily controlled the how . . . [a] phone and an e-mail address and maybe a 'Chat now' button.

"Then in the 2000s, that's when social media, I think, really started to change that dynamic. And that's why we used that Bezos quote.

"And so when we started Assistly, the original idea behind it was this profound belief that customer service would go from a department to a philosophy, that it would force companies to embrace this idea of a customer being an atomic unit of their success and a partner in their journey, and it would force them actually because of this amplified customer voice.

"The solution from Assistly was to take all of the ways that your customers can communicate to you and to add social media channels as first-class citizens. So it helped businesses listen, engage, [and] interact much more dynamically, whether it was on a phone call [or] whether it was a tweet, a Facebook post, [or] an e-mail address, and it unified all that into one place."

The questions for all business leaders when it comes to peripheral vision are: What major trends are changing the landscape for your customers? and How will you adapt your business to take advantage of these trends and remain relevant?

CommsChoice: Changing the Telecoms Game[23]

Grant Ellison, CEO of Australasian-based telecommunications ser-vices provider CommsChoice, uses peripheral vision as a core to his company's competitive advantage. When we conducted a customer culture assessment in 2011 we found a very strong future orientation embedded in peripheral vision and customer foresight supported by strong strategic alignment and collaboration. This was not surprising when you understood its business model—a service provider where the value-add is the selection, provision, and management of an opti-mal mix of telecoms networks for business customers that help them adapt to the future.

From his experience in London working with Vanco, a value-added network provider linking data communications across the world for multinational companies, then setting up its offices in Chicago, Tokyo, and Sydney in early 2000s, Grant understood how customers can benefit by outsourcing their telecoms services.

In 2008, when he launched CommsChoice, he says, "I wanted to build a business from the ground up that was totally aligned with customers' current and future needs. Traditional telecoms compa-nies have the legacy of a huge investment in a specific network and shareholder pressure that compels them to push their own products and services to get satisfactory returns. I saw that with network inde-pendence and a clear vision of the future we could provide superior advice and professional services to those businesses that don't have a specialist 'owner' of the telecommunications decisions. The explosion of technology and choice has created confusion for customers. Our aim is to demystify the decision for customers and deliver the quality of service that enables them to get on with competing in their core business."

CommsChoice helps its customers not only by reducing costs of telecommunications (by configuring a better combination of ser-vices closely aligned with their needs) but also through the effective application of latest technology like video to uses such as selling, recruiting, and reporting, which is a competitive advantage. It provides flexibility by enabling customers to quickly switch networks and technologies as their needs change.

Grant says, "We are constantly scanning the horizon for products and services that can give our customers a competitive advantage. We have a team of professionals who are passionate about their customers and want to help them keep ahead of the game."

CommsChoice has embedded peripheral vision as a discipline for technology and service innovation for customers. The planned daily "water cooler" meetings are designed to get everyone up to date on anything new in 10 to 15 minutes. The frequent "walk and talk" lunchtime meetings in groups of two or three staff members provide an informal environment to talk about what they are learning from customers and what it might mean for future needs. The monthly innovation meetings are planned to discuss in more depth what new innovations are on the horizon and which customers might benefit from them. These meetings also cover what future customer needs are emerging that require a search for possible solutions. All of these practices are focused on designing and delivering a superior customer experience.

CommsChoice is an example of a company that is changing the telecoms game by using peripheral vision and customer foresight as central to its customer culture. It enables their customers to see the "whole playing field" and the appropriate choices for meeting their current and future needs.

CHAPTER SUMMARY

Why is peripheral vision important to customer-centricity?
Peripheral vision enables a company to sense shifts in the way in which value through new business models will be designed and delivered to customers to meet their needs in the future. The essence of customer-centricity is to understand and act on future customer needs. To do this, peripheral vision as a discipline is central to customer-centricity.

What is peripheral vision?
Peripheral vision is the extent to which employees monitor, predict, and make decisions in consideration of emerging trends in the business environment that have the potential to impact customer needs and the value being offered by the organization.

Why is peripheral vision a cultural discipline?
It is not enough for leaders to identify the need for massive change. An entire organization must have the mindset and capability to carry it through. Even Intel took five years or more to "get it" after it was first identified by its CEO. Kodak, Motorola, and Nortel failed to "get it." For organizations to transform, like Markit, salesforce.com, and Nike, they must build peripheral vision into their customer culture.

What behaviors lead to peripheral vision?
Activities that proactively sense, identify, monitor, and understand market shifts being driven by change in the external environment are those that lead to strong peripheral vision. When these signals and insights are widely shared and also generated by many people in the organization, the peripheral vision becomes a discipline and enables the business to act quickly and successfully to preempt or respond to market shifts.

Leader's Guide to Peripheral vision

Peripheral Vision: *Does the company monitor, understand, and respond to the political, economic, social, environmental, and technological trends emerging on the periphery that could affect its customers and its business? Are all staff members encouraged to scan their respective fields of expertise for new ideas relevant to the changing external environment? Does the company act on this flow of new ideas?*

Rate where *you and your team* stand on peripheral vision by checking the relevant box in answering each question.

(Continued)

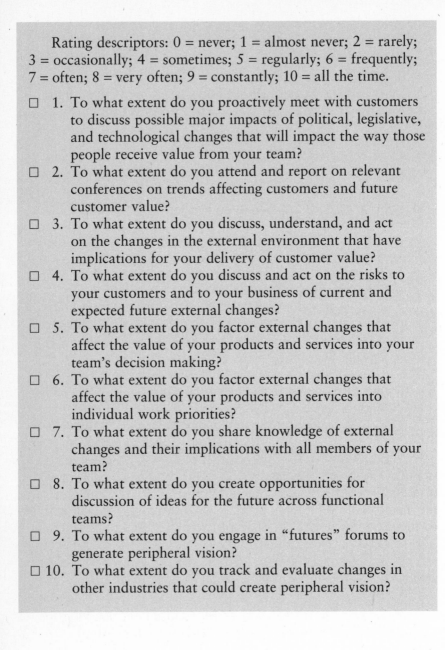

Rating descriptors: 0 = never; 1 = almost never; 2 = rarely; 3 = occasionally; 4 = sometimes; 5 = regularly; 6 = frequently; 7 = often; 8 = very often; 9 = constantly; 10 = all the time.

☐ 1. To what extent do you proactively meet with customers to discuss possible major impacts of political, legislative, and technological changes that will impact the way those people receive value from your team?

☐ 2. To what extent do you attend and report on relevant conferences on trends affecting customers and future customer value?

☐ 3. To what extent do you discuss, understand, and act on the changes in the external environment that have implications for your delivery of customer value?

☐ 4. To what extent do you discuss and act on the risks to your customers and to your business of current and expected future external changes?

☐ 5. To what extent do you factor external changes that affect the value of your products and services into your team's decision making?

☐ 6. To what extent do you factor external changes that affect the value of your products and services into individual work priorities?

☐ 7. To what extent do you share knowledge of external changes and their implications with all members of your team?

☐ 8. To what extent do you create opportunities for discussion of ideas for the future across functional teams?

☐ 9. To what extent do you engage in "futures" forums to generate peripheral vision?

☐ 10. To what extent do you track and evaluate changes in other industries that could create peripheral vision?

Chapter 7

The New Math: 1 + 1 = 3 or 4 or even 10

Alone we can do so little; together we can do so much.
—Helen Keller

In a recent project with a large energy company, we were working with the senior management and staff to help develop and embed a customer-centric culture. It is the managers' belief and ours that a customer-focused business will drive ongoing prosperity. In our research, along with that of many others, we have found that an important factor in enabling a customer culture to become embedded is internal cross-functional collaboration. We found senior and middle managers in the energy company were stymied in their attempts to focus on customers by having to respond to e-mails and attend informational meetings, which dominated their workday. Functions were working in silos with very little cross-functional collaboration involving customers and ways to increase customer value.

This is typical of so many large organizations. In organizations of all sizes we see silos, lack of collaboration, infighting, and much worse—all to the detriment of the customer and the business. Why does this happen? In part it comes from the fact that people in organizations have different backgrounds, different levels of experience, and training in different disciplines. It exists most strongly when the organization does not have a cultural focus on the delivery of superior value to customers.

Consider all the "fighting" that often goes on between marketing and finance in a business. This occurs when focus on the marketing and accounting disciplines overshadows the focus on customer value. It is typified by the following fable:

> *The marketer decided to take the afternoon off ("Doesn't that*
> *happen all the time?" says the accountant) and go for a*
> *ride in a hot-air balloon. He took off in the balloon just*
> *north of San Francisco, but suddenly a strong southerly*
> *wind pushed the balloon rapidly toward the Napa Valley.*
> *Feeling disoriented, he decided it was time to bring the*
> *balloon down, and he managed to land it in a vineyard.*
> *A bit shaken, he got out and saw a stranger walking in the*
> *vineyard and called out:*
> *"Can you tell me where I am?"*
> *"Yes," said the stranger, "you are in the center of a*
> *vineyard!"*
> *"That's interesting," said the marketer. "You must be an*
> *accountant"*
> *The stranger replied, "As a matter of fact. I am. How do*
> *you know?"*
> *"You have given me absolutely precise information of no*
> *value whatsoever!"*
> *The accountant replied, "You must be a marketer."*
> *The marketer replied, "As a matter of fact, I am. How do*
> *you know?"*
> *"You don't know where you are, and you won't accept the*
> *facts!"*

The way to solve these different views of the world is to make the customer the focus of attention. Then the questions asked by both accountant and marketer become:

What value do we need to give customers so that we satisfy
  and retain them and make them advocates? (Retained loyal
  customers are much more profitable, and they create new

customers much more often than do casual customers who buy only on price.)

How much investment is needed to provide that value and customer experience (in terms of product, service and information), and what is the likely return on investment?

How can we work together to ensure that the new product will reach the market as planned so that we can enhance value for customers and return satisfactory sales and profits?

While working on answers to questions like these can bring accountants and marketers together, similar questions can be used to connect sales and marketing, HR with IT, and operations with customer service. The common factor is the culture that focuses on customers, customer experience, and delivery of value by all functions of the business. When this happens our "worst enemies" progressively become "best friends" with a shared sense of purpose and a common cause.

Nokia is an example of success breeding complacency and a bureaucratic culture that has inhibited change in a fast-changing, competitive mobile-phone marketplace. In the last two years under a new CEO there has been an effort to decentralize decision making, reduce layers of management, and refocus on innovation.

Once the world's dominant mobile-phone maker, by 2013 Nokia had fallen behind Apple, Samsung, and other competitors in the global handheld device market. In 2013 the company went through a significant change program focusing on better behaviors in terms of accountability and responsibility, urgency and speed, and empathy— by being less arrogant and listening to consumers.[1]

But will this be enough? Apparently not! In September 2013, Nokia announced the sale of its phone business to Microsoft.

In order to survive and prosper against Apple and Samsung in the smartphone market, Nokia needed a customer-focused culture throughout its entire business (not just at the front end) to drive innovation and sustained growth and profitability. This required embedded behavior change that goes beyond restructuring, a refocused strategy and decentralized decision making. It required a completely new mindset where there is an understanding and belief, translated into behavior, that's what's best for the customer is best for the business. This needed cross-functional collaboration with the common focus of innovating to create more value for customers.

The Business Case

Imagine This Situation
Imagine you are facing these existing or potential threats:

- Customers complaining about lack of communication between people they are dealing with in the company's business
- Different messages from different parts of the business to the same customers
- Customers unable to get a solution to their problem
- New-product or service delays giving competitors an advantage with the company's customers

What's Your Response?
Is it to tell customers you are fixing the problems and hope their complaints go away?
Or
Do you initiate customer-focused collaboration across functional groups to address customers' complaints and competitive threats?

What's the Difference?
Organizations with strong customer-focused cross-functional collaboration generate continuous alignment that creates a multiplier effect on performance. It results in higher customer satisfaction, innovation, new-product success, sales growth, profit growth, and profitability than their competitors.

Link to Business Performance
This measures a business's ability to leverage its resources and advantages across its organization to deliver differentiated value. This impacts customer satisfaction, innovation, new-product success, sales growth, profit growth, and profitability. It has medium to longer-term impacts on business efficiency and profitability.

Link to Strategy
Strength in this discipline is relevant to all business strategies by enhancing *delivery* of value to customers and strengthening competitive advantage.

Figure 7.1 highlights cross-functional collaboration as the focus of this chapter. The goal is for companies to improve their absolute and relative strength in this discipline. The score of 100 percent means that a company is above all others in our MRI global database in terms of cross-functional collaboration behaviors.

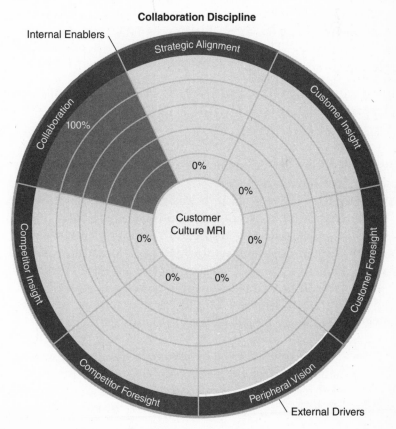

Figure 7.1 Collaboration discipline

What Is Cross-Functional Collaboration?

Cross-functional collaboration is a discipline of workforce behavior that enables a strong customer-centric culture and makes it possible for the company to transform the information generated by the externally oriented activities into value for customers and shareholders. Without strong collaboration within a business, valuable information is squandered and business opportunities are lost. Also the impact of value delivered to customers is reduced.

Cross-functional collaboration is the extent to which employees interact, share information, and work with colleagues from other work groups and assist them; the focus is on creating value for customers. This discipline is critical to the successful delivery of value for customers. When information, insight and customer requests are shared across functions it has a positive multiplier effect on the value that is created for customers. Employees must interact effectively across boundaries. They also must work together with a unity of effort and common goals.

Why Is Cross-Functional Collaboration a Cultural Discipline?

Customers receive value from a product or service through their experience of buying and using it when it meets their needs better than alternatives. Everyone in a business contributes toward the delivery and maintenance of value for customers. Marketers and salespeople create relevance and connection of customers with the brand by providing valuable information. Production and operations people affect the product and service quality. IT staff affect the ability of customer service people to solve customer problems using information systems as well as creating valuable online experiences. Finance people affect customers through their billing service and credit management processes. R&D people affect customers through the creation of new products to meet new needs. HR staff members affect the ability of all functions to deliver customer value through their recruitment effectiveness, learning and development programs, and reward systems. When these functions collaborate effectively with the customer as the common focal point and delivery of superior value as the common goal, customers will receive exceptional experiences.

Westpac Bank has five organizational values, one of which is "One Team," which is about working collaboratively together as one team regardless of department for the sake of the customer. By having this as a corporate value, Westpac recognizes this as a cultural discipline. Leaders are regularly brought together at all levels to participate in strategic discussions. Increasingly, people are moved about in different parts of the organization to cross-fertilize knowledge and build networks among divisions. The bank undertakes social and community activities to build personal relationships among divisions. Westpac has internal social media systems that enable people to share ideas, suggest innovations, and work on cross-functional projects designed to improve customer experience. These initiatives have increased value for customers as measured by customer satisfaction scores and reduced customer complaints.[2]

By contrast, the authors were working with a U.S. health insurance organization to help build a customer culture across the business. Corporate marketing had been centralized away from the business units as part of a restructure to increase synergy, reduce costs, and build a stronger connection between customers and the brand. It was found that lack of trust and strong divisional self-interest had taken the focus away from collaboration to benefit customers. This was resulting in declining customer satisfaction and lost customers, with negative impacts on revenue and profit. It was essential to bring these teams together and show the personal benefits as well as business gains that come from collaboration around customers. It also involved personal coaching of some of the leaders to help them regain trust and the confidence to work together. This was the start in building a collaborative culture.

A team of Harvard psychologists surveyed and interviewed teams of analysts in the U.S. intelligence services to find out what determined their level of effectiveness.[3] By far the strongest predictor was the amount of assistance that intelligence analysts gave each other. Collaboration in the form of coaching and consulting with their colleagues was the decisive determinant of high- and low-performing teams.

The importance of helping-behavior for organizational effectiveness stretches far beyond intelligence work. Our research demonstrates that collaborative behavior within teams and across functions that focuses on the customer correlates with important business performance outcomes: customer satisfaction, new-product success, and revenue and profit growth,

The implications of low performance on cross-functional collaboration have a significant impact on businesses, as they simply are not able to effectively deliver value to customers. All people in the business need to know how they contribute value for the customer and how they impact the customer's experience. In addition they need to work together to do it consistently. For these reasons, it is a cultural discipline to be created and nurtured for competitive advantage.

Who Has It?

Ikea is one of a handful of successful global retailers. It is a privately held home products retailer that sells a wide range of well-designed flat-pack furniture, accessories, and bathroom and kitchen items. The story of Ikea began in 1943 in the small village of Agunnaryd, Sweden, when Ingvar Kamprad, the founder, was just 17. Since then, the Ikea Group has grown into a global retail brand with 139,000 coworkers operating 330 Ikea franchised stores in 44 countries, which generate annual sales of more than 27 billion euros.

Ikea's former CEO, Anders Dahlvig, puts the collaborative culture as central to the company's success. He says: "As a company grows, the earlier you build cross-functionality, the more effective you will be. You have to be very decisive and strong and cross this river—that is a really tough process. We managed to do that because we set our minds on it. It was a 10-year process and I'd say we are still not through it yet. But I think the key thing was this: You have to be prepared *not* to promote strong performers who are great alone but not great collaborators. I see that all the time: People who are good at optimizing themselves but cannot work with others. It's really tough to say, 'You have to go.' But if you don't get rid of these people, you will never overcome your demons."[4] This is a key learning from Ikea. It is one that is practiced by Virgin in that company's recruitment approach. It is one that is embedded in Intuit and Westpac, where collaboration and teamwork are cultural values.

Dahlvig says: "While it's tempting to imagine that exhortation alone will force people to collaborate, it won't. You need the right structures. You need the right people." He says that the traits that stand out are energy, social confidence, common sense, and the ability to learn from experience and work with people.[5]

When you think that Ikea is integrated along the value chain from furniture production through to selling through its franchised retail stores, you can imagine the level of collaboration needed to be successful. This includes cocreation of products with customers, customer feedback from stores in 44 countries, back to production and distribution of products consumers want to buy. A central part of Ikea's culture is workers helping each other and working together and being a part of the Ikea "family."

How Do You Get It?

At its heart, creating a collaborative culture is about recognizing the value of different types of expertise and experience. It requires a willingness by leaders to bring people together to come up with better solutions than can be done in isolation.

There are many ways to nurture collaboration. The most effective is to bring people together when a major business issue needs to be addressed. If this is done as the normal way of working, then cross-functional collaboration around solving customer problems becomes a discipline. Two examples illustrate how this is developed.

HP: Innovative Strategy from Cross-Functional Collaboration

During the early 2000s, HP decided to move into the high-growth digital camera market. Demand for digital cameras was exploding at the time, and there was a rapid transition away from the traditional film equivalents. At the time it appeared like a natural fit: HP was a major player in the inkjet printer market, and consumers were using these products to print their own photos at home. By providing a digital camera and inkjet printer, HP could provide a more holistic solution and compete more effectively with Canon and Kodak, which had gone down this path.

Chris Brown, the marketing director for HP at the time, and his team was given the challenge to successfully launch the new camera line in the Australian marketplace. One of his product managers was given the portfolio, and he went about the business of developing a go-to-market strategy for the launch. He began by meeting with HP's largest retailers and wholesalers to discuss the new line and the possibilities.

After one of these visits the product manager came around to Chris's desk looking distraught. "Our largest wholesaler just told me they are not going to carry the camera line," he said. "In fact, the managing director told me flat out that HP should not even be in that business, and we are wasting our time! What are we going to do? They have more customer reach than any other partner." The role of the go-to-market operation of HP was to take products successfully to market. They could not go back to the R&D organization and tell them, "We can't launch because there is no market for HP digital cameras in Australia."

Chris decided he needed some broader team inputs, so he pulled together a small group of people from sales, operations, finance, and marketing. The goal was to lay out what they thought were the launch options available and to brainstorm some more ideas. The results of this meeting were sensational. It was as though many of these team members had never been asked their opinion before. The ideas were creative, and there was a lot of energy in the room about solving what seemed to be an insurmountable problem.

The result of this collaboration was a successful launch via an exclusive retail channel partner, which was not a genuine consideration prior to the meeting. One of the participants had deep knowledge of this partner and the value it could bring. The finance member of the team was able to model the costs of using this channel in real time. With a cross-discipline approach the problem solving was faster and more effective.

Within 12 months HP was within the top 5 digital camera players for market share from a total of more than 15 players and ahead of long-established players such as Panasonic and Fuji. From a customer standpoint, HP was able to provide an integrated and optimized solution that allowed a direct connection between the HP digital camera and printer.

Not only was the collaboration a successful one for the company and ultimately customers but also it ensured commitment to a successful launch by key players that needed to be on board to maximize the chances of success.

Fairfax Media: Building Customer Culture through Collaboration

Nic Cola, CEO of Marketplaces, the online businesses of Fairfax Media, wanted to benchmark the company's customer culture in 2012. It was found that cross-functional collaboration could be leveraged to the benefit of customers and the businesses.

Nic launched what is called its "Customer First" initiative. Workshops were held with cross-function and cross-business participation to identify how more value could be created for customers in each business through sharing of knowledge. These businesses included online dating, real estate, car sales, and travel accommodation. From these workshops it was found that benefits could be gained from forming several cross-functional teams to work on a number of initiatives that were common to these apparently disparate businesses. These included customer metrics and feedback systems, embedding user experience and customer involvement into the product development process (much of which involved IT innovations), development of a customer service charter to be tailored to each business, and an internal communication program to share experiences, best practices, and innovative customer solutions. These teams were guided by a group steering committee that allocated resources as required. One outcome from these initiatives was the creation of panels of customers who are drawn into the businesses as collaborators on new-product and service developments.

Kirsty Shaw, director of marketing and strategy at Fairfax Media, says, "This has also created a common language across the businesses with the customer at the forefront. You need to keep talking about it and point out slipups by saying, 'That's not very customer-first!' "[6]

As Fairfax Media's customer culture has strengthened and collaboration across businesses has become part of the culture, the Customer First initiative is now led by a group of about 16 people from all functions and levels, including the CEO of the digital businesses division.

Kirsty says that the various businesses in the division have become more customer focused, adaptive, and competitive as a result of strengthening the collaborative culture.

Our experience with Fairfax Media and other companies highlights the value of people working outside their boundaries as well as inside. They seek senior management support; search for information on customer needs, competition, and external impacts on customer value; and look for pockets of expertise within the organization on which to build. They foster external ties to go beyond their boundaries, coordinate their activities, and adapt over time. They also develop exchangeable membership to include members who come in and out of the teams and rotate leadership. We have seen this work well in operating business units as well as in shared service functional groups, such as finance, operations, human resources, and product development. These companies discovered that by taking a more external approach it enabled them to substantially improve their business performance.

This thinking and these approaches apply directly to sharing knowledge about customers and competitors. Effective use of communication technologies has a substantial impact on innovation, competitiveness, and customer value if it is directed toward sharing across the business a deep understanding of customers, competitors, and the changing market environment. This strengthens an organization's customer culture, which in turn will drive future growth and profitability.

What Behaviors Draw Out Cross-Functional Collaboration?

Organizations with strong cross-functional collaboration generate continuous alignment and communicate across groups. In turn, employees do not strictly confine their work and responsibilities to group boundaries. They share knowledge and ideas openly, they share resources, and they develop relationships across the organization. They work in cross-functional teams to improve value for customers.

These are mechanisms for sharing knowledge, skills, and experiences cross-functionally that produce customer-centric behaviors:

- Joint projects to simplify processes for customers
- Storytelling sessions of customer experiences to share best practices
- Discussion forums for sharing ideas and brainstorming innovations
- Movement of people across functions to gain multiple skills and broader perspectives
- Cross-functional problem-solving sessions that provide improved solutions for customers
- Social interaction and events that enhance and deepen cross-functional personal relationships
- Sharing technology, know-how, and resources

Most people in a business enjoy the satisfaction that comes from being part of a winning team. If they contribute to do good for customers, they are likely to stay on and do well for themselves and the business. That satisfaction and prosperity comes from customers who are loyal advocates.

What Are Some of the Best Practices?

Those companies that have strong collaborative behaviors as a discipline are very successful at gaining competitive advantage. The following examples of collaborative practices show how cross-functional collaboration strengthens customer culture.

BlackRock: Linking Operations and Client Service

When BlackRock benchmarked its customer culture it found that there was substantial room for improvement in cross-functional collaboration. At BlackRock, its Service Alpha initiative implemented in the United Kingdom and Australia brought teams together to create a unified customer mindset and skills across the business through a series of workshops that linked "operations" and "client service" functions around the customer. These were designed to create substantially enhanced service for customers in terms of what customers wanted and expected. Customers participated in and contributed to these BlackRock workshops to infuse a customer viewpoint. As a result, the shared view of jointly solving the customers' problems led to more relevant and timely information as well as joint proactive ideas to lift customer service.[7]

By bringing in customers and exposing all parts of the Black-Rock business to them, employees could see the bigger picture of how their work positively or negatively impacted those customers. By having customers describe their challenges and what they need from BlackRock, employees were motivated to collaborate more effectively around what was needed.

Salesforce.com: Born to Collaborate— It's in the Software

Salesforce.com is ranked number 27 on *Fortune's* 2012 list of the 100 Best Companies to Work For. David Kaplan describes what happens inside the company.[8]

He explains that salesforce.com's new social-networking app, Chatter, functions like a Facebook inside a company—and enhances corporate culture. Chatter is a dynamic and collaborative tool; e-mail, by comparison, is static and private. Employees can share work and ideas in real time on projects, analyze reports, and compare progress. Marc Benioff, CEO and founder of salesforce.com, has said that he "learned more about his company in a few months through using Chatter than he had in the previous three years."

At salesforce.com itself—where there are more than three thousand daily Chatter posts, and where internal e-mails have decreased substantially since Chatter went live—there are groups such as Tribal Knowledge and Airing of Grievances designed to get employees across functions and ranks talking to each other about their work. Kaplan reports that employees who have worked at Google and Facebook say there is "less politics" at salesforce. com and it generates a degree of cooperation unseen at most large organizations.

When you think about it, by providing business software on the web as its core mission, the collaborative model that the company has with its customers engenders cross-functional collaboration with each customer as that person uses the salesforce.com software. Modeling use of these collaboration tools by the senior leadership is crucial to enabling their use and deriving the collaboration benefits.

NatWest: Collaborating to Lift Customer Experience

Brian Hartzer, former divisional head at the Royal Bank of Scotland, describes how a collaborative effort solved a long-time problem of poor retail customer experiences in the group's NatWest's 110 Greater London branches.[9]

When Brian and his team spent some time looking through the raw data, metrics, and customer feedback, they found that the customer satisfaction scores were much lower in Greater London than in the rest of the company. They had an executive at the meeting who said that people in his business, the John Lewis department stores in Great Britain, had the same experience—customer satisfaction scores lower for the Greater London area. His interpretation was that in London people are grumpier, logistics are more difficult, and there is more movement of staff.

Brian tells the story this way. "If we could do something about this, what would we do? Someone said we'd appoint a manager to focus on the Greater London area bank branches to fix it. So we did and told him to assess what he needs and we will support him with resources and backing. He came back and said, 'I need 100 new tellers and 80 new machines to enable automated customer deposits plus a small budget for property improvement.' He said they would focus on shortening queues in the London branches, which was a source of major customer complaint. Also he said that London had not followed the procedure for new-hires screening because it took too long to hire people and it was always urgent to quickly find replacement branch staff. So staff hires had not been screened for attitude and frontline staff psychological profiles. He noted we've found 16 branch managers who have been consistently underperforming with poor service quality scores, so we will move them out. Also we have found 30 teller staff whose customer feedback indicated that they actively turned customers off. They were to be moved out. We will go through the proper screening process for hiring new people.

"The local HR people came up with an idea for an ad. They placed posters in the underground tube stations showing a smiling face of a NatWest teller saying:

> Are you the person who gave up your seat for someone else on the tube?
> Are you the person who helped the lady with her pram on the escalator?
> Are you the person who picked up the child's glove?
> If you are, we want to talk to you."

Brian noted: "We ended up hiring 85 new tellers from 1,500 employment applications. We replaced the 16 branch managers . . . put in new machines to enable customers to make deposits and help shorten the queues.

"The first meeting had been in January 2012. The advertising started in February. The new tellers, branch managers and machines were trained and all in operation in early April 2012. This collaborative effort involving the new Greater London retail manager, HR, branch managers, front-line bank staff, and senior management encouragement and support led to a much better customer experience. The customer satisfaction scores had traditionally been in the low 60s. By June 2012 these had risen 13 percentage points for the Greater London NatWest branches."

Virgin Group: Collaborating to Innovate for Customers

Virgin Group companies are part of one big family rather than a hierarchy. They are empowered to run their own affairs, yet the companies actively help one another, and solutions to problems are often sourced from within the group. In a sense they form a commonwealth, with shared ideas, values, interest, and goals.[10]

The Virgin Group has taken its lead from Richard Branson, founder and CEO. Among his leadership attributes that are embodied in Virgin's culture are delegation, listening to others, and collaboration. He personally interacts with employees on a regular basis, discussing ideas and getting feedback. With a flat hierarchical structure, the organization works as a community rather than a corporation by promoting interaction between all levels, which increases effective communication and collaboration. Reward for great performance is mainly nonfinancial, with benefits such as social activities, company-sponsored weekend getaways, and impromptu parties. For example, the heroic efforts of all employees at Virgin Trains (mentioned in Chapter 9) were rewarded with a huge party for all at Richard Branson's English home in Oxfordshire in September 2013.

The mantra of "business as a force for good," now becoming more visible through the nonprofit Virgin Unite, is creating collaborative efforts across and between Virgin businesses to use their strengths to help solve some of the world's most difficult problems and provide real value to local communities. The people at Virgin Unite have the breadth of connections across industries, communities, and geographies to enhance the collaborative skills and experiences of Virgin people in their respective businesses. It spurs the collaborative mindset and skills that Virgin employees can use to innovate for their customers and the good of wider communities.

Intuit[11]: Collaborating to Solve Customers' Problems

Brad Smith, CEO of Intuit, says that he has always valued and encouraged teamwork, and that collaborative spirit of "we" versus "I" is central to Intuit's success. Smith says: "Innovation has been part of Intuit's DNA for nearly 30 years. We pride ourselves on two core capabilities that differentiate us and allow us to deliver solutions that truly change people's financial lives." He says the first process is customer-driven innovation, which involves a mindset and methodology that helps companies uncover important customer problems, described in Chapter 3.

Smith says the second process, Design for Delight, enables Intuit to create better ways to deliver what's most important for customers. This approach is based on deep customer empathy, with rapid experimentation of potential new products with customers.

Smith believes that "regardless of whether you are leading a large enterprise or a small team, you need to remove barriers to innovation and get out of the way." He says that customers are at the heart of everything done at Intuit and it is essential to give employees opportunities to collaborate on new ideas to solve customer problems. Smith says they use the "Two-Pizza rule," making sure product development teams are no larger than what two pizzas can feed. He believes it is about empowering individuals to contribute ideas and make an impact and setting goals that challenge them. Says Smith: "The best reward for employees is seeing the profound impact of their work on the lives of our more than 50 million customers."

Intuit embodies collaboration around the customer as a cultural discipline. When combined with strength in the other cultural disciplines it provides an innovative force that is irresistible. It forms the basis of a sustainable business where 1 + 1 = 10 or even 100 in terms of its multiplying effect on business performance.

CHAPTER SUMMARY

Why is cross-functional collaboration important to customer-centricity?
Cross-functional collaboration is critical to a successful focus on customers. Information, insight, and requests from customers must be shared across work groups and functions in order for customer responsiveness and value to be created. Employees must interact effectively across boundaries. They also must work together with a unity of effort and common goals.
High levels of cross-functional collaboration have been found to positively impact innovation, customer satisfaction, sales growth, and profitability.

What is cross-functional collaboration?
Cross-functional collaboration is the extent to which employees interact, share information, and work with colleagues from

other work groups and assist them; the focus is on creating value for customers. This discipline is critical to the successful delivery of value for customers. Information, insight, and requests from customers must be shared among work groups and functions in order for customer-centricity and value to be created.

Why is cross-functional collaboration a cultural discipline?
It is a cultural discipline because it requires cultures like those of the Virgin Group, Intuit, and Ikea, where collaboration is a deliberate strategy supported by senior management, organization structure, and cultural values that promotes sharing, teamwork, and innovation for the benefit of customers.

What behaviors lead to cross-functional collaboration?
Organizations with strong cross-functional collaboration generate continuous alignment and communicate across groups. In turn, employees do not strictly confine their work and responsibilities to group boundaries. They share knowledge, ideas, and resources openly, and they develop relationships across the organization. Companies need to look for mechanisms for cross-collaboration such as joint projects, discussion forums, cross-functional problem-solving sessions, and social interaction that enhances cross-functional relationships and solutions.

Leader's Guide to Cross-Functional Collaboration

Cross-Functional Collaboration: *Do colleagues from different work groups share information and work together? Are silos tolerated or even encouraged? Are your people working cross-functionally to solve customer problems and deliver better service to customers? Are mechanisms in place to encourage cross-fertilization of ideas, practices, and value creation? Do staff members receive individual recognition for initiating end-to-end solutions for the customer? Is internal competition managed in a way that creates better customer solutions rather than destructive silos?*

(Continued)

Rate where *you and your team* stand on cross-functional collaboration by checking the relevant box in answering each question.

Rating descriptors: 0 = never; 1 = almost never; 2 = rarely; 3 = occasionally; 4 = sometimes; 5 = regularly; 6 = frequently; 7 = often; 8 = very often; 9 = constantly; 10 = all the time.

☐ 1. To what extent do you have cross-functional teams collaborating on creating more value for customers?

☐ 2. To what extent do you have cross-functional discussion forums designed to generate new ideas for continual improvement for customers?

☐ 3. To what extent do you engage in cross-functional problem-solving sessions that provide improved solutions for customers?

☐ 4. To what extent are people moved from one function to another as a means of creating fresh perspectives on adding value for customers?

☐ 5. To what extent is coaching of teams used to enhance collaborative efforts?

☐ 6. To what extent do you share technology, know-how, best practices, and resources across functions?

☐ 7. To what extent do you share good and bad customer experiences across functions as a means of generating collaboration?

☐ 8. To what extent do you facilitate social interaction across functions that enhances personal relationships?

☐ 9. To what extent do you create opportunities for cross-functional teams to work together on their own innovations for future customer benefit?

☐ 10. To what extent do you encourage employees to both seek and provide help with people from different functions?

Chapter 8

How Leaders Get Their Ducks in a Row

Leaders establish the vision for the future and set the strategy for getting there; they cause change. They motivate and inspire others to go in the right direction and they, along with everyone else, sacrifice to get there.

—John Kotter

David Thodey, CEO of Telstra, tells the story of the challenges in creating strategic alignment around the customer in a large, dynamic, complex business. In early 2012 a cathartic experience by senior executives illustrates what it means to put customers first. At the time, executives were asked to telephone three customers who had rated them 10 out of 10 for customer service experience and to call three who had rated them 2 or 3 out of 10. The executives were asked to report what they had learned at a meeting.

A senior planning director reported his experience as follows. He had called a 10-out-of-10 customer who explained that he could not fault the service he had received. It was simply excellent. When the director asked if there was anything more he could help the customer with, the executive heard the following story. This same customer two weeks earlier had visited a Telstra shop to set up a mobile plan with a new smartphone for his wife. He committed to a two-year plan. A week later his wife died. He went back to the shop and was told that it would cost more than AU$2,000 (US$1,900) to waive the contract. This unfortunately was the company's policy. At this point of the story the planning director did not know what to do or what was the right course of action.

David Thodey asked the question, "How would you like it handled if it was you?"

The executive replied, "Well, I think I would like it waived at no charge."

David then asked, "Why do you think we wouldn't do that?"

"Well, because of the policy we have." David said, "Our values of treating customers fairly would override any policy, wouldn't it? There's a higher purpose for what we stand for."[1]

Creating alignment around what's best for the customer is easier said than done in businesses that are making the transformation toward a customer culture. All levels of the business need to understand in tangible terms what actions to take that support the company's values, vision, and strategy and that back the customer as the focal point of the business. Empowerment must be given to staff to override the rules if they are not in the customer's best interests or seem to be totally unfair in a specific circumstance. In many moment-of-truth interactions with customers it is better to not ask management for permission and later, if necessary, beg for forgiveness. For people to be empowered they need to trust that they will not be punished for doing what's right for the customer.

Internal focus on operations, processes, and working in silos creates habits that can be hard to change. As companies grow complexity increases, silos develop, and clear communication becomes a challenge. Processes develop to enhance efficiency and become hard to change when new circumstances have made them redundant. Internal politics can shift focus to self interest away from customer interests. This can happen in small and medium size businesses as well as large ones. Lack of strategic alignment around what's best for the customer is perpetuated by a number of factors prevalent in large organizations.

One factor is short-tem focused behavior driven by investor priorities for favorable quarterly results. This leads to a focus on profit and revenue to the detriment of customers, and it reflects actions taken in all levels of the business to achieve short-term numbers. A strong customer culture that drives a sustainable business leads to integrated thinking and reporting. This is based on medium-term performance trends and shifts focus to longer term relationships with customers rather than one-off transactions.

This is frequently reinforced by compensation schemes that work against the best interests of customers. We have seen this happen in the financial services market where sales people have had incentives to sell mortgages or car loans to people who could not afford them. Such schemes lead to customers not having their real needs met. Compensation programs that reward people at all levels in a business based on customer metrics (for example, lifetime value of customers that measures the average length and financial value of customer relationships) work to align interests of customers, staff members, and business. Also linking remuneration to customer advocacy metrics, such as the net promoter score, reinforce the importance of positive customer experiences and their role in generating business growth.

Another factor is lack of big-picture understanding by staff members about how they contribute to value for customers. Without that mindset and tangible connection there is a focus on function and process for its own sake. Many of today's professionals are specialists with highly developed technical skills in their areas of expertise. This leads to a narrow focus without a broader understanding of the business environment and how those specialists affect the value received by customers. Some professionals even view customers as inhibitors to getting their jobs done—an annoyance to minimize. Examples are the busy legal expert in a company that must redraft contracts in plain English or the accountant who must oversee a new billing system to simplify processes and enhance customer understanding often lament the influence of customers. Some professionals focus on profit to the exclusion of customer interests. When this attitude takes hold in organizations it becomes a major roadblock to a customer culture regardless of what the mission states. When staff members do not understand or care about the company's strategy and how what they do contributes to delivering value to customers, this leads to the customer receiving mixed service and conflicting messages.

This can be overcome by senior leaders taking an active role in clarifying and "living" the company's values and vision that incorporate customers at the core. It takes a big effort by leaders at all levels to inspire their teams to engage with customers and experience the satisfaction that comes from positive customer feedback and endorsement.

A further factor is the walls created by functional silos, where there is lack of cross-functional collaboration and unclear customer "ownership" creates problems for customers. For example, we have all experienced frustrations of talking with several people in an organization, none of whom will take ownership of our problem and fix it. This leads to customer frustration and lack of credibility in the customer promise. (Breaking down silos and creating companywide collaboration as a cultural discipline was discussed in Chapter 7.)

The Business Case

Imagine This Situation
Imagine you are facing these existing or potential threats:

- Customers' expectations that are unfulfilled due to lack of engagement of employees
- Products and services delivered to unprofitable customers
- Customers confused by ineffective service delivery
- Lack of understanding of which customers to target
- Different staff members giving customers different answers to the same question

What's Your Response?
Is it to blame it on incompetent staff or unreasonable customers?
Or
To investigate the source of the problems and act to create clear strategic alignment in terms of clarity of communicated vision, values, goals, and strategy?

What's the Difference?
Organizations with clear, well-communicated, and understood vision, values, goals, and strategy in all levels and parts of the business generate continuous alignment, which results in higher customer satisfaction, innovation, new-product success, sales growth, profit growth, and profitability than their competitors.

Link to Business Performance
This measures a business's ability to leverage its resources and advantages across its organization and throughout its value chain to deliver differentiated value. This impacts customer satisfaction, innovation, new-product success, sales growth, profit growth, and profitability. It has short-, medium-, and longer-term impacts on business effectiveness and profitability.

Link to Strategy
Strength in this discipline is relevant to all business strategies by enhancing *delivery* of value to customers and strengthening competitive advantage.

Figure 8.1 highlights strategic alignment as the focus of this chapter. The goal is for companies to improve their absolute and relative strength in this discipline. The score of 100 percent means that a company is above all others in our MRI global database in terms of strategic alignment behaviors.

What Is Strategic Alignment?

Strategic alignment is a discipline of workforce behavior that enables a strong customer culture and makes it possible for the company to create and deliver value for customers and shareholders. Without strong alignment within a business, there are inefficiencies that affect customers and lack of employee engagement that affects business performance and customer satisfaction.

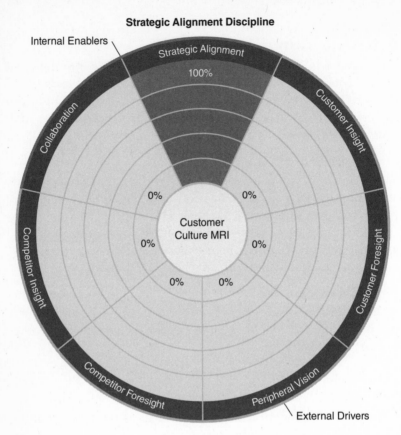

Figure 8.1 Strategic alignment discipline

Strategic alignment is the extent to which employees understand and enact the vision, mission, objectives, and strategic direction of the company.

In order to make the most of value creation efforts, groups must align their efforts with the strategy of the organization. Strategy must not only be known and understood by employees, but it must be actively aligned to as well. Groups with strong strategic alignment discuss company strategy; align with its goals and objectives; eliminate nonvalue activities, efforts, and projects that do not align; and quickly adjust when strategy changes.

The alignment of an organization to a shared vision and values, common goals, and a clear strategy requires that every person from the board to the back room understands the strategy and how his or her actions contribute to creating value for customers. It requires a shared understanding and commitment at all levels and in all functions of the organization.

The Stelter Company of Des Moines, Iowa, is a family business that takes its customer culture seriously. It is in the business of helping its customers achieve their charitable missions by providing unique insights into the world of personal philanthropy. Stelter helps companies such as the World Wildlife Fund and the Make-A-Wish Foundation reach their supporters via a deep expertise in marketing and an understanding of what encourages people to support their favorite causes.

The CEO, Larry Stelter, leads by example when it comes to making customers a priority. He personally calls all new customers and thanks them for their business and regularly connects with many of the more than 1,800 customers Stelter supports across the United States.

Stelter leaders Wendi Lanning and Dawn Solis Toledo have led the charge to continue to enhance the company's customer culture by creating a new set of values for the organization to live by. Described as the "secret sauce," it includes values that are important to Stelter's ability to service its customers.

These values were developed and agreed upon by the whole organization and provide the foundation to maintain its strong customer-focused culture for the future.

This, coupled with a deep understanding of the different types of customers Stelter serves, has allowed it to align its services with customers that are the best fit. In practical terms this means providing high levels of service to those customers that want a strategic partner–type of relationship while responding to the needs of other customers in a more tactical manner.

Nathan Stelter, a third-generation family member and vice president of business development, describes the organization's approach to hiring as follows: "We are very careful about who we hire. We hire for culture fit first rather than skill set. While high-level skills are important, we know we can develop skills but cultivating the right attitude towards customers can be harder." This ensures new hires are aligned with the company's vision, values, and customer culture.

This is a clear responsibility of company leaders. If staff members are not "getting it" there is a breakdown in leadership.

Another story, from Telstra, illustrates the importance of leaders understanding their responsibility to support staff members to enable them to become aligned. In late 2011, as the senior executives sat around in a circle in the first of many workshops to be rolled out across the company, they heard a recording of a Telstra rep trying to appease an irate customer. Try as he might, he could not satisfy the customer who became more outraged and frustrated. In the end, the customer slammed down the phone. There was stunned silence in the room full of executives. At that moment they realized the lack of support being given to the front-line reps in dealing with serious customer service issues.

The executives then asked, "What can we do to help the rep satisfy the customer's problem? How can we create a situation where the rep and the customer do not have to experience such anguish?"

This landmark experience by senior executives illustrated the heart of the problem they were facing, and it created in them a determination to fix it.

Why Is Strategic Alignment a Cultural Discipline?

Our research shows that low scores on the strategic alignment discipline of customer culture have a major impact on business performance, as a business is simply not able to effectively deliver value to its customers.

When strategic alignment is low, we have found that employees are not fully engaged with the business purpose or delivering value to customers. They lack a higher purpose, and work has no meaning. They remain in the job for security.

Perhaps many in their company have experienced the fate of jumping circus fleas. We are told that a flea can jump to a height 150 times its own size. To train circus fleas to all jump to the same height in unison to music they are placed in a large jar with a lid that acts as a glass ceiling. They don't like to bump their heads (apparently even fleas get headaches), so they jump just short of the top, and once they are trained that way, the ceiling is removed. The same happens in business: even when the "ceiling" is lifted and people are empowered to make the right decisions for customers, many find it difficult to change. They may lack confidence, skills, or tangible guidance necessary to make the shift. Also business process transformation is often necessary to help empower employees to help customers.[2]

But we have found that high strategic alignment focused on delivery of superior customer value is positively associated with higher employee engagement. In one customer culture initiative we conducted we found that high strategic alignment around the customer in one part of a business also showed much higher employee engagement than in other parts of the business where strategic alignment was lower.[3]

Strategic alignment and employee engagement are major challenges for senior leaders. According to recent studies, two-thirds of corporate strategy is never executed. Senior leaders might be clear on their strategy and their goals, but if you check what people are doing on a day-to-day basis there is often a big gap between what they are doing and what is required to execute the strategy.[4] There needs to be focus and discipline to create alignment between organizational vision and strategy and what people in the business do day to day.

Strategic alignment requires all employees to be positively engaged. Yet a variety of reports tell us that up to 70 percent of employees in the United States are not engaged or are actively disengaged. Also about 70 percent of people who leave their jobs in the United States do so because of their boss.[5] Stan Phelps, in his latest book, *What's Your Green Goldfish,* describes the practices that companies have found successful in engaging employees, from AnswerLab's one-on-one "walk and talk" with the CEO to Intel's greeters and gifts for new hires. It is based on the premise that happy employees create happy customers and that employee engagement is a commitment, not a campaign—it is a cultural discipline. Engaged employees are aligned to the strategy, actively involved in its execution, and seeking to innovate and improve value for customers.[6] Everyone in the business needs to know how she or he contributes value for the customer and the business through the company's strategy.

Even the iconic Japanese company Toyota can falter. At Toyota the concept of "the next process is the customer" has played a significant role in defining the company culture. "The next process is the customer" means that everyone treats all downstream processes as if they were the final customer, all the while emphasizing that the final customer deserves and demands perfection. But something went wrong in 2010. Toyota, a guiding example of strong customer culture, suffered not only losses but humiliation at a U.S. congressional hearing in February 2010 when it failed to accept that some of its models had safety problems. This was a failure of strategic alignment in which the famed Toyota quality control was not questioned. That, despite substantial customer feedback of problems experienced by American customers. There also appeared to be reluctance by American executives to report these problems back to the corporate center in Tokyo. Akio Toyoda, president of Toyota, was driven to make a televised apology to the American people, a "loss of face" striking at the heart of Japanese culture.[7] The impact of this breakdown has continued to the present day with the recall in June 2013 of about eighty-seven thousand 2010 Toyota Prius and Lexus HS 250h vehicles because of a brake problem.[8]

Strategic alignment requires inspiration from leaders. It comes from helping people believe there is no limit to what they can achieve if they believe it. It requires a change in mindset from "I'll believe it when I see it" to "I'll see it when I believe it." It is about painting a vision and making it tangible. Storytelling is a powerful method of inspiring and creating an understanding of what it means to deliver on the company's strategy.

The power of personal stories is illustrated by the experience of John Hooper, the CFO of Ergon Energy. He tells of his journey to climb Mount Kilimanjaro (19,340 feet, or 5,895 meters, high) in Tanzania, Africa, during the end-of-year holidays of 2012. John uses this story to align the thinking and actions of his staff to a customer culture. In his own words he recounts his experience.

"I had put in a lot of training for this adventure," he says, "so I dearly wanted to make it to the top, but could I? Climbing high mountains plays on you both physically and mentally. On the lower parts of the climb I kept hearing stories of how hard it is to reach the summit. I saw people being rapidly brought down the mountain suffering from altitude sickness.

"After five days of climbing, we set off with our guides at 11 p.m. for the remaining 3,000-foot climb to the summit. [Deprivation] of oxygen at that altitude impacts the body and the mind. I was feeling tired, but good. The Tanzanian guides were continually encouraging us—'go slow. You're doing great!' At one point a guide came back to me and suggested he carry my backpack. I felt OK and said I could carry it myself. The guide persisted and said he would only carry it as far as the next rest stop. When we arrived at the next rest stop, I could see that the guide had carried an additional three packs apart from his own. When I approached him, the guide said he would just carry it a little further for me.

"We reached the summit at 7.30 a.m. the next morning, and the guide was waiting for me with my backpack. I was exhausted. Who knows whether I would have made it carrying my own pack? But the guide could sense that I [might] have [had] difficulties making the top—not only in the first part of that summit climb, but for the last bit of it. He was thinking ahead of his client's future needs. He was almost literally 'walking in my shoes.' He was checking with me to understand how I was feeling and sensing what else he could do to help me achieve my goal. Most of all, he was thinking of me as a human being. I experienced immense gratitude towards this guide—an emotion that will remain with me lifelong."[9]

When a story like this (like the one recounted by Chris Zane of Zane Cycles in Chapter 1) relates to your business, it is even more powerful in communicating the customer mindset and alignment needed in a customer-centric business.

Stories, of course, must be backed not only by the action of leaders communicating the vision, value, and strategy by stories and illustrations but also by their decisions, recognition, and reward programs and their commitment to staff to help them by reducing irrelevant bureaucracy and improve processes. When all of these things happen, strategic alignment is created as a discipline that benefits customers, employees, and the business.

Who Has It?

Every Friday an e-mail sits in the in-box of every Virgin Group employee across the globe. It is from Josh Bayliss, global chief executive of the Virgin Group from the head office in Geneva. His e-mail tells his team what he is doing and asks for their thoughts and

feedback. He says: "I believe in personal accountability, accountability to the business. It is absolutely critical to being successful."[10]
Bayliss follows closely Richard Branson's advice to "delegate and
listen." Branson says of him: "He's become good at getting teams
to run things. He also sees the bigger picture and understands the
brands."[11] Josh Bayliss has brought focus back to where Richard
Branson comes from by reinforcing the vision, values, and strategic
alignment to guide the strategies and behaviors of each of the Virgin
businesses.

The Virgin Group has a clear vision, set of values, and working principles that create strong strategic alignment across its diverse
businesses. It states:

> Virgin believes in making a difference. We stand for
> value for money, quality, innovation, fun and a sense
> of competitive challenge. We strive to achieve this by
> empowering our employees to continually deliver an
> unbeatable customer experience.

> Virgin Group companies are part of one big family rather
> than a hierarchy. They are empowered to run their own
> affairs, yet the companies actively help one another, and
> solutions to problems are often sourced from within
> the Group. In a sense they form a commonwealth, with
> shared ideas, values, interest and goals. At our core we
> believe business must be a force for good and use its
> influence and resources to help find solutions to some of
> the world's major issues.[12]

It is one thing to espouse these values and goals. It is another to
live it and do it. Mark Gilmour, head of global brand development
for the Virgin Group, says that the powerful use of language helps
create alignment across and within Virgin businesses at all levels.[13]
He says each Virgin business seeks to be "purpose-driven"—a purpose for good that goes beyond profit with a focus on people, planet,
and profit. He describes Virgin's customer culture as "brilliant basics
with magic touches" where the individual is expected to connect

with a customer "beyond the rulebook." Mark recounts a story that illustrates this as follows.

Virgin Holidays in the United Kingdom had sold a holiday package to a family. When departing on holidays, the young daughter of the family left her favorite doll at the airport on departure. Virgin Holiday staff made contact with the family and told the daughter that her doll was having a wonderful holiday while they were away—doing all kinds of exciting things. The child was very relieved and happy that her doll was being cared for—and the family had a memorable holiday. This story illustrates the "magic touches" that strike an emotional connection with customers that results in a powerful bond with the brand. The story ended up on social media and further enhanced the values espoused by the Virgin brand—care for customers.

Some of Virgin's values are reinforced with memorable symbols that are a talking point inside and outside the business. In one of the Virgin offices in the bathrooms where the toilet roll is on the wall you will see above it the words "this is the only place you will be ripped off at Virgin"—reinforcing the value for money positioning of all Virgin businesses. With food service on Virgin Atlantic, you will find appealing salt and pepper shakers. These seem to be taken frequently as souvenirs by customers, and replacement costs became an issue. Instead of removing these items from airline stock, Virgin decided to print on the bottom of them the label "Pinched from Virgin"—reinforcing the sense of fun at Virgin.

Mark says that people recruited to Virgin are those who have a natural *insatiable curiosity*. The ethos is, "We value you as a person for who you are. We allow you to do what's right for the customer and do what needs to be done to satisfy the customer."

"A goal of Virgin is to not just play the game," says Mark, "but change it for *good*." In such a diverse range of industries, how is strategic alignment of the Virgin brand ethos maintained? Mark says the key way to get brand alignment is with the right selection of leaders, teams, and people that already "get Virgin." This applies whether the Virgin Group has substantial ownership in a business or no ownership at all.

The Virgin vision, values, leadership, recruitment approach, symbols, and language all support a strategic alignment that results in superior value and experience for customers delivered by passionate people who believe, above all, in doing good for others. Mark Gilmour is a great example of the Virgin ethos.

How Do You Develop Strategic Alignment?

Ian Grace, CEO of Virgin Radio,[14] knows how to create strategic alignment. He has successfully launched 19 separate radio stations in seven countries over the last 12 years. Each station has to start with and maintain strategic alignment in terms of Virgin vision, values, goals, strategy, product offering, and customer.

Setting up the Lebanon station in May 2013 shows how it works. Prior to establishing the station in that country there was extensive consumer research and evaluation of the advertiser market from which a launch strategy was developed around program format, brand positioning, and timing. The station director, program manager, sales director, and finance manager were relocated from Virgin Radio locations elsewhere to form the management team for the new Beirut radio station. Strategy and consumer market-share goals were set as well as advertising customers and revenue targets. Local people in Beirut were recruited to staff the business. Often these people knew about Virgin from other businesses and were soon oriented to the Virgin philosophy and culture. It helped that total staffing of a station is 30 to 50 people; all would become known to each other personally and quickly form camaraderie as the new station launched and went to air. Richard Branson arrived for the preparty launch, and he acted as the figurehead of the business. In his memorable way he reinforced the Virgin values, goals, and strategy by meeting with staff members, showing personal interest in them as people, and inspiring them to do a great job.

After the launch, weekly consumer research measures preferences and listener market penetration were collected to identify trends and see if changes should be made to program format. These metrics keep people on their toes and aligned to the strategy and goals.

The same approach was adopted previously in launches in Bangkok, Delhi, and Dubai. Virgin held the number-one market-share position in its target segment in those three markets within six months of entry, and it has since held on to it. Advertising revenue has followed to make for sustainable, profitable businesses.

What Behaviors Draw Out Strategic Alignment?

Brian Hartzer, chief executive of Australian financial services at Westpac Bank, says the role of senior leaders is to be customer-centric and to exhibit those behaviors. They need to look through the customers' eyes, walk in the customers' shoes, and put themselves through the customers' own experiences. They need to make it a discipline.

He says: "The companies that have done well at this are those where the senior managers have been happy to go out and experience what customers are experiencing. They are prepared 'to eat their own dog food' and find out what customers are experiencing and then to do something about it."[15]

Brian attends lunches with customers, does customer visits and branch visits, and talks with staff members about their experiences with customers. He calls loan officers with low service-quality scores and also those with high scores. He writes his own blog on his experiences of talking with staff and what he learns from it, describes best practices he has seen at the bank, and shows his personal interest and intervention to help and coach where needed. Brian says, "You need a narrative that inspires buy-in. I look for symbolic acts and stories which illustrate and show people what it means to be customer-centric."

He repeats an illustrative story in a video conference, on his blog and to a group at a town hall meeting. He uses video to show people who are doing it well to act as peer advocates. He identifies what Malcolm Gladwell in his book *The Tipping Point* calls the "mavens"—that small number of people whom it is vital to get to.[16] In a bank it is the branch managers. So Brian does road shows with the branch managers.

Strategic alignment requires communication approaches that are clear and effective within a team and between groups so that objectives, strategies, and priorities are well understood. Communication systems and methods should be reviewed periodically for their effectiveness in supporting strategic alignment.

These are examples of strategic alignment behaviors:

- Clear and repeated communication of the company's vision, mission, and strategy
- Monitoring customer-centric behavior in all functions
- Measuring and benchmarking progress of customer-centricity against targets
- Recognizing employees who act in a customer-centric way
- Rewarding customer-centric behavior
- Aligning work with the company's goals and objectives
- Adjusting focus and priorities when strategies change
- Eliminating projects and activities that do not contribute to strategy execution
- Sharing stories of great customer experiences brought about by customer-centric behavior
- Planning, implementing, and embedding a customer-centric culture

Senior leaders need to ensure not only that many of these systems and processes are in place but also that they are well understood and work properly for staff to feel empowered, aligned, and excited to do what's best for the customer.

What Are Some of the Best Practices?

Those companies that have developed strategic alignment as a discipline make them very successful at gaining competitive advantage. The following examples show how strategic alignment practices strengthen customer culture.

Salesforce.com: V2MOM, a Powerful Alignment Tool

When we asked Alex Bard, a senior vice president and general manager at salesforce.com how to grow rapidly and still retain a high level of customer-centricity he pointed to their internal system designed to create alignment.

The process is called the V2MOM and was developed by the founder of salesforce.com, Marc Benioff. It is a methodology that Alex describes as the key ingredient to creating alignment in the fast-paced, ever-changing technology business.

Alex describes the value of the process as a new leader in sales-force.com as follows: "There's a lesson that I learned when I became part of Salesforce, which is you can't send a bulleted list without people looking at it as though it's in priority order. So everything that we do—even the V2MOM specifically sets this tone—that, if something is the first bullet, that means it is the most important. In fact, when shaping the V2MOM, there'll be conversations where we say, 'Is that more important than this?' So it helps us as a leadership team to quickly get on the same page and prioritize."[17]

The V2MOM acronym stands for "Vision, Values, Methods, Obstacles, and Measures." The process begins with Marc Benioff reviewing his V2MOM every six months. He presents it to the top team members, they debate and refine it, and it rolls down. But it is not only a top-down approach. The corporate V2MOM is shared on salesforce.com's internal idea exchange platform to solicit and gather input from all employees.

Once the corporate V2MOM is set, every executive develops his or her own V2MOM that references the corporate V2MOM. Every employee develops a V2MOM as well.

"It takes time, but it's a very worthwhile investment, because coming out of it, everybody's crystal-clear on exactly what the priorities are for the company, for your group, for yourself individually as a contributor to those things."

As Alex mentioned to us, Marc Benioff's latest revision of the vision statement says it all, with its first sentence beginning with "Create wildly successful customers."

What are you doing to align people around the idea to create wildly successful customers at your organization?

Virgin Trains: Creating Alignment Around Customers

The CEO of Virgin Trains, Tony Collins, has a unique approach to creating strategic alignment around the customer. He has taken British Rail from an old-fashioned, poorly regarded company with a command-and-control structure (where leaders are to be feared and obeyed) to one where customers love it so much they have campaigned to keep it running routes. It has been a remarkable cultural transformation over a 12-year period; it shows the true value of employee engagement and customer connectedness in transforming business performance.

At Virgin Trains, they had to break down all those barriers of a command-and-control culture, build trust, and excite the employees about the future of the business. They began a huge exercise to develop the mission, vision, and values by going out to the 3,000 staff members and holding workshops anchored around "putting our customer first in everything we do." It addressed the implications of changing from a command-and-control, inward-looking organization to a company that is empowered and innovative, that has more open communication and transparency, and that has staff members treated with equality and fairness. It took a long time for this to come to fruition, but Tony felt that the value of employees developing their own vision was well worth it. He said this also encouraged people to challenge upward and disagree with managers as a way for keeping an organization "real."

His view was that to be able to succeed a leader needs to assemble a team with passion. The second step involved identifying people at all levels with leadership and customer-centric skills and engaging them in workshops to understand how they could align closely with the company's strategy and the customers' needs. Tony also reshaped the recruitment policy to recruit for attitude, because he believes that you can give people skills, but people either have a great attitude or they don't.[18] These people were supported with coaching and tools to help them act as role models throughout the company.

A third step was to encourage people to nominate others for awards for their activities around customer-centricity and recognition for engaging in the core behaviors of collaboration, open communication, building of relationships, promotion of teamwork, and respect. All of these things were necessary to develop a customer culture in Virgin Trains.

What Virgin Trains has achieved is described in a case study in the next chapter.

Telstra: The "One Telstra" Alignment

David Thodey, CEO of Telstra, knows about the challenges of getting strategic alignment in a large business with 60,000 staff members and full-time contractors. Earlier he was recruited from IBM to head one of Telstra's most important, rapidly growing business units with a lot of autonomy and run it as his own business and be accountable for growth and profitability. David developed a customer culture in his unit, and he says that he didn't care too much about what was happening in other business units.

But when he took over as CEO, he realized that for Telstra to prosper in an increasingly competitive environment it needed to become aligned as one company around the customer. Telstra had been a very silo-based organization.

David says: "Having the focus on the customer has been really important in breaking the silos down. There is only one arbiter—the customer. We needed to bring all of Telstra, the old and the new, into the new world together—as one Telstra. So, we had to get our people to believe that Telstra can become an admired company. Give them the confidence to talk about where they work at BBQs and take a positive view with friends that if they have had a bad experience, we really care and we will find a way to fix it. The employee referral scheme was implemented to enable staff to get direct help for a customer."[19]

A big part of the process of getting alignment was achieved by conducting workshops that were titled "Our Customer Connection" (OCC). Leadership alignment was the number-one objective. Rachel Sandford, an organizational development lead in Telstra's Culture Advocacy Program, describes this as a massive impact program to create both customers and employees as advocates.[20] She says the first two-day workshop, OCC1, was for engaging 3,500 people leaders and was designed to create alignment with Telstra's vision of committing to customers. It immersed people in what it was like to be a customer and in making a personal commitment to creating a "movement" with their teams. This was followed by the OCC2 workshop for leaders and individuals in key collaborative roles. These two-day workshops were attended by more than 7,000 employees and business partners across the business in Australia and the Philippines.

Peter Wheeler, a partner at PricewaterhouseCoopers, helped facilitate this program, which was designed to explain the customer advocacy system being introduced in the business, identify relevant behaviors that drive advocacy, and show methods of cascading this mindset and tools to teams in the business.[21]

Every workshop was opened by a member of the Telstra executive team, and their deputies facilitated many sessions. Just concluded in mid-2013, the workshops have revealed to both Rachel and Peter what a substantial impact they have had. They report that virtually everyone understands customer advocacy, there has been a doubling of internal people as advocates inside Telstra, and the energy and commitment of people is evident. Role modeling by leaders is making good progress.

In addition, Telstra has implemented the Net Promoter System (NPS) as the key customer metrics against which everyone in the company benefits financially if targets are achieved. The OCC workshops have been designed to enable all leaders to tell their Telstra story, to explain how advocacy and the NPS system work, and to use their skills to work with their teams to align them around Telstra's vision, values, and strategy. Team meetings, known as "T-Time," are held at least monthly for teams all across the business to review customer feedback and act to improve the customer experience.

These elements are acting to create strategic alignment in Telstra and strengthen customer culture.

JetBlue: Eating Your Own Dog Food

We're not certain where the expression "eating your own dog food" originated. What we do know is that Lyndon Prowse, a South African living in Australia, became famous when he started his own pet-food company called Luv Pet Foods in the 1960s. Not because he produced good pet food, but because he ate his own dog food on television in commercials and interviews. It was rumored that as a supplier, to have any success in selling anything to Lyndon you had to sit down with him and eat a can of Luv dog food.[22]

This expression has come to mean that you need to experience your own product or service just as your customer does to really understand their perception.

At JetBlue, founder David Neeleman travels at least once a week to several destinations in a day, serving customers on the flight, talking to every one of them, asking them questions about their experience, and talking with crew members and answering their questions. He almost single-handedly creates and maintains strategic alignment within the business and with customers.[23] He said he had three rules for employees: show up on time, take care of your coworkers, and take care of customers. He explains: "When customers fly JetBlue they feel special. You feel like the people serving you are actually pleased to have you on board. It's okay to use the flight attendant call button. We relish the opportunity to serve."[24] On June 13, 2012, JetBlue ranked "Highest in Customer Satisfaction Among Low Cost Carriers in North America" by J.D. Power and Associates, a customer satisfaction recognition received for the eighth year in a row.[25] Neeleman's biggest worry is dilution of the customer-focused culture, and he personally works hard to keep his organization strategically aligned with customer needs.

This example illustrates the importance of senior leaders getting out in the field and experiencing what customers experience, talking with staff, understanding how they can be better supported to serve customers, and continually reinforcing the alignment of everyone in the business with customer experience.

CHAPTER SUMMARY

Why is strategic alignment important to customer-centricity?
Strategic alignment is critical to a successful focus toward customers. In order to make the most of value creation efforts, groups must align these efforts with the strategy of the organization. Strategy must not only be known and understood by employees but also actively aligned.

High levels of strategic alignment have been found to positively impact innovation, customer satisfaction, sales growth, and profitability.

(Continued)

What is strategic alignment?

Strategic alignment is the extent to which employees understand, and enact the vision, mission, objectives, and strategic direction of the company. It is a discipline of workforce behavior that enables a strong customer culture and makes it possible for the company to create and deliver value for customers and shareholders. The alignment of an organization to a shared vision and values, common goals, and a clear strategy requires that every person, from the board to the back room, understands the strategy and how his or her actions contribute to creating value for customers.

Why is strategic alignment a cultural discipline?

According to recent studies, two-thirds of corporate strategies are never executed. Senior leaders might be clear on their strategy and their goals, but if you check what people are doing on a day-to-day basis there is often a big gap between what they are doing and what is required to execute the strategy. There needs to be focus and discipline to create and maintain alignment between organizational vision, values and strategy and what people in the business do day to day. This means it has to become part of the customer culture.

What behaviors lead to strategic alignment?

Strategic alignment requires communication approaches that are clear and effective within and between groups so that objectives, strategies, and priorities are well understood. Communication systems and methods should be reviewed periodically for their effectiveness in supporting strategic alignment. Groups with strong strategic alignment discuss company strategy; align with its goals and objectives; eliminate activities, efforts, and projects that do not align; and quickly adjust when strategy changes.

These behaviors are focused on activities that execute the business's value proposition with a priority on meeting changing customer needs and responding effectively to customers' problems.

Leader's Guide to Strategic Alignment

Strategic Alignment: *Is the firm's strategic direction discussed regularly with all employees? How quickly are work-group priorities changed when the firm's strategic plans change? Do staff members fully understand and buy in to the company's vision and see how it relates to them personally and how they work? Can everyone in the business tell you how he or she is working differently to implement a customer-focused strategy? Are people adapting their behavior in line with their business unit's strategy?*

Rate where *you and your team* stand on strategic alignment by checking the relevant box in answering each question.

Rating descriptors: 0 = never; 1 = almost never; 2 = rarely; 3 = occasionally; 4 = sometimes; 5 = regularly; 6 = frequently; 7 = often; 8 = very often; 9 = constantly; 10 = all the time.

☐ 1. To what extent is there clear and repeated communication of the vision, values, and strategy throughout all parts of the business?

☐ 2. To what extent is customer-centric behavior monitored in all functions and business units?

☐ 3. To what extent is customer-centricity measured and progressively benchmarked against customer culture targets?

☐ 4. To what extent is work aligned with the company's goals and objectives in all parts of the company?

☐ 5. To what extent are priorities and focus adjusted when strategy changes?

☐ 6. To what extent are projects and activities eliminated that do not contribute to strategy execution?

☐ 7. To what extent is there recognition of employees who act in a customer-centric way?

☐ 8. To what extent are individuals and teams rewarded for their strong customer culture?

(Continued)

☐ 9. To what extent is storytelling used to strengthen and reinforce customer culture across the business?

☐ 10. To what extent is there ongoing planning and embedding of deeper levels of customer culture throughout the business?

Chapter 9

How to Make It Happen

Focus on your customers and lead your people as though their lives depend on your success.

—Warren Buffett

In large organizations and even in midsize companies it is easy for us to feel that we cannot do what's right for customers as well as what's right for the business. It may be that the processes are against it. It might be that others don't care. It might be that our manager doesn't "get it." But it has been proven by companies like Amazon.com, Starbucks, salesforce.com, and Virgin that what's best for the customer is also best for the business. Customers are happy. This makes staff, as well as stockholders, happy. Of course, these companies don't always get it right, but they are guided by a culture that expects that when they fall short they quickly acknowledge their mistakes and make things right.

How do these companies do it? They have been able to infuse everyone with a mindset and set of skills that focus on providing a superior customer experience. Every individual is given permission to lead with the customer, and the goal is to win with the customer.

It starts at the top with the CEO and senior management. Leaders need a clear corporate vision and goal, awareness of how to compete with a clear strategy, and training and practice so that they embed customer behaviors into their own DNA and, of course, in to their teams, so that that everyone in the organization has "buy-in." In any organization, leaders must engage and inspire all staff to lead the customer experience race.

Business Case

Imagine This Situation
You kick off a new initiative to drive improvements in your company's customer-centric culture.

What's Your Response?
You take an ad hoc approach with no real plan. You and your leaders are diverted by a new priority or a short-term focus. The initial investment is lost, staff members become cynical, and the business continues the way it has always been.
Or
You have a powerful vision and values of what you want the organization to become, you have a clear long-term strategy, you have a road map of how to get there and a commitment from the senior leaders to follow it through, no matter what it takes.

What's the Difference?
If senior leaders are indifferent to customer culture or delegate the leadership of this process, it will get lost in the bowels of the organization and be sidelined by shifts in short-term priorities and day-to-day operations. Without a clear, communicated vision and road map, the initiative is doomed to be just another management fad.

For it to work, the CEO and senior leaders must be invested in it, to have "skin in the game."

A road map, lined up with the company's vision and strategy, followed by committed leaders who are prepared to stay the course despite short-term setbacks, will create a strong customer culture that delivers superior business performance over the long term. In our experience, most companies need to be transformed to have a resilient customer culture and need a road map to embed it. But a special few are born with it and are able to maintain it over a long period of time.

Is a Customer Culture Born or Made?

Customer cultures are both born and made. We see companies that started with a strong customer culture, fused within the vision of the founder, and have kept it over many years; others that were born with it, lost it, and regained it; and other, well established companies that have undergone a complete transformation to get it. They all have two things in common. First, they are crystal clear on their vision and purpose that goes well beyond the goal of providing good returns for their shareholders. Second, they have a belief in a higher purpose that transcends the products and services they provide—a purpose that inspires employees to want to be a part of it and contribute something of real value as a legacy for current and future generations.

Born with Customer Culture
Some companies were born with a customer culture and have maintained it over many years. In earlier chapters we tell some short stories of Amazon.com, salesforce.com, Virgin, and Markit to illustrate what these companies have as a durable, adaptive customer culture. We use Amazon.com in this chapter as the example of the quintessential customer-centric business that was born that way and has maintained it throughout its 18-year life.

Had It, Lost It, and Regained It
We use Starbucks in this chapter to illustrate what it takes to regain a customer culture once you have lost it. Starbucks was born customer-centric, lost it, and needed a massive effort to regain it,

showing that you must be vigilant to keep a customer culture once you have it. In fact, you need to continuously keep strengthening it.

Transformation from Low Customer Focus to a Strong Customer Culture

We tell four stories of companies committed to undergoing a customer-centric transformation and what they have done to get there. All companies are in different phases of the transformation process, and they tell us what they have done to be where they are. We look at a postal/parcel freight service, a telecommunications company, a bank, and a rail company—each one an iconic company in its own industry. These large businesses have a long history and have come from a legacy of being internally focused and in some cases from original legislated monopolies or regulatory protection. These have been selected because of the massive change that has been required to transform them and the success they are making of it. They are the most challenging to change and are useful in guiding us with a practical road map and showing us what it takes to build a customer culture from an entrenched, internally focused culture.

A Road Map to Customer Culture

This chapter provides a four-phase road map with associated actions and processes for changing a company, business unit, function, or team from one with low customer focus to a strong customer culture. Our examples in this chapter relate to the entire organization, but the road map can be equally applied to a business unit or to a function. For example, Fairfax Media initially transformed its Online Marketplaces businesses to a customer culture before initiating this process through its mainstream newspaper and magazines businesses.[1] Telstra's Finance group undertook a customer culture transformation prior to the whole organization making a long-term commitment to becoming customer-centric.[2]

What we do in this chapter is provide a framework and a road-map for you to undertake this journey in your business.[3]

The Big-Picture Road Map

It is our aim, based on our research and experience, to provide a framework for leaders to take the customer culture journey following several clearly defined steps. In each case you will need to adapt this road map to your own situation. Where your company is in terms of its current level of interaction with customers, feedback systems and processes, customer culture level, and clarity of vision and strategy, will determine both the priority of things to be done first and the order of the steps. The firm's competitive situation and the urgency related to survival will also determine which customer culture disciplines are the most important to build or strengthen first.

The first thing to recognize is that customer-centricity is a journey that takes companies from one level of customer culture to a higher level and then on to a higher level again. It is a continuous journey of improvement, vigilance, and discipline that creates an innovative, adaptive culture able to transition market shifts, competitive disruption, and future customer needs. Figure 9.1 depicts this as a continuous cycle moving from lower levels of customer culture to higher levels over time.

At the higher levels, customer culture is more firmly embedded in the DNA of the organization, and the behaviors, skills, processes, and customer engagement move companies to a level where their customers view the brand as the center of their world for that type of product or service. That is, customer advocacy and loyalty is "off the charts" along with long-term profitability and growth.

Our research and experience show that throughout this journey there are four phases to getting and keeping a customer culture. We have called these:

- Engage
- Ignite
- Embed
- Fortify

Figure 9.2 shows these phases as a sequence. In reality they reflect a continuous cycle. When major changes in strategy occur as a result of major shifts in the competitive environment, a need arises to realign the organization behind the strategy. Sometimes this may

190

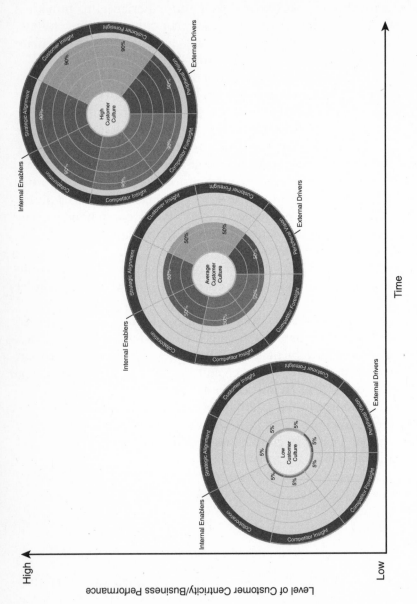

Figure 9.1 Levels of customer culture over time

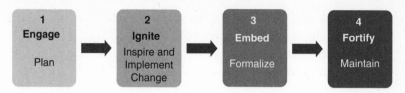

Figure 9.2 Four phases of the journey

involve a modification of vision and core values, as is described in the Westpac Bank case in this chapter. So a new cycle will occur to reengage, reignite, and further embed a stronger customer culture.

The Four-Phase Road Map

At any level, when leaders decide to create or strengthen a customer culture they will take their organization through four sequential phases of transformation. How long each phase takes will depend upon its current customer culture foundation, the size and diversity of the business, and the urgency with which the transformation is undertaken.

For each phase we identify

1. The most important customer culture disciplines to develop
2. The critical actions, processes and outcomes that must be achieved to successfully move on to the next phase

We also assess the benefits that have resulted from the company's customer-centric journey.

Phase 1: Engage and plan: This involves development of a customer-focused vision, values, and strategy. It includes an assessment of the current level of customer culture, buy-in of the senior leadership team, development of and commitment to a plan that goes beyond the annual planning cycle, and allocation of the resources needed to carry it through. *This starts with a focus on building customer insight and strategic alignment.*

Phase 2: Ignite to change: This involves all people leaders communicating and translating the vision and plan, getting buy-in across the business, developing a customer mindset, and understanding the customer behaviors involved. It includes the development of customer metrics and a strengthening of customer feedback systems and processes. *This focuses on building strategic alignment of the vision, values, and strategy and developing customer insight and foresight through increased collaboration, and then adding competitor insight.*

Phase 3: Embed and formalize: This phase aims to make the changes stick by embedding customer-centric disciplines and formalizing, recognizing, and rewarding customer culture behaviors across the entire business at all levels. It includes the formalization of customer metric systems, reward and recognition systems, customer relationship management systems, and simplified customer processes that encourage and support customer-centered behaviors. *This focuses on creating strategic alignment; strengthening customer insight, competitor insight, and strategic alignment; then adding the future-oriented disciplines of customer and competitor foresight supported by cross-functional collaboration.*

Phase 4: Fortify and maintain: This phase involves monitoring, measuring, and benchmarking customer culture and introduces actions to refresh and revitalize customer culture behaviors and processes within the business. It recognizes continuous improvement needed just to maintain a strong customer culture. *This phase focuses on strengthening all disciplines with an emphasis on competitor foresight and peripheral vision.*

The Four-Phase Road Map: Steps in Each Phase

Figure 9.3 depicts the four phases in a sequence, with the most critical steps to be taken at each phase. It also shows what disciplines to build in each phase as a general guideline.

These phases will vary by organization, depending on each one's starting situation. Sometimes we see activities occurring in different phases than what has been depicted in Figure 9.3. Nevertheless, there are some steps, such as vision development and strategy, that should occur before other steps can be effectively executed. Also we see different disciplines being more important than others, depending upon the company's business strategy. But these differences serve to remind us that there is not a hard-and-fast formula, and companies will tailor this process and discipline building to their own needs and competitive conditions.

Phase 1: Engage and Plan: Getting Senior Leadership Buy-In to a Plan

It is essential to plan a customer cultural change effort. Companies that adopt an ad hoc approach usually fail to gain the momentum needed for the change to stick. But there must to be an impetus for a customer culture change to be initiated. This usually occurs when the board, a CEO, or several key stakeholders recognize the need for a change from an internally focused, often politically charged culture to a more open, externally oriented one. *The most critical elements are CEO leadership, a vision with the customer at its center, and values that include the customer and collaboration. Key disciplines to develop with the senior team are strategic alignment and customer insight.*

The Trigger for Customer-centric Change

The trigger is usually created by real or perceived external threats from market shifts, competitor inroads into the business, or disruptive technology, which are negatively affecting business performance. An internal trigger is the appointment of a new CEO. A strong and determined leader must recognize the effects of this actual or imminent challenge to business viability and the urgency for action and be willing to take the journey. The leader must lead the change, not delegate it.

The Three Things You Must Do

1. Develop a customer-centered vision, values, and strategy: The vision must go beyond products and profitability to provide an inspired view of what the organization wants to become. The executive leader and team need to craft and refine the vision, values,

Phases	What You Must Do for Success	What Disciplines to Build
Phase 1 Engage and Plan	• Customer-Centered Vision, Values, and Strategy • Buy-in, Commitment, and Focus of Senior Leaders • Develop a Plan and Announce It	• Strategic Alignment • Customer Insight
Phase 2 Ignite Change	• Communicate and Interact • Translate Vision and Values into Meaningful Action • Customer Mindset, Process and Skills Workshops • Cross-Function Collaboration • Market Intelligence and Information-Sharing Systems	• Strategic Alignment • Customer Insight and Foresight • Competitor Insight • Collaboration
Phase 3 Embed and Formalize	• Develop Customer Culture Behaviors • Formalization Through Symbols, Rituals, and Rewards • Measure Customer Culture and Customer Experience Progress • Ongoing Orientation, Coaching, and Training	• Strategic Alignment • Customer Insight and Foresight • Competitor Insight and Foresight • Collaboration
Phase 4 Fortify and Maintain	• Reinforce and Revitalize Vision, Values, and Strategy • Refresh People Leader Skills, Tools, and Peripheral Vision • Monitor Culture, Customer, and Business Performance	• Strategic Alignment • Customer Insight and Foresight • Competitor Insight and Foresight • Collaboration • Peripheral Vision

Figure 9.3 Road map to customer-centricity

goals, strategy, and priorities. *The vision and values must include the customer as central elements.*

This step needs to have within it a sense of urgency that can be easily communicated and understood by everyone in the organization. The Westpac Bank vision is an example: "To be one of the world's great companies in helping our customers, our communities and our people to prosper and grow." This aligns staff to "helping customers prosper and grow." Values must include "customers" and "collaboration." Again, Westpac includes among its five values "delighting customers" and "one team." The strategy must be defined clearly so that staff members know the value proposition for the business overall and for each major market segment. It must define the competitive advantage that will deliver superior value—whether it be relational value (customer relationships and superior service), product value (superior products as perceived by the customer segment), or price value (the lowest price as perceived by the customer segment). Also the goals must be clear (for example: acquire new customers and increase revenue in this segment; retain customers in that segment; innovate with new products, services, or convenience in that segment).

2. Gain the buy-in, commitment, and focus of senior leaders: The CEO must have a highly committed and collaborative senior leadership team. When a major change, such as the move to customer-centricity, is decided, some leaders will leave. New ones will need to be appointed. Those appointed should already have made the commitment to customer-centricity and become strong advocates and role models for its implementation.

Two initiatives can help to gain buy-in and commitment. One is a program of customer immersion in which all senior leaders interact directly with customers and report on customer feedback they receive and what it means for the business. Also by directly experiencing the company's products or services as a customer, senior leaders get to know what it's like to be a customer. The second initiative is to benchmark the company's customer culture and identify strengths and weaknesses. This identifies which customer culture disciplines are strong or weak and which ones are most critical to its strategy. This provides senior leadership focus for strengthening customer culture across the business.

3. Develop a plan, and announce it: You must have a plan that presents a road map of key initiatives to build a strong customer culture over a minimum two-year period with resources and budget allocated to support it. This will usually include four types of initiatives:

- Building or strengthening customer culture
- Developing and improving customer metrics
- Improving customer processes and support systems
- Making structural changes in the business

The CEO will need to lead a team that includes his or her senior leaders plus any influential advocates as a group to guide the overall progress of the transformation. This group has been given different names such as Customer Engagement Council or Customer Transformation Team. This team will make decisions, allocate resources, and guide the overall initiative.

Phase 2: Ignite Change: Getting People Leaders' Buy-In and Action

There are five key actions to take during the *change* stage. Although shown as a sequence, some of these steps will occur simultaneously, and some will be in a different order. *One of the most critical elements is to get involvement and buy-in by people leaders of the vision and values so they can translate these for their teams. Another is communication through a common "customer" language. Evaluation of where you stand in terms of customer culture and customer satisfaction helps identify priorities for action. Key customer culture disciplines to develop are strategic alignment, customer insight and foresight, competitor insight, and cross-function collaboration.*

The Five Things You Must Do

1. Communicate and interact: Implementing culture change needs a memorable watershed event where the vision is clear, the stakes are raised, the leader leads, and the experience is emblazoned in people's minds. Sometimes referred to as a demarcation event, it is usually done as a major town hall event. This must be skillfully executed to maximize staff engagement. The goal here is to get public buy-in from the people leaders and generate momentum for change. This may have occurred in phase 1, but it is more effective if it is done when the senior leaders have a plan so as to reduce the uncertainty as to what will happen next.

Throughout this phase, clear communication builds clarity and confidence that the senior leaders know what they are doing and why they are doing it. What people see and hear needs to create a sense of fun and excitement for them to connect with the new cultural expectations. Stories are the conversations that create shared experiences and produce a common cultural bond between people. This is reinforced by communication of quick wins and shared stories at mini–town hall meetings and by internal social media.

2. Translate vision and values into meaningful action: The desired new culture needs to be made real. People need to see it, "feel" it, and emotionally connect to it. They have to see it will benefit them, and they need to have the skills and confidence to enact the new behaviors. In Virgin Trains in the United Kingdom, small cross-functional teams worked to develop their own meaning to the vision and values identified by their leadership and what this meant in everyday work practices. The language is developed about customers, clients, advocates, or even "fans."

3. Conduct customer mindset, process, and skills workshops: A large proportion of, if not all, people leaders attend workshops to help them understand what a "customer mindset" is and to practice behaviors that make customer culture tangible and relevant. Often workshop participants are cross-functional to reinforce the customer mindset and importance of organizationwide delivery of value to customers. In large corporations, workshops may start with the top few hundred leaders and then cascade down into their teams.

What is crucially important about these workshops is that they contain simple customer-oriented processes that every team within an organization can implement. Without these processes the skill development does not have a framework for ongoing use and implementation. In other words, one of the reasons new skills are not easily transferred into organizations is that they do not tie into processes.

What are these customer-oriented processes? The first one is for every team to understand how it creates value for internal customers and ultimately external ones. While this may sound obvious, many teams have not mapped this, and in today's organizations this is a moving target with customer expectations moving quickly. Existing processes become outdated quickly and need to be reviewed. For example, customers in many industries expect faster response times than in the past and broader accessibility to support services anytime, anywhere.

Another key process is for every team to gather specific feedback on what other teams within the business expect from their team and how that relates to the ability of the organization to serve customers better. These are not difficult processes to implement, but they do require some level of focus, and leaders need to reinforce their importance to improving the customer culture of the organization.

4. Collaborate cross-functionally: Teams work together cross-functionally to strengthen customer focus. Cross-functional work teams come together to create or strengthen systems, tools, and processes to increase customer engagement. These include processes such as user testing during the new-product process, customer feedback systems, metrics, and tools to improve at customer touchpoints value that is found to be lacking. It includes customer-focused innovation initiatives designed to reduce cost, speed up value delivery or service response, or enhance two-way communication with customers.

Several activities are initiated to reconnect with customers and the marketplace. These include customer immersion of executives and non-customer-facing people. The power of the immersion program is when it challenges people's perceptions of who their customers are and how they use their products. A key benefit of immersion is its ability to create a culture of customer-centric thinking within the organization from top to bottom. There is nothing like the personal customer insight and impact to be gained from interacting with customers. You get the raw emotion of a frustrated customer appealing for help if you listen in to customers describing the problems they are having with your product or service to a call center rep. It can have even greater impact if you watch customers trying to buy your product and experiencing increasing frustration from time-consuming processes or unwieldy websites.

Firsthand experience and advocacy by senior executives dramatically enhance a customer culture in the organization. Companies best internalize the consumer perspective when leaders at all levels can experience its impact. It fosters a greater appetite for customer understanding. It ultimately leads to an improved customer experience.

5. **Build market intelligence and information-sharing systems:** Customer and competitor insight and foresight come from access to meaningful and shared market intelligence. This necessitates development of customer feedback systems and competitive intelligence analysis. It requires tools for sharing this information and creating collaborative teams that generate insight and foresight for their areas and the business overall.

Phase 3: Embed and Formalize: Making Change Stick

The focus of this stage is on institutionalizing the customer culture through supporting systems, ongoing training, increased employee empowerment, and accountability of all individuals and teams for delivering an improved customer experience. *The most critical element is tying customer culture behaviors and customer feedback metrics to recognition and reward. Key customer culture disciplines to strengthen are customer insight and foresight, competitor insight and foresight, and strategic alignment and collaboration.*

The Four Things You Must Do

1. **Develop customer culture behaviors at leader and individual levels:** Key performance indicators measuring the level of customer behavior disciplines are formalized for performance reviews and designing personal development programs. These criteria are included in recruitment processes and orientation of new staff into the business. Many companies now hire for "cultural fit" to ensure reinforcement of the culture.

The power to make decisions on behalf of the company shifts to all employees within an agreed framework. This new empowerment and accountability is sometimes hard to accept by long-standing employees. Some companies have used a "buddy" approach to help less-experienced staff members gain new skills and confidence.

2. **Formalize customer culture through symbols, rituals, reward, and recognition and visual signs:** This step often includes organizational structure changes, more open office designs, images of customers taking precedence over images of products, customer invitations to corporate meetings, and cross-function teams evaluating new

market opportunities. Recognition of outstanding individual customer service and customer-inspired innovation acts as a symbol of customer-centered activities. Leaders use public forums to recognize and reward people who are taking a lead in adopting the values and norms in their work to deliver more value for customers. The most powerful recognition is interpersonal, with senior leaders showing approval, support, or disapproval of employee actions or comments at particular venues such as mini–town halls and corporate events.

Remuneration systems and promotion is formally tied to customer culture behaviors and customer engagement performance and customer feedback metrics.

3. Measure customer culture and customer experience progress (customer satisfaction, loyalty, and advocacy) against targets: Culture change is not a "bolt-on" process; it is a "built-in" one. Effectively done, it can't be "unbolted." Measurement covering the breadth and depth of the organization is necessary to determine to what extent customer culture has been built in.

Ongoing measurement is part of customer culture embedding and provides a frequent benchmark of customer engagement performance. It guides how the organization needs to adapt to changing market trends and customer needs.

4. Conduct ongoing orientation, coaching, and training: This is valuable for two groups: new and recent hires and groups within the organization found to be lacking a customer mindset and relevant skills. At some point, coaching dissenters and blockers of change ceases and their removal becomes the focus. Senior leaders need to be removed if they are obstacles to change. At the same time hiring criteria and orientation training of new staff members reflects the new values and norms and infuses customer culture and relevant customer engagement skills. Documented case studies of successes and learning are often used to demonstrate successful customer engagement experiences.

Phase 4: Fortify and Maintain: Reinforcing and Revitalizing Customer Culture

Our research and experience show that you cannot assume that a customer culture will be retained without continual nurturing and reinforcement. Sudden changes in the external environment can have a major impact on the business's performance as can an exodus of several senior leaders around the same time. This is the time to be vigilant and make sure that the strong customer culture, which has been embedded, is reinforced by the leadership. *The most critical element is leadership. On the one hand a strong customer culture should become independent of who the CEO is. On the other, a new CEO or business unit leader can quickly destroy customer culture by reverting back to a short-term focus driven by financial goals. It is important to revitalize and refine all seven customer culture disciplines, putting a particular emphasis on peripheral vision.*

Once customer culture is embedded as the normal way of doing business it is important to be vigilant and reinforce it. With success comes arrogance, and with arrogance, complacency. There are many examples of previously successful companies that have fallen into that trap.

The Three Things You Must Do

1. Reinforce culture and revitalize: Leaders should use new technologies to reinforce customer culture and revitalize staff. These may include real-time observation of customers buying their products and real-time social media commentary on the company's service. Paying particular attention to negative customer experiences and comments helps to avoid complacency. As firms adapt to change, employees are faced with changes in processes that can affect customer culture. This is extreme when a company acquires another business that has a different culture. These changes make the company susceptible to new management fads that may run counter to its customer culture. The role of cultural "flame keepers" is to ensure that these changes do not negatively affect the company's core customer culture. Sharing customer and competitor insights across the business acts as a vehicle to engage all staff members in innovative activities that realign the business with its changing market and competitive landscape.

2. Refresh people leader skills, tools, and peripheral vision: Leaders need continual refreshment of their leadership and collaborative skills through wider exposure to the next practices and tools used in other organizations and industries. This strengthens their peripheral vision and brings new excitement and enthusiasm back into the business. Attendance at global conferences on customer-centricity and customer experience as well as executive development programs help to reinforce customer-centric thinking and practices.

3. Continuously monitor customer culture, customer performance, and business performance impacts: Companies need to look for new ways to improve their measurement of customer culture and customer-focused business performance. In particular, models for identifying the drivers of future performance can act as early-warning signals for adaptation. The Market Responsiveness Index (MRI), which measures the drivers of future performance, and the Net Promoter Score (NPS), which measures advocacy, are two complementary measurement tools that provide early-warning signs of future performance.

The major purpose of a strong customer culture is to enable a company to adapt to external change in a way that produces sustainable revenue and profit growth. By measuring the profit impacts of its customer culture and improved customer experience and the costs of any missteps, a company reinforces the value of having a strong customer culture.

Strategy and Customer Culture Disciplines

Specific business strategies need different customer discipline capabilities for their successful implementation. Some of those, such as market share and customer retention strategies, require emphasis on disciplines that create customer and competitor insights. Other strategies involving high levels of innovation for new products and services and attraction of new customers need strength in more future-oriented disciplines, such as customer and competitor foresight. Figure 9.4 illustrates four common growth strategies and the capabilities required from the relevant customer culture disciplines. Your company's strategy will determine which disciplines must be developed as top priority and the ones to be developed in the future. Irrespective of which strategy is adopted, a high level of strategic alignment and cross-functional collaboration must support them.

Market Penetration Strategy

This strategy focuses on existing markets and customers with current products and services. The aim is to retain existing customers and market share and increase revenue and profitability by creating more customer advocates that buy a wider range of products or services. Customer insight and competitor insight are the disciplines required to make this strategy most effective.

Market Development Strategy

A strategy to gain new customers and enter new markets with the company's current products or services is reliant for success on customer insight and foresight and competitor insight disciplines. Strength in these disciplines support the market growth strategy and increase the chance of successfully achieving revenue and profit growth goals.

Product Development Strategy

An innovative new products strategy designed for current markets and customers needs strong customer foresight and competitor foresight disciplines for success. Strength in these disciplines will result in sales revenue growth and market share gains being achieved.

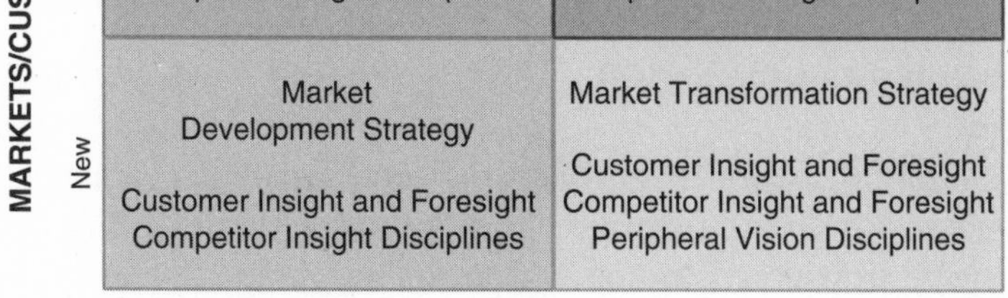

PRODUCTS/SERVICES/SOLUTIONS

	Present	New
Present	Market Penetration Strategy Customer Insight Competitor Insight Disciplines	Product/Service Development Strategy Customer Foresight Competitor Foresight Disciplines
New	Market Development Strategy Customer Insight and Foresight Competitor Insight Disciplines	Market Transformation Strategy Customer Insight and Foresight Competitor Insight and Foresight Peripheral Vision Disciplines

(MARKETS/CUSTOMERS)

Figure 9.4 Strategy and customer culture disciplines

Market Transformation Strategy

This is the highest risk strategy, and success is reliant on strength in all five externally oriented disciplines. The goal is to gain new sources of revenue and profit growth. Innovation with new products in new markets may be a conscious strategic choice for expansion and growth or may be the result of a tectonic shift where current markets and products are becoming eroded or obsolete. Peripheral vision is particularly important to identifying and acting on the opportunities emerging from transformational market shifts and business model changes required. Customer and competitor foresight are essential to understanding and acting on the new forms of value that must be created to successfully bridge the shift in the market and competitive environment.

Case Studies

A corporation that has done a great job at developing and maintaining a strong customer culture throughout its many different businesses is the Virgin Group. Its Head, Richard Branson has been able to embed strong customer cultures in many Virgin companies. The company operates in businesses as unrelated as railroads and banking and serves as proof that a focus on creating a powerful customer culture is a successful way to differentiate and profit. In this chapter we tell the story of one such business, Virgin Trains, and Chapter 10 relates the story of Tony Collins, CEO of Virgin Trains, which illustrates the decisive influence of the CEO in developing a customer culture.

Our case studies begin with a company that began with a customer culture in its DNA and has kept it. This is an example of a business that is among those that have the strongest customer culture in the world.

Born with a Customer Culture

The Amazon.com Vision: "Earth's Most Customer-centric Company"

From its earliest beginnings Amazon.com has sought to align how it does business with its customers' best interests in mind. Amazon.com is a customer-obsessed company that believes that over the long term the interests of customers, the company, and investors align.

What does this mean in terms of how it operates as a business? One of the most poignant examples of its customer culture comes from an April 2013 letter from CEO, Jeff Bezos, to shareholders.

> When you pre-order something from Amazon.com, we guarantee you the lowest price offered by us between your order time and the end of the day of the release date. "I just received notice of a $5 refund to my credit card for pre-order price protection. . . . What a great way to do business! Thank you very much for your fair and honest dealings." Most customers are too busy themselves to monitor the price of an item after they pre-order it, and our policy could be to require the customer to contact us and ask for the refund. Doing it proactively is more expensive for us, but it also surprises, delights, and earns trust.[4]

Is your company willing to invest back in customers in this way to build long-term trust-based relationships? Situations such as the one described by Jeff Bezos are moments of truth for the leadership of a business. These types of decisions will say more about the company and its values than millions of dollars spent on advertising.

Amazon.com does not just talk about being customer focused, it takes action everyday to remain focused. The decisions the company makes always begin and end with the customer in mind. In fact, Amazon.com is building automated systems that allow it to proactively reach out to customers when it has not lived up to its promise. A great example of this comes from a customer who received the following message: "We noticed that you experienced poor video playback while watching the following rental on Amazon.com Video On Demand: *Casablanca*. We're sorry for the inconvenience and have issued you a refund for the following amount: $2.99. We hope to see you again soon."

This proactive approach to doing what is in the best interests of customers in the short term costs Amazon.com millions of dollars, and it has been heavily criticized by some observers. But the critics miss the point; this type of behavior from companies is unexpected, it builds a strong foundation of trust and loyalty, and it results in increasing both the number of Amazon.com's customers and the amount of money they spend.

Amazon.com, like other truly customer-centric businesses, has an intense focus on the customer experience. It goes to great lengths to understand how its customers interact with the company's services at every touchpoint. By stepping into the customer's shoes, people at Amazon.com are able to use this understanding to innovate in a way that customers will find most valuable. A large part of the value Amazon.com brings is designing services that make it easy for customers. The company offers low prices, vast selections, fast delivery, and convenient buying and returning.

Amazon.com's innovative ideas have resulted in price guarantees, price change alerts, the recommendation engine, and 1-click purchasing, among many other things. The depth and detail that customers go to in providing product reviews is unparalleled. This creates value for potential customers as they use the site as a research tool across an ever-increasing range of product categories.

Amazon.com has even demonstrated an ability to innovate beyond its core website by creating new platforms to access content, such as the Kindle e-reader, the Android Appstore for Android, and the Amazon Instant Video on-demand movie-streaming service. These innovations provide solutions for customers that will also drive future revenue, share growth, and eventual profit growth for the company.

Transformation to a Customer Culture: Engage Phase

Australia Post: Competing for its Future[5]
When Ahmed Fahour was appointed managing director and CEO of Australia Post (AP) in February 2010, the Australian postal delivery service was facing a tectonic shift. Its core letters business was declining rapidly, its parcel business was growing, and the online revolution was affecting them both. The following quotes come from the customer reviews for Australia Post on the product ratings site www.productreview.com.au:

Haven't been able to find 7 kg parcel for a month
Rating 1.0 Star - Terrible
Cons - Unreliable, expensive, nonexistent customer service, totally uninterested staff

Maybe if Australia Post went back to just providing postal services they might actually be able to deliver mail in a reasonable amount of time. They have lost a 7 kg parcel which of course they blame on the sender as they always do & to make it even worse they have 22 days after USPS lodged missing mail request to find it. Amazing how many times they can stuff up but still refuse to ever take any responsibility. They excel at blaming everyone else even when it's proven to be their fault.

At the time, Fahour saw that his company was "a 200-year-old business and potentially facing extinction." However, Australia Post has been able to turn itself around: "When I started," Fahour continues, "it was a letters business with a growing parcels element. Now, in 2013, it is a parcels and communication business." As CEO, he has been able to change Australia Post's direction and is building momentum for growth.

A key part of the journey has been driving a culture change in the business towards customer-centricity. This case illustrates what needs to be done in a company with a long history that must be transformed to remain viable and prosper. It is in the earlier phases of building a customer culture.

The history of Australia Post is closely aligned to the history of European settlement in Australia. The first settlement of Europeans in Sydney, in 1788, was in one of the most isolated places on earth, and when the six-month supply ship arrived with mail, riots broke out as people desperately sought news from home. Mail was often stolen and lost during the mayhem. To create some order the governor of 10,000 soldiers, free settlers, and convicts who were living alongside small communities of indigenous Aboriginals opened Australia's first post office in 1809 near the current-day Sydney Harbour Bridge. The postmaster would board ships before they docked, collect the mail, and distribute it from his office.

The monopoly of the letter service (known as the Reserved Service) has been held by this government-owned corporation ever since, but like all postal services around the world, Australia Post is experiencing a huge market and technology shift. The rise of the digitally enabled economy is the biggest challenge Australia Post has seen in its 204 years of history. Ahmed Fahour, CEO, says, "Australia Post has always been at the center of the Australian community, forming a critical communications link for people. That central communications role remains, but the characteristics of the services that our customers need from us have changed and continue to change rapidly." Independent research studies of corporate reputation show Australia Post is the most trusted Australian company. However, the customer review quoted previously, which is not unusual for large companies facing massive change, reflects the task faced by this iconic company and its leadership.

Soon after his appointment, Ahmed proposed, and the board endorsed, three strategic goals:

1. Build a sustainable communications business—both physically and digitally.
2. Offer a world-class parcels business—with excellence in service performance—that leverages the trend to online shopping.
3. Expand the range of trusted services and enable customers to access these services through stores and online.

By 2013, it was a parcels and communications business. "Parcels are more than half of our revenue and profit," says Ahmed. "Letters are declining more rapidly than even our most pessimistic forecasts, but the demand for secure digital communications is emerging strongly."

He remarks that the changes over the last three years have been difficult, as Australia Post has "first had to stabilize the company because it was on a downward profit path that would leave us unable to reinvest. We have then been rebuilding the company to make it relevant to the needs of contemporary Australian consumers, businesses, and government organizations—this work is ongoing. We are about to launch into a new growth phase, built around new investment in areas that our customers want—parcels and digital communications."[6]

The Challenges of Reinventing Australia Post

In Ahmed's words: "The biggest challenges have been those inherently involved in turning around a big ship. Our staff recognize the need for change, and they are willing participants. However, we are financially burdened by the need to provide the loss-making Reserved Service [the regulated monopoly on the delivery of standard letters], and the enormous fixed costs involved in meeting our obligations.

"We have started to overcome the challenges through extensive research into what our customers want. We are instigating a $2 billion [that is, AU$2 billion, or US$1.9 billion] investment program in parcels processing and enhanced delivery facilities and leading the push for a secure digital mailbox for every Australian, launched in 2013. We are driving a program of culture change in the business, which emphasizes our cultural pillars of: Safety, Accountability, Customer Focus, and Speed of Action.

"We are looking for ways to reduce the cost of the Reserved Service while continuing to provide an acceptable level of service for the entire Australian community."

One of his challenges is to work closely with the Communications Union to agree on changes that will come about as the mail service continues to decline, which impacts the benefits to employees, costs of the service, and the service levels provided. This needs to be balanced with the needs of the Australian government as sole shareholder and guardian of the mail service to the Australian people.

John Stanhope, chairman of Australia Post, has a key role in ensuring that the needs of the government are met. He says, "I see the government as a customer whose current and future needs we have to understand and ensure that we meet them."

Strategy focuses on Australia Post developing deeper connections with its customers and consumers so it can better understand and respond to their needs now and in the future. There is a need to provide greater convenience, access, and choice. The core commitment is to provide a reliable service accessible to all.

Building Customer-centricity

Ahmed says: "Australia Post has always had a strong sense of servicing its customers. Our emphasis on customer-centricity was less about introducing the concept than about sharpening it, refocusing it, and helping our people to deliver on it. The majority of our current business, and all of our future growth, is in competitive markets. If we do not continue to improve our focus on customer-centricity, we will not succeed. The first step has been to recruit a senior team who understand the need for a customer-centric approach. I have then supported them by sponsoring a comprehensive internal program to explain and reinforce our cultural pillars and by showing my own commitment to them. We have also emphasized customer outcomes and collaboration in the incentive systems for all our managers."

Ahmed believes the biggest impact on people's behavior is being honest and emphatic in communication with all employees about the importance of the cultural pillars and making clear the extent of direct and indirect competition (such as electronic substitution) faced by Australia Post.

What Has Australia Post Done to Improve Customer Experience?

The sales and marketing function in Australia Post has the mandate to oversee the development of customer-centric capability. The recently revitalized team has built a sales and marketing infrastructure involving a new structure, new sales and marketing processes, sales and marketing education academy, centralized communication capability, a market segmentation framework supported by extensive market research, a governance process for monitoring and managing, job descriptions and career paths, and training needed. This is a massive effort in moving from a public service legacy toward an innovative, proactive customer service organization.

The team has focused on building and documenting an infrastructure and capability so that the whole value chain from enquiry, leads, selling, sale/contract, delivery, service, and follow-up is standardized. From this the customer touchpoints and customer experience can be assessed. With systems, processes, and procedures in place, customer-facing people can help customers and solve issues. Sales and marketing people have gained skills. This groundwork is part of the first "engage and plan" phase of the customer-centricity model.

There is now a strong willingness to be customer focused, as evidenced in the last engagement survey. Staff members now need to be enabled to harness the capability and organizational support to be customer focused. Customers should get a common and consistent service no matter which channel they use to engage with AP. In a buying process, a customer may use several different channels before they buy something—a digital ad, a phone call, your website, a Google search for alternatives, another phone call, a field sales visit. This must be synchronized and consistent.[7]

Australia Post is now ready to roll out an initiative involving education, customer feedback, and empowerment of staff to make customer-focused decisions. The Net Promoter Score is being used to measure advocacy along with other customer surveys. Customer journey maps are being designed to identify typical combinations of touchpoints for assessing and monitoring customer experience.

What Have Australia Post's Steps Been?

1. The CEO and board have set clear direction, goals, strategy, and cultural values for change.
2. The CEO has a leadership team who understand the strategy and follow the CEO's lead in living the values that include customer focus.
3. The goals, strategy, and values are clearly communicated and reinforced by senior management across the business.
4. It has introduced a range of new services designed to provide consumers and organizations with enhanced access, convenience, and choice from its retail and parcel distribution networks.
5. Substantial effort has been made to improve the capability of sales and marketing, including market segmentation, sales and service processes, and customer feedback systems.
6. Customer metrics are being initiated with links to employee remuneration.
7. There is willingness by employees to become more customer focused. Some parts of the business are ahead of others, so there is a need to embed a consistent customer culture across the entire organization.

Where is Australia Post in its Customer-centricity Journey?

With its improved customer culture, customer reviews for Australia Post on the product ratings site have reflected this positive change. For example:

Excellent
Rating 5.0 Stars - Excellent

They have very good services. I can pay all my bills at the stores. I can buy stationery that I need for my son for school. They sell learning books that I can only get for my son at Australia Post. The staff are very friendly and very helpful. My local Australia Post knows me by my name and they are very good.

Pros + I really like Australia Post. They are quick. It's delivered straight to my door. . . .
Cons - No cons. They are very good.

There are many positive comments like this one, but there are also many negative customer reviews, which shows that Australia Post still has a lot of work to do.

The company has a clearly communicated customer-centered leadership direction, goals, strategy, improved processes, and customer interaction—all part of the "engage and plan" phase of our model. The most critical part of this phase has been achieved—clear strategy, vision and values, and a committed CEO who is leading by example and connecting with his employees. He reads all mail that arrives addressed to him from customers (happy or otherwise) or from staff members. Having actively encouraged staff members to share their feelings about the company, he gets plenty of direct feedback.

Ahmed spends more time out of head office than might be expected of a CEO. He got a motorbike license, so he could act as a "postie" and understand what that's like. He also spent time working in the processing centers. He wants as far as possible to live out the experience of his workers. It helps him see how the cultural pillars apply to different roles in the business.[8]

As of June 2013 Australia Post is in the early stages of phase 2 in the journey—"inspire customer culture change" throughout all people leaders. Ahmed Fahour sees embedding a safe, fast, customer-focused culture as an imperative for transformation to the future. He says: "I don't believe that there is an end point to cultural transformation where one can say 'job done.' There is always further room for improvement. Also customer needs are always changing. We have made great progress, and the feedback I get from customers (both individuals and large business customers) is evidence that they feel it too. Ultimately, as our letters business continues to decline and our Parcels and express business grows (a fully competitive market), the proof will be whether we service our customers well enough for them to choose us instead of the competitors."

What Is the Business Result?

From a business that was failing and in danger of suffering massive losses, Australia Post's financial results are improving. It grew its overall net earnings 17 percent, to AU$281 million (US$267 million), in 2012, providing a foundation for future investment.

Transformation to a Customer Culture: Ignite Phase

Building Telstra's Future on Advocacy: Customers and Employees[9]

David Thodey, since his appointment as CEO of Telstra in May 2009, is successfully doing what most people thought was impossible—transforming Australia's telecommunications giant from a lumbering monopoly into a leaner, more customer-focused, more profitable growing business. By his own admission there is still a lot of work to be done to become a fully customer-centric organization; he says they have "just finished the swim leg of a triathlon." But he has created momentum that is already reaping rewards in revenue, profit, and stock price growth.

This case illustrates the tasks undertaken to develop a customer culture across a large, fast-changing, complex technology business. It has completed the first two phases of our model and is entering the third phase: "embed and formalize."

Getting in Tune with the Customer

At 7.30 a.m. every morning, CEO David Thodey and his senior executive team individually receive a data message on their smartphones summarizing the previous day's customer advocacy scores—one score for the overall company, and separate scores for end-to-end customer experience and one-off customer interaction experiences. These are based on ongoing market research using blind surveys and e-mail surveys of 40,000 customers daily. This provides a profile as to how Telstra is performing based on what percentage of customers are "promoters," "passives," and "detractors" of the company.

At the same time feedback from those 40,000 customers, including verbatim comments, is sent to company staff and contractors from where the service originated for their review and action for improvement. These are sent almost in "real" time, promoting immediate action to follow up with customers, if necessary, and to improve performance with them. At frequent T-Time meetings small teams review their customers' feedback and plan changes to improve the customers' experience.

All of this is the outcome of a plan, initiated by the CEO and endorsed by the board in 2011, to transform the culture of this large telecommunications organization to a customer service business using the concept of customer advocacy to drive it. Customer service is the number-one priority for the company, and all decisions are framed in terms of the impact an initiative will have on customer advocacy. The strategic aim of this transformation is for Telstra to achieve market leadership in all the markets it is currently in and in which it chooses to be in the future.

"We Had Lost Our Focus on the Customer"

When appointed CEO of Telstra in May 2009, David faced some serious problems. In his first 18 months he had to issue profit downgrades on three separate occasions. At the end of his first full year in office, customers were fed up with high premiums for mobile and fixed broadband services and began leaving in droves; the decline in Telstra's once lucrative fixed-line telephony business was accelerating; and large segments of staff were disenchanted. The relations with the Australian government were poor; in fact, Telstra was being excluded from negotiations for a new national broadband network and under threat of being broken up.

His strategy to attack these issues was to make the customer number one and embark on a journey that would make the customer the focus for making decisions. He realized this initiative was about much more than changing processes and getting customer feedback. It needed to involve a customer culture developed in all functions at all levels based on a belief and vision that Telstra could be one of the world's most admired companies by its customers and its employees.

David says: "We focused on customers, on growing our customer base with new products and services, bringing new innovative products to the market and at the same time simplifying the business. We had to find ways to change things that were getting in the way of good customer service. The strategy involved spending $1 billion [that is, AU$1 billion, or US$950 million] to win back customers with new products, [increasing] mobile phone subsidies, [lowering] prices, [simplifying] the business, and [focusing] on the customer. At the end of the day it's about picking a strategy and executing it consistently."

He says, "Our strategy has been very consistent over the last three years [and focused] around better customer service and customer growth, simplification, and [growth of] the business."

David believes that market intelligence is key. Under the director of research, insights and analytics, Liz Moore, the value of market information is converted into insights, and a huge investment has been made in gathering, collating, and disseminating market information to all parts of the business. Liz says: "The research model has changed from being an accurate rear-vision mirror to headlights on the future. You need to bring the consumer 'alive' into the organization. This makes insight alive in the business. With our access to a large panel of customers we can get feedback about a particular issue or opportunity within 48 hours."

Particular attention is paid to identifying unarticulated needs and likely future needs in the market. Customer and competitor foresight that comes from analysis and discussion is communicated across the business. There is a competitive intelligence section on the intranet that enables staff to post observations and warning signs of future competitive intent. Liz says that the whole focus of her team is to undertake research, do analysis, and bring the right people together to create insights.

Customers are an integral part of new-product design in which 40 people from different functions are brought together to talk with customers as they go through the product development process. This has enhanced Telstra's success with new products.

Telstra's analysis has shown that creating customer advocates is good business because the advocates spend 15 percent more of their disposable income with Telstra than the average customer, they use 30 percent more of Telstra's products, and the loss rate of advocates is about 0.1 percent compared with an average of 1 to 1.5 percent loss of nonadvocates.

Building the Advocacy System

In 2011, Telstra made the shift from measuring customer satisfaction to measuring *advocacy* using the Net Promoter System (NPS). John Parkin was tasked with directing the development and embedding of the system with its measurement (scores), feedback loops, tools and training around advocacy along with almost real-time scores. Incentives and contracts are aligned to advocacy as is onboarding of new staff.

The NPS provides a strategic score for the company based on "blind" surveys using market research and operational scores at two levels based on an e-mail survey of 40,000 customers daily out of 5 million points of feedback occurring daily. One level is the end-to-end experience; the other is the interaction experience based on a single interaction or touchpoint.

John Parkin says, "Our priorities are customer service and a customer culture first, financial performance second, and great place to work third. We have rallied people around these three priorities by linking their remuneration based on achieving annual goals set for these."

At the same time costs have to be cut out of the business. The slogan in Telstra is "Simplify to save to serve." This means that by simplifying the business it will cut costs and at the same time improve service.

David Thodey says: "You should always start with the view that the customer has the right intent. I have found NPS to be helpful because it gets our staff to think about how they can help the customer in a way that they feel good about the service and will want to tell others about it positively."

Igniting Employee Change Through People Leaders

Telstra has taken several steps in 2011 through 2013 across the entire organization to create a single focus on the customer. Even support groups such as finance, legal, engineering handling and support functions and purchasing are engaged to identify a "line of site" to the customer in which they focus on providing valuable service to those groups who support the customer directly. This includes the following elements:

1. During 2011–2013 two sequential workshops titled "Our Customer Connection" were rolled out to 9,500 people leaders in Australia and the Philippines. These included all partner leaders and contractor leaders. They were delivered in two parts: the first directed at "shaking up" attitudes and defining what a customer mindset is and how it is reflected in what people do; the second at what to do and how to do it. This second part is anchored around core NPS advocacy results and what to do to improve them. It involves all leaders developing a point of view and sharing their Telstra story, creating meetings to review customer data and decide what to do to improve customer experience, and finally coaching and highlighting positive improvements and sharing of best practices.
2. A customer feedback system has been developed to provide ongoing customer information to all levels of the business.
3. Every Friday night an executive report is sent to the top 300 executives. It includes examples of people described as heroes. They look for those people and teams who are doing it time and time again and highlight those who have shown the greatest improvement.
4. The quarterly advocacy meeting involves the senior management team meeting with the CEO to report. They are evaluated based on "ownership" and "NPS results."

5. Strategic and operational NPS advocacy scores were aligned with many of Telstra's incentive programs for the 2012–2013 financial year. The corporate short-term incentive (STI) program, which covers the majority of employees up to and including the CEO, has up to 40 percent weighting that is based on advocacy scores. Those employees not on the STI program had the opportunity to earn a bonus of up to AU$5,000 (US$4,750) based on the achievement of Telstra's 2012–2013 advocacy goals.
6. An economic model has been developed that identifies drivers of customer behavior and the NPS impacts on the lifetime value of customers. This shows the financial impacts of successful cultural transformation at Telstra.

The emphasis during this phase has been to engage all staff members in sharing their Telstra story and how they can individually make it better for the customer. Leaders are encouraged to highlight and share positive improvements and to coach their team members by example.

Introduction of the Yammer internal social media network has provided a voice for Telstra employees. Now almost 30,000 have logged in.

Telstra's intranet now provides an executive summary of NPS results each week and highlights customer service heroes for everyone to see. Its home page at the top shows live NPS scores changing daily. Farther down is the daily stock price. This is a subtle but important signal of the company's top priority—customer service and advocacy. John says, "You can't run away from performance. It's highlighting those areas we have to fix. It will find out the leaders in the company and their ability to change the customer experience and advocates."

The "line of sight" approach is particularly helpful for support teams that identify the business units and teams they support who are dealing directly with customers. For instance, the legal group, by assessing customer complaint feedback, has looked for ways of simplifying the legal contracts that customers must sign and consultants must explain.

Embedding Customer Culture across the Entire Workforce

In 2013 and 2014 the emphasis is on embedding customer culture disciplines across the full workforce—phase 3 in our model: "embed and formalize customer behaviors." In this phase, in its early stages at the time of writing, leaders who have been through the OCC workshops are to meet with their teams at least monthly (called T-Time and T-Solve meetings) to review NPS results and their relevance to the team, and to focus on continual improvement based on identifying and resolving issues based on customer feedback. Lists are drawn up of actions to take to implement the changes. Also to be worked out are what the leader and his or her team can do and what support is needed from the company to help the team improve. A survey taken in early 2013 showed 69 percent of leaders were doing this.

If all teams were doing this, it would become the culture that binds the people together as one company. Employees are encouraged to help customers who voice a problem when they are outside of work hours (for example, they hear about it on the train or plane) and can refer that person to the Telstra Employee Referral Scheme to get it solved.

What Have Telstra's Steps Been?

1. The CEO and leadership team have a clear, consistent strategy supported by a customer-centered vision and values that are consistently communicated throughout the business.
2. The CEO and leadership team believe in and embody the values and follow through to improve customer experience.
3. Telstra has built a dynamic NPS measurement and customer feedback system that ties to business performance and employee remuneration.
4. There has been major investment in winning the hearts and minds of people leaders and providing the skills to help them develop customer behaviors in their teams.
5. There has been a massive investment in simplifying systems and processes to enable staff members to help customers.
6. Having a focus on the customer has broken down silos through recognition that there is one arbiter—the customer.

Where Is Telstra in Its Customer-centric Journey?

The company has completed phases 1 and 2 in our model and is embarking on phase 3: "embed and formalize" customer culture across all employees. This is the phase that, with successful execution and persistence, will result in a much more consistent level of customer service and much higher advocacy. Telstra, like almost all large businesses, still has many detractors who experience the frustration of a breakdown in customer service. The company stills get a lot of one-star (out of five-star) reviews for its service.[10] As David Thodey says: "There is still a way to go in embedding change, which relies not only on cultural change but also investment, where necessary in systems, so that staff can do their jobs better and are not frustrated by complex, consumer unfriendly systems. It has to be made easier for people to do their jobs better. The regular T-Time sessions by teams are designed to work out how to simplify processes, take on customer feedback and implement improvements. *The key is to stay focused and stay the course.*"

What Is the Business Result?

Telstra has reversed the downward trend in sales and profit affected by the substantial decline in its highly profitable fixed-line business with sales and profit increases in 2012 and 2013. Stockholders are again confident in the company's future, with its share price increasing steadily from AU$2.56 (US$2.43) in July 2011 to over AU$5 (US$4.75) in 2013.

Transformation to a Customer Culture: Embed Phase

Westpac Bank: Journey to Customer-centricity[11]

When Gail Kelly joined Westpac, Australia's oldest bank and ongoing business, as CEO in February 2008, she knew what she needed to do—to transform this longstanding organization to a more innovative, adaptive, customer-centric business. She had just spent five years as CEO of the smaller St. George Bank, where she had successfully embedded a customer-centric culture at the heart of its customer service strategy with impressive financial results. From experience she knew it would be a long journey as Westpac had many traditional systems, processes, structures, and legacies that would be hard to change. Also she knew that Australians had a long history of "hating" their banks, especially the large four, of which Westpac was one. This case traces the journey that has taken Westpac through three phases of the customer culture journey.

The Demarcation Event

Soon after joining Westpac as CEO, Gail Kelly prepared her first communication to go out to all Westpac staff. Her communication staff at Westpac who were used to preparing all previous CEO communications bulletins were concerned when they saw a reference to "delighting customers." They told her, "We don't do 'delight' here at Westpac; we just aim to 'satisfy.' " But the bulletin went out unchanged.

At her first People Leaders' conference a month later in March 2008, Gail told the story that in an earlier "life" she had been a teacher of Latin and that the word *satisfaction* is derived from the word *satisfactus*, meaning "made enough" or "good enough." To simply "satisfy" or be good enough, Gail said, is not enough. She said we need to delight customers, to make them advocates, because they will then spend more with us, stay longer, and promote our brand to others.

This set the tone for a customer-centricity journey that has lifted Westpac's performance and ranking in the Australian banking industry and set it on the path to leadership.

An Early Revelation

As a new vision and values were being developed over several months there was a lot of discussion with many groups in all the divisions of the company. It was pointed out by staff members that the key values of integrity, high performance, and teamwork were more about "us," and there was nothing as a value about customers. This revelation across various parts of the business made it easy then to incorporate "delighting customers" as a high-order value, a set of behaviors and principles and actions to run the business.

It resonated with staff that "delighting customers" as a value was reflecting a vision with a higher-order purpose—something they could buy into. By May 2008 the vision, strategy, and set of five values, including "delighting customers," was approved by the board for the period 2008–2012.

Starting the Journey to 2017

To mark the change that was to take place, it was named the 2017 Strategic Program—a name with significance because on April 8, 2017, Westpac becomes 200 years old. This was nine years out and enabled people to visualize what the bank could be in 2017 without being restricted by what the bank was like in 2008. This program was approved by the board in July 2008.

Then began extensive communications and training around advocacy and its measurement and how it differed from satisfaction measures. This had to break through the rational, risk-averse mentality that is the hallmark of most bankers with a "prove it works" approach for the bank and an understanding of the net promoter score as the basis of advocacy and how it can be used.

Refining the Vision

The vision went through a few iterations, the last being in 2010 before it was agreed as "To be one of the world's great companies in helping our customers, our communities and our people to prosper and grow."

This created a focus for Westpac staff around "helping customers . . . to prosper and grow." To be a great company meant benchmarking on a balanced scorecard against the world's best—the most-loved companies. This also reinforced why advocacy was important.

After the first two or three years in which emphasis was on the NPS scores, the mentality had moved to focus on whether customers are *really* advocates—"would you recommend Westpac to your family and friends?" This required bankers to look beyond the scores and ask customers questions such as, "Is there another part of your business we can help you with? Is there anyone of your friends or colleagues who would benefit from my expertise?" This required bankers to connect at a more personal level with their customers. For bankers to be able to ask these types of questions of customers they needed to develop a relationship based on trust.

Transformational Shift—"I Am Westpac"

Extensive reviews of customer feedback showed that those customers who rated Westpac highly, "loved" their banker and always named a person. Those who had complaints and were detractors never referred to individuals but only to functions such as the credit department, the customer service system, or the mortgage group.

The "I am Westpac" program for delighting customers was launched with all customer contact people to reinforce the importance of the individual taking personal ownership and addressing the emotional connection with customers.

The insight was that the customer might hate the bank, but many loved their banker.

So in late 2009 a transformational shift was made to "Westpac Local," where previously centralized decisions were handed back to the local branch manager who could then make decisions for the customer—joining the bank and banker together as one in the eyes of customers. In effect, you are the "Gail Kelly" of your branch, and you should make the same value-based decision for the customer that you think she would make.

Extensive training took place using "moments of truth" as a way of demonstrating how to address customer emotions and create an authentic connection with customers that would result in advocacy. This meant putting trust into the front-line people that they will do the right thing.

This shift required a change to 4,000 roles with substantial pressure to change processes, service standards, decision rights, and customer-facing technology to simplify things for customers.

Injecting Innovation

Jason Yetton initiated an innovation system, called Mr. Easy, in 2003 within a division of Westpac to enable staff members to feed in well-thought-out ideas for continuous improvement that could be evaluated and prioritized by Jason and his senior team. This system was extended across the entire bank in 2009 to enable staff in Westpac to provide ideas for change and improvement. Ideas that benefit the customer and the business are structured, costed, and proposed, and a senior management panel evaluates, prioritizes, and approves. This was enthusiastically adopted by staff and resulted in many new ideas being proposed across the business. Jason said. "There were a lot of great ideas put forward and the panel had to sort out which ones were best aligned with Westpac's strategy and future direction. Then, these had to be prioritized, put into a timetable and resourced." This has become a powerful engine for new-idea development, cross-functional collaboration, and transparency for all staff members to see which ideas are prioritized and implemented.

Embedding Customer-centric Behaviors

During 2011–2013 Westpac had been embedding a customer culture across the entire business. Jason Yetton explains the activities that are embedding customer culture disciplines. He says, "The *customer principles* are embedded within our vision and values framework, and customer relationships are explicitly called out as one of our five key strategic priorities. In terms of metrics, internal and external customer satisfaction and advocacy (net promoter score) are measured across customer segments, products, and channels. Customer complaint information is collected and acted on. Mystery shopping of Westpac and competitors, industry benchmarking reports and brand awareness, brand consideration, and propensity to buy are tracked. Market research is conducted on future customer needs and through online customer feedback groups.

"The *competitor disciplines* are supported with a range of competitor tracking tools around customer tracking and market share reports, competitor advertising and press tracking, analyst presentations, and competitor mystery shopping. In terms of potential competitors, we keep track of developments in international markets and regularly monitor alternative payments providers such as PayPal, Google, Apple, and mobile phone carriers as well as review related financial services industry providers in Australia."

Jason has seen *collaboration and strategic alignment* strengthen over the last two years. He says: "Westpac has five organizational values, one of which is 'One Team,' which is about working collaboratively as one team, regardless of department, for the customer. The Westpac vision, values, and strategy framework is communicated through a variety of mechanisms to all staff in the group, and we test how well this resonates with our people through an annual staff perspective survey. Results from this survey indicate a very strong understanding and belief in the Westpac vision, values, and goals, as well as very strong alignment to how the work of each individual contributes to these goals.

"As part of the strategic planning process, investment spending is prioritized to key strategic objectives and measures. In terms of people and collaborative work processes, we regularly bring leaders together at all levels to participate in strategic discussions and increasingly move people around different parts of the organization to cross-fertilize knowledge and build networks between divisions. We undertake social and community activities to build personal relationships between divisions. We have talent management and development tools to ensure alignment of best resources to best opportunities, whilst also facilitating individual career development objectives."

Where Westpac Is in 2013

By 2013, five years after its initiation, the vision, values, strategy, and 2017 mantra are embedded and give staff members a framework to do their job and make customer-centric decisions. But it is recognized that the job is not yet done. The transformation has gone through the first three phases of engage, inspire, and embed, but in the last year advocacy has plateaued. Customers are saying, "You have improved," but there are still more detractors than advocates. There has been a feeling that maybe you won't get customers to love their bank. But there is still some way to go to get to the advocacy levels of the most-loved companies in the world.

Jason's assessment is that the "what we do" rational part of the process has dramatically improved, but the "how we do it" emotional part is still lacking and there is significant variability in customer experience across the business. Jason says "we are engineers" more so than "designers" concerned with usability and how customers feel. The company is not yet delivering on its vision of "helping people to grow and prosper" through strong emotional connections.

This requires Westpac staff members to change their language from "we're selling you a mortgage" to "we're helping you to buy a new home." In helping the new migrant "we're helping them to establish a new life in Australia" rather than "setting up a bank account." Start with what's important to your life.

On the appointment of Brian Hartzer as head of Australian Financial Services of the Westpac Group in July 2012, there is an impetus for renewed effort to focus on deepening customer relationships and lifting the customer culture to a new level. A new strategy for the period 2012–2017 encompassing a stronger customer-centric culture was approved by the board in September 2012.

What Have Westpac's Steps Been?

1. The CEO created a memorable demarcation event that led the way for development and buy-in by people leaders of a clearly understood customer-centered vision, values, and strategy. This was a way of embracing a common culture across the several bank brands that make up the Westpac Group.
2. Customer insight was used to make major decisions such as the decentralization of decision making, simplification of customer processes, and development of customer disciplines by branch managers and their teams with the creation of the Westpac local bank.
3. Customer culture disciplines have been strengthened and embedded through training and skill development, collaborative forums and projects, innovation systems, and customer metrics.

Where Is Westpac in Its Customer-centric Journey?

Westpac has been through the first three phases of our model and is still in the embedding phase across the entire business. Jason Yetton believes there is still inconsistency of service across the business, and this is borne out by customer complaints logged internally and also made public on the product-rating site www.productreview.com.au. *The perception of banks by consumers and small businesses is also colored by their interest rate policy. Westpac still has work to do to strengthen its customer culture disciplines if it is to achieve its 2017 goal. This is recognized by senior leadership, and it is embarking on a further effort to lift the level and consistency of customer experience across all market segments.*

What Is the Business Result?

All big four Australian banks are highly profitable. Westpac Group revenue has grown 9 percent since 2009 and profit before tax by 45 percent.[12] Stock price has risen from AU$15.84 (US$15.05) in July 2008 to over AU$36 (US$34) in October 2013.[13] This has been a good performance given the uncertainty surrounding the global financial system during this period.

The Way Ahead

Westpac's competitive position in 2013 is number two in retail banking and in a strong challenger position to the retail leader, Commonwealth Bank of Australia (CommBank). In the business market, National Australia Bank (NAB) is a clear leader, with the other banks being some way back. Westpac can be a strong challenger in the future. In its quest for overall leadership in the Australian retail and business banking markets Westpac must lead, innovate, and take risks. This requires "courage" to take it to a new level of customer culture, and it is starting the transformation cycle again in 2013.

In its journey to 2017, Westpac is replacing one of its values—"One Team," that is now well embedded, with a new value—"courage." The creation of customer-centered design teams (which had worked well in Jason's earlier work in a Westpac division) that focus on customer experience and usability is an important step toward creating stronger emotional connections with customers. This is being formed across the entire bank in 2013. An extensive training program of all leaders from all parts of the business that covers customer-centric behaviors and customer-inspired innovation, translating vision into action, and leading commercially is underway in 2013.

April 8, 2017, looms large in the Westpac timetable, and there is a new sense of urgency to achieving its vision.

Transformation to a Customer Culture: The Full Journey to Fortify Phase

Virgin Trains: Customer Advocacy Saves the Business[14]

In August 2012 Virgin Trains (VT) lost its bid for extension of its government franchise for the train service from London to Glasgow it had held for the previous 15 years. This tells why Virgin Trains overcame the odds. It was the passion for customers through trust in the staff combined with courageous leadership that had created the Virgin Trains legacy. The customer culture that had been developed from 1997 to 2012 translated into such strong customer advocacy through dramatically improved customer experience that it created the impetus leading to the decision being overturned.

On September 10, 2012, Sir Richard Branson was at Euston Station, London, meeting the staff of his Virgin Trains franchise. Station manager Anita Brown and her staff gave Branson an emotional welcome. This was no ordinary meeting. He was there to support them in a time of difficult transition, and they were also there to support him.

A short time later Branson; his CEO of Virgin Rail, Tony Collins; the commercial director, Graham Leech; and the Stagecoach (49 percent owner of the West Coast franchise) cochairman, Martin Griffiths, were all together answering questions at a parliamentary enquiry initiated by Branson. This was about the awarding of the West Coast train franchise (London to Glasgow) to a competitor, FirstGroup—a franchise that had been held by Virgin Trains for the previous 15 years.

Branson said, "We submitted a strong and deliverable bid based on improving the customers' experience through increased investment and innovation." He added, "Our team has transformed the West Coast line over the last 15 years from a heavily loss-making operation to one that will return the taxpayer billions in years to come."

Noting how passenger numbers have risen from 14 million to 31 million since Virgin Rail began running the services in 1997, he reminded the government that critics used to say that doubling traffic on the route was "mission impossible." He drew comparisons with recent failures on the East Coast Main Line, where both GNER and National Express walked out on the contract after their bids proved too optimistic. He claimed Virgin was the runner-up both times with realistic bids.

Critics say there is a distinct possibility that FirstGroup will abandon the franchise before the contract ends in 2026, pointing to the transportation company's recent decision to take advantage of a clause that effectively allowed it to hand back the Great Western franchise three years early after the economic downturn rendered its £1.1 billion contract uneconomic.

Branson, who had considered abandoning the rail industry in Britain after this fourth unsuccessful bid (second each time), decided to put up a fight this time. It was not because of the money—he has plenty of that—it was because of his values and beliefs and the customers and the staff of Virgin Trains.

Buoyed by 170,000 passenger signatories to an e-petition supporting the company, rallying support from unions and staff, he and Tony Collins decided to press the government for an investigation into the transport franchise tendering process and how decisions were made. When asked on September 10 by a member of the parliamentary inquiry why he was objecting, Branson said, "The customer is the heart of our business. Our staff are committed and excited and our passengers love it." He went on to say that customers and staff had given overwhelming support to him and the CEO, Tony Collins, and he did not want to let them down. The growth of over 10 percent per annum in passenger numbers over the previous 10 years was testimony to the customer appeal and quality of the service provided. So too was the daily feedback from happy customers to frontline staff and a 91 percent satisfaction rate (the highest ever achieved by a long-distance rail operator) in the National Passenger Survey.

This is a man who believes that the most important thing in business is to have satisfied customers and fully engaged, happy staff around a customer culture that delivers increasing value to all stakeholders.

Virgin Trains' Customer-centricity Journey

Virgin Trains won the right to run the West Coast Line in 1997 from British Rail. It took over all the staff, the equipment, the systems, and the processes and set on the task of making it a Virgin business. It had been run as a hierarchical and bureaucratic command-and-control culture, typical of the public service at that time, and it was one of the few Virgin businesses that had not been built from the ground up. When Tony Collins was appointed CEO in 2004, after joining the company in 1999, he set about building the culture of the business in line with his belief that it is in the "customer service business." At the outset he presented some nonnegotiables to Virgin staff: the train line must be safe, it has to be profitable, and the Virgin brand must be managed and protected. In addition, staff members must be open and honest with each other and be prepared to speak up if things are not working. The context for building the culture was around providing the very best customer service that created the desired experience for customers.

Before Tony Collins's tenure as CEO, Virgin had tried a "10 customer commitments" (10CC's) process, but soon realized that people will not have their heart in it if they are told to interact according to a strict set of processes.

In a conversation with Richard Branson, he said: "We've got carried away with all the new trains and PR events and forgotten why we are here, and that is to provide a great journey experience for the passenger. We need time—time to engage and involve the whole company in developing a vision we can all believe in and get behind."

Branson agreed.

So Collins exhorted staff to think about how each of them, individually, could provide better service to customers, to get to know customers, and to let executives know what they needed to help them service customers better. He believes you must be flexible and adaptable to changing customer needs.

Developing a Shared Vision

Tony Collins realized that it was not enough for the senior leadership to develop a vision. For people who had been used to a command-and-control structure, to have a passion for customer service and the confidence to deliver it, they needed to develop their own vision. So over two years he and his team with a group of organizational psychologists worked with everyone in the business to help them develop their vision in line with the CEO's nonnegotiables—safe, profitable, open and honest, and focused on customer service. They worked with groups of 10 to 12 staff members from mixed disciplines and functions over three days.

Tony says: "We asked them to come up with their vision for their part of the business and what values did they as a group hold dear and were important to them as individuals. We acted as facilitators and coaches, giving them the skills to challenge their colleagues and us in an appropriate way, and receive challenge—importantly, to be able to challenge upwards, to challenge people who they saw as senior to them. We developed their abilities to give feedback and express their views clearly. Right at the end of the session we shared our vision. Perhaps not surprisingly the two were very similar, including the nonnegotiables and values. But there was one big difference— the vision they took back to the workplace was theirs and not ours imposed upon them."

The Vision workshops were very effective because for most people it was the first time they had been asked for their views and senior leaders had actually listened. The cross-functional grouping meant that many created new relationships and friendships and a new sense of collaboration. They returned to their part of the business with their own vision and new skills to work with colleagues to apply that to the business.

Tony says: "Imagine how powerful and empowering it is for everyone in the company to have developed and created their own vision for the company and then given the freedom to deliver it. In fact, what I am arguing is to reverse the traditional process: have the front-line teams develop their goals and objectives first based on their vision; then it becomes our job to make sure they are aligned across the business."

He continues: "You can design the very best processes, the very best business plans, and have the very best equipment, but this will all come to nothing if you do not have enthusiastic and passionate staff. We look for people who love the product we are trying to deliver, people who have a passion for providing fantastic customer service. Our recruitment team have a very simple approach—recruit for attitude first and experience second."

Fortifying Customer Culture and Customer Experience

By August 2012, Virgin Trains had a strong customer ethic, staff members were highly engaged, customer satisfaction ratings were well above those of its competitors, the business was continuing to grow and increase profitability, and Virgin Trains was the benchmark for how to run a rail operation in the United Kingdom in which all key stakeholders benefited. There was also interest from Europe as to how to operate a train business successfully. Then an event occurred that would test the resolve of the leaders, the staff, and the customers.

On August 15 it seemed that all of this would be lost overnight. The Department for Transport (DfT) awarded the franchise for the next 14 years to FirstGroup over Virgin Trains. The executives at VT couldn't believe it when the details of both bids were released. There seemed to be something badly wrong. The VT bid was clearly sustainable for the government and for rail customers. VT's record was proven. It appeared that the hard work to develop a good business for customers, staff, and the shareholders would be lost.

Against conventional wisdom that "you'll never beat the government," they believed that they had to fight the DfT decision. On August 28 they applied for a judicial review just hours before the new contract was to be signed by FirstGroup. Virgin's lawsuit claimed that the DfT's procurement process did not correctly assess the risk of FirstGroup defaulting, with guarantees far below the premiums it would have to pay otherwise.

This message by the senior leaders reinforced their beliefs and signaled them to their employees and their customers. It acted to fortify and revitalize the customer culture and why Virgin Trains existed. It signaled by the leaders' actions that they want people in Virgin Trains to be courageous and take risks.

As a result of this challenge the government overturned the decision to award the franchise to FirstGroup, citing errors in calculations and lack of transparency by DfT in making its decision. Subsequent negotiations between Virgin Trains and the DfT ended on December 8 with VT being awarded a 23-month contract to continue operating the West Coast line until November 2014. Subsequently it was extended to April 2017. Immediate steps were taken to thank Virgin's customers and the staff with thank-you signs and ice creams handed out during the London Olympic Games period. Richard Branson invited all staff members to his home in Oxford for a party in 2013.

What Have Virgin Trains' Steps Been?

1. The CEO invested substantial time and money to change a culture from command and control to an open, empowered, and collaborative customer culture through alignment of team visions and values around customer service.
2. The CEO and senior leaders spent a lot of time listening to front-line staff members suggest how they could improve customer experience and provided the support for them to do it.
3. Customer culture disciplines have been strengthened through skill development, collaborative projects, acting on customer feedback, and customer satisfaction metrics.
4. A strong customer culture has been fortified through the actions of leaders in fighting the bid decision and winning the franchise extension.

Where Is Virgin Trains in Its Customer-centric Journey?

Virgin Trains has made a remarkable transformation from the internally focused, hierarchical, silo's command-and-control structure of the previous operator—British Rail. With basically the same workforce it has been through all four phases of our model and is in the "fortify and maintain" phase. But Tony Collins wants to lift the company to a new level on the customer culture spectrum. The next two years will focus on lifting the customer experience much farther. This will involve going through a new cycle of engage, ignite, and embed the strengthening of the customer culture. It will occur right across the entire business, including a shared vision, open and collaborative communication, and alignment of all staff in all functions around the belief that "what's best for the customer is best for the business." His messages to staff will be: "We are the best train service. Be proud of yourselves. Let's look forward and work out how we can make a difference."

Senior management will spend a lot of time in 2013 and 2014 engaging with staff and inviting them to feed ideas and experiences on how service and value can be improved for customers from all parts of the business and work individually and in teams to implement improvements in their own areas.

This will prepare the company to win the competitive bid in April 2017.

What Is the Business Result?

Passenger growth and customer loyalty has shown continuing growth over the past 10 years. Net earnings increased from a £3 million (US$4.8 million) loss in 2007 with a steady increase to £142 million (US$227 million) profit in 2012. In that year the British government received a franchise payment of £110 million (US$176 million). Virgin Group and Stagecoach shared £32 million (US$51 million).

Retransformation to a Customer Culture: Recovery

Starbucks Transformational Mission: "To Inspire and Nurture the Human Spirit"

Starbucks has a long history of growth and success, yet somehow during the period after Howard Schultz retired from his role as CEO in 2000 things began to head in the wrong direction. Arthur Rubinfeld, one of the key executives responsible for Starbucks's successful retail expansion from 1992 to 2002, was asked by Howard to return to Starbucks in 2008.

Howard described to Arthur what he felt had happened to Starbucks as a gradual unraveling of the core principles that Starbucks had been founded on. There was nothing specific to point toward— only a gradual shift, a subtle change in emphasis, and a slow erosion of the core customer experience that had made Starbucks such a powerhouse.

When a company loses sight of its purpose, takes its eye off customers, and emphasizes growth and profits over and above everything else it pays a big price. Most of Starbucks's problems during the period from 2002 until 2008 were self-inflicted, and they were about to become exacerbated by the worst global recession since the great depression.

Arthur characterized Starbucks as having been a business that offered a "third place" for people, a place between work and home to connect people with their neighbors and support community building In the early 1990s. Starbucks had restyled the romance with coffee and ambiance of the traditional Italian coffee bars for the American public. By the mid-2000s success had created a focus on growth, improved efficiencies, and a focus on same-store quarter-on-quarter revenue increases.

Arthur describes the "Starbucks Experience" as beginning "with the moment of connection that occurs between our baristas and our customers. It builds an emotional human connection with customers, a powerful experience that strengthens customer loyalty through relationships". During the late nineties, faster espresso machines had been introduced to reduce waiting times, but the effect (due to their height) was to create a barrier between the barista and the customer. Another concern related to the introduction of breakfast sandwiches, a profitable line of products, which resulted in a change to the aromas in stores. Instead of the smell of freshly ground coffee, the smell of burned cheese was overpowering in many stores. More troubling was the fact that bad habits had developed in many stores relating to the foaming of milk, an essential component in many of the key Starbucks beverages. Baristas had taken to steaming milk and letting the pitchers sit, which allowed the milk to break down. The creamy, thick, and sweet consistency was lost, and the quality and taste of Starbucks's core latte beverage suffered as a result.

This erosion of the customer experience is subtle, and over time customers notice and their ties to the stores weaken, their connection is lost, their daily habits change, and they look for alternatives. The impact on the business is obvious through reduced customer traffic, fewer repeat visits, and lower revenues.

Howard Schultz knew the organization needed to be transformed, and in January of 2008 he resumed his former role as CEO. For the first time in its history Starbucks began missing its growth numbers and started seeing its same-store sales decline. Arthur was given the task of leading the effort to determine which stores would need to be closed and rightsizing the portfolio to set Starbucks back on course. It had never before had to close more than a handful of stores, and this was a massive disappointment and took an emotional toll on all the leaders involved in having to make those decisions. In fact, many customers actually petitioned the company to keep stores in their towns open, because they had become part of the fabric of their communities. But the stark reality was that it would take a long time for many of these stores to be economically viable.

The Transformation Begins

Companies don't transform over e-mail. Leaders need to get clear on the issues they are facing, tell the truth about those issues, and gain alignment around what it will take to change course.

Engage

"When did we stop hearing our own music? . . . When did we forget our business is about the customer and our love and passion for the coffee?"[15] Howard Schultz wondered aloud to an audience of the top 200 leaders from all parts of the world in March 2008. Schultz had just returned as CEO, and it was time to share some hard truths and begin the process of reengaging the leadership around the issues that needed to be addressed.

When companies have lost sight of their customers and their purpose the first step is to face these tough realities. Starbucks did this via a three-day leadership offsite where they looked to gain the buy-in and involvement in a refreshed vision and transformation agenda for the company. Howard and his top team had been developing their ideas over a number of months, and now it was time to share them with the team who could execute and make them a reality. This process involved a lot of discussion, some debate, and ultimately refinement of a "seven big moves" transformation agenda that would guide what the company needed to do to regain its soul.

An example of one of these big moves was to "ignite the emotional attachment with our customers." This was a recognition that the customer experience mattered and all programs, innovations, and new products would need to prioritize customers' needs and more importantly how they would make customers feel. The ultimate litmus test was whether customers would be surprised and delighted by new offerings.

Arthur, one of the key executives that helped lead the turnaround, suggested that at the time Starbucks needed to go back to its core. That meant framing everything around enhancing the "Starbucks Experience" to meet customers' updated needs.

A display was created at the event as a customer immersion exercise. It was a powerful reminder for the leadership of the connections people make every day over a cup of Starbucks coffee. The display showed 100 Starbucks Grande–sized coffee cups in alignment across a wall. Each cup had a moment of customer connection described. One outcome of the leadership offsite in March 2008 was the decision to revise the mission in a manner that reinspired the leadership and would provide a touchstone for the future. This newly updated mission statement became "to inspire and nurture the human spirit one person, one cup, and one neighborhood at a time."

Ultimately the leadership walked away from the event aligned around what needed to be done, documented in the transformation agenda, and why it was important to do it, revealed in an inspiring mission.

At the beginning of a customer-centric transformation it is crucially important to get all leaders reconnected with customers, with the core of what the business is really about. Various forms of customer immersion exercises will help people remember what it is like to be a customer again.

Ignite

In October 2008, Starbucks held an extended leadership team "demarcation" event designed to ignite and inspire the broader leadership team: 10,000 North American regional, district, and store managers. This event included mini-workshops, discussion panels, and interactive displays all based around the transformation agenda. The schedule also included community volunteer events to foster collaboration and give back to the New Orleans community that had been hit hard a few years earlier by Hurricane Katrina.

It was a galvanizing event designed to create buy-in and ignite the desire to execute changes that had to be made to be successful.

These types of events demonstrate to all staff members that the leadership is really serious about making changes and they help people become clear about their role in the change process. The goal is to have people emotionally engaged so they can feel and then take ownership of what needs to be done to execute change.

Embed

During that time Starbucks took concrete steps toward embedding new behaviors that would reignite the core customer experience. Specifically, they took the decision to close all stores at once to retrain baristas in the art of coffee and espresso making. This was a bold move, given the potential business and reputation risks. But ultimately it sent the right message to customers: we are serious about coffee, and we want to make the perfect cup every time. A crucial leadership lesson from this exercise was the message Howard gave baristas during this time. He gave them permission to pour out any espressos that the baristas just felt were not up to the Starbucks's standard and what customers would expect and start again.

This was also a time when Starbucks decided to implement a loyalty program to reward customers who were frequent visitors. This would also allow Starbucks to get a better understanding of their most loyal customers' purchasing behavior. What were their favorite drinks? How often did they visit the store? Store managers could build stronger connections with their loyal customers and plan their operations more effectively.

During this time Arthur described the other changes that were implemented. One of the first was the installation of the latest espresso machines that would make consistent high-quality espresso shots and sit lower on the counter, allowing the baristas to connect with the customers.

Starbucks worked on its food and developed a breakfast offering with a cheese that did not overwhelm the coffee smell in stores. These were a few of many touches that allowed them to retain the store ambiance and still meet the needs of customers who were looking for a substantial morning meal in the store.

Also during this time Arthur undertook a major review of the stores' overall design and aesthetics. It was evident that the stores were looking a little tired, and new store designs were more of the same. Arthur described how he and his team responded to this customer feedback: "We created a platform for future store design, based on a 'modern organic aesthetic,' to include stone, metal, wood, recyclables, all rooted in organic materials. We then combined those broader design themes to the store's physical design, we looked at relevant furniture, fixtures, and lighting to create a very unique customer experience aligned with our company's history as well as the organic nature of coffee. We knew that our customers expected more, and we raised the bar by declaring that company-owned stores would be designed and constructed to leading energy and environmental design standards."[16]

Fortify

How do we know that Starbucks is really back on track?

One of the proof points comes from Starbucks's success in launching its instant coffee brand VIA in 2009. At the time it was seen as heretical by many commentators and even some insiders. However, Schultz and his leadership team knew that Starbucks could reinvent the category by making a high-quality instant coffee that was incomparable to existing products in the market, but with Starbucks unique flavors. By doing this they would be able to attract new customers to the Starbucks brand and tap into the growing trend of always on, always now culture driven by technology and instant access to everything. Arthur described one frame of reference that was used in every new innovation at Starbucks as whether the new innovation would make partners proud. In other words, could everyone at Starbucks get behind this innovation, and would it fit in with what Starbucks stood for—bringing the romance of high quality coffee experiences to the world.

Howard Schultz credits this type of innovation as helping to reinspire the organization, reminding everyone that Starbucks could continue to challenge the status quo, push the boundaries, and elevate the coffee experiences for an even larger number of customers worldwide.

What Were Starbucks's Recovery Steps?

1. Creation of a revised mission- centered on the customer and strategic alignment around what was to be done from customer feedback and reconnection with customers.
2. A demarcation event to ignite and inspire all leaders in the business to collaborate and execute the changes to be made.

3. Strengthening the customer experience through product quality consistency, store layout, and redesign and a customer loyalty program that recognized loyal customers and provided inputs to customer insight and foresight.
4. Innovative new products that extended the boundaries and inspired people in the organization to greater experiences for more customers.

The Future: Roy Street Coffee & Tea

Starbucks has been experimenting with different store concepts in order to build out a range of different experiences beyond those in their traditional stores. A great example of this is Roy Street Coffee & Tea, which is a store concept "inspired" (and owned) by Starbucks located in Seattle. As Arthur describes it, "The ultimate service of a coffee house is to promote intellectual thought in terms of literature, film, and music." What makes Roy Street different from the traditional Starbucks store is that it caters to a broader range of experiences, where it attracts customers in the evening as well as the morning and midday. It is a place where independent filmmakers gather and listen to live musicians as well as savor customized blended coffees, unique pastries, and specialty beers and wines.

Starbucks's customer-centric culture, clarity of vision, and leadership will ensure it continues to thrive and grow as it fulfills its mission to inspire and nurture the human spirit.

SUMMARY

There are four clear evolutionary stages that most organizations go through in transforming from an internally focused to externally customer-centered business. Each of these includes steps that form a road map to becoming customer-centric.

Some organizations that are strongly internally focused must go through all of them. Others that are already well down the path of customer focus will bypass some steps and speed up the implementation of others.

Finally, success will be dependent on five main factors:

1. The CEO and senior executives leading the change and continually reinforcing the customer disciplines through personal action and following a road map to execute change
2. Engaging all staff in all functions and at all levels and empowering them to put the customer first
3. Providing support structures and processes that enable staff to deliver increased value to customers
4. Measuring the progress of both customer culture and customer experience
5. Tying employee recognition and reward to customer culture and customer feedback metrics

This process does not stop after one cycle. For companies to maintain their competitiveness and negotiate market shifts and disruptive changes in the environment they will need to engage in this process of continual strengthening of customer culture.

Chapter 10

Leaving a Legacy

The great use of life is to spend it for something that will outlast it.
—William James, American psychologist and philosopher

Donald Williamson, an extraordinary leadership coach, believes that the concept of "customer" has very wide application because when a person thinks of another person —a colleague, boss, partner, or buyer—as a customer, it acts as a way of developing relationships between people. He says, "If you want to be a leader you first have to be an authentic person. To be *customer-centric* you must be person-centric."[1]

Williamson believes that this touches on a fundamental human truth: "that if people are responded to as humans inside and outside a business, that is, to be seen and heard, it creates such a strong connection as to engender a powerful loyalty."

Richard Branson agrees, and has said, "A company is people. . . . Employees want to know . . . am I being listened to or am I a cog in the wheel? People really need to feel wanted."[2]

If an organization's culture is based on these fundamentals, and of course if it delivers products or services of perceived value, then it will have very loyal employees and customers. We have seen that some companies, such as Virgin and salesforce.com, have employees and customers who are fiercely loyal.

In this chapter we draw lessons from customer-centric leaders who have been able to leave a legacy in their organizations that will last. In particular, we report on those who have been able to create and embed a customer culture that is bearing long-term fruit for their organization's value, their employees' welfare, and their customers' loyalty. This chapter includes short stories from interviews with successful business leaders who have created, or are creating, customer cultures—either from the very beginning to a global business like Markit or through transformation of a rail company like Virgin Trains. It includes leaders from different industries, including financial information services, telecommunications, technology, transport, and retail.

These customer-centric leaders, we have found, have several characteristics in common:

- They are authentic, *people-centric leaders* who strive for some higher purpose beyond profitability while recognizing that businesses must be profitable and grow.
- They take a *longer-term view* and want to leave a legacy of sustainability of their businesses that will go well beyond their life's work.
- They do not let their egos get in the way of *inspirational leadership, collaboration, and creating value for customers.*
- They are very *good listeners* and are prepared to learn from others.
- They are good at *synthesizing* the information they have and can make difficult decisions that they follow through with conviction.
- They do not believe in the "cult of the leader," which overshadows the culture of the organization and makes it susceptible to the "next management fad."
- They have the *belief, conviction, courage, and resilience* to carry it through despite criticism, setbacks, and resistance. They are also prepared to take calculated risks.
- They continually spend time listening to and talking with customers. For most of them, *interacting with customers* has been a lifelong habit, the value of which was learned at an early age.

- Many come from humble beginnings and they all remain grounded and realistic when they achieve success. They are lifelong learners and believe that they and their organizations can always do better—for customers and the business. Through that humility they inspire others and have become successful long-term leaders.

All of those reported in this chapter are impressive for their business performance in leading their organizations, but they are even more impressive in the legacy they are leaving—a sustainable customer culture. We review all these leaders and consider what we can learn from them to lead our own customer culture transformation.

Tony Collins, CEO, Virgin Trains, England[3]

"I've never looked for a career. I've always looked for a challenge."

Tony Collins got his wish for a challenge when, as CEO of Virgin Trains, the company lost its bid for a 14-year extension of the West Coast (London to Glasgow) train franchise from the British government on August 15, 2012. Virgin Trains (VT) had operated the franchise since 1997 and transformed the business from a loss-making government-owned command-and-control organization with poor customer service to a growing, profitable customer-focused service organization with passionate staff and loyal customers.

Tony had been CEO of Virgin Trains for nine years, and it was almost as if his whole working life had prepared him for this challenge—the biggest one he had ever encountered.

"Put your trust in people, not in processes."

Tony Collins believes that if you have the courage to put your trust in people, they don't want to let you down. For the last six years at Virgin Trains he has led a change in the culture in line with his belief that the company is in "the customer service business." The context for building the culture was around providing the very best customer service that created the desired experience for customers. He has created a culture in which staff members are open and honest with one another and prepared to challenge their bosses.

He says that the test of a culture is when things go wrong and people are brave enough to say, "It's not working." He says leadership's role is like helping children learn to "ride a bike"—they will fall off from time to time, and you have to help them get back on and try again. You allow them to make mistakes, develop, and to do their very best.

When asked what was the basis for his commercial success at Virgin Trains he says it is people who have had a passion to give great service to customers. The leadership has freed up that passion by providing a broad framework with the nonnegotiables and allowed the staff members to engage with customers in their own style. For example, he says the London, Liverpool, and Manchester train crews each have their own natural style of providing service to customers. The common link is having the right people with the right attitude and skills to do the job well. Recruiting for attitude, not skill, is important, as people can learn new skills. He says if you, as a leader, want to know what's working and what's not, talk to the people who are dealing with customers. He said his role was to get to know his staff individually and put his trust in individuals and they will not let you down. That was a tall order with 3,000 staff and it required more than half of his time engaging with staff.

"We must fight this! We will fight tooth and nail to right the wrong."

When the government bid for an extension of the rail franchise was awarded to a competitor, both Tony Collins and Richard Branson believed there was something wrong. Buoyed by 170,000 passenger signatories to an e-petition supporting the company, and rallying support from unions and staff, they decided to press the government for an investigation into the transport franchise–tendering process and how decisions were made. They had not challenged their lost bids previously, but now they felt they had to do so. Customers and staff had given overwhelming support to Collins and Branson, and the leaders did not want to let them down. But this took courage and was a high risk in terms of cost and reputation.

A government investigation into the bid evaluation process and decision found flaws, and the decision was overturned. An extension in the franchise was awarded to Virgin Trains on December 8, 2012, until 2014, then extended farther, until April 2017.[4]

"I loved roller-coaster rides as a kid."

Tony Collins has been supported by Richard Branson to become a CEO his way, and he has learned that he can trust people just as Branson trusts him. He has been able to shift the culture in a way that has given the staff the resilience to handle the uncertainty created by the bid fiasco.

He described this experience between August 15 and December 8 as the biggest roller-coaster ride he has ever been on. From one day to the next he did not know where it was heading, and he thought it might come to a crashing halt. His feelings on achieving the 23-month extension were relief (Virgin Trains still exists), annoyance (VT should have had a 14-year contract, because it had the superior bid), and eagerness to plan for the future (a need to get the team refocused on the customer and ways to lift the customer experience to a whole new level).

"I have always realized that a customer service culture is good for business."

When asked about his success in Virgin Trains, Tony believes the people to have been the key—the right people with the right attitude. They have had a passion to give great customer service. Leadership throughout the business has freed up that passion and provided a framework for honest and open discussion and challenge.

He says that what is remarkable is how the same people who delivered the service under British Rail, seen to be disinterested and cold toward passengers, are the same people who now deliver industry-leading customer service. He believes the passion was always there, but it had been destroyed by a command-and-control structure driven by process, status, and fear. So the challenge was how to release this energy for the good of customers and the business. He says the people in the business need to have a vision: "What do we exist for? What is it we want to do for our customers?"

"A leader needs passion, courage, and an ability to listen."

Tony Collins has developed his philosophy from two long-standing mentors who have been open and honest with him in their advice. They have been good listeners and caring people who took the time and effort to develop him as an individual and a leader. Also working with his organizational development coach and his senior executive team and with Richard Branson have enhanced the value of trust and the absence of egos to achieve outstanding results. He believes the business will take its persona from its leader.

Leaving a Legacy

Collins sees his legacy as the people he has influenced. His greatest pleasure is to see individuals succeed and go on to greater success inside or outside Virgin.

Our observation is that his leadership during the bid saga and an ability to overcome the odds has created a legacy for all individuals at Virgin Trains that will be talked about for years to come. We expect it will inspire others to have the courage to take risks to do the right thing.

How Does Tony Collins Inspire a Sustainable Customer Culture?

Under high stress Tony inspires support from people (staff and customers) through his empathy, ability to listen, and clear communications of his support even when the future is very uncertain. He consistently leads customer culture thinking by example, and he inspires trust and an openness that enable staff members to challenge his viewpoint. He empowers people to excel. He puts people ahead of processes and systems and believes in the power of personal interaction to create superior customer experiences.

Lance Uggla, CEO, Markit, England[5]

"The thing I love most is that we are in an exciting, dynamic environment that is constantly changing."

The first thing you notice when meeting Lance Uggla is his energy and urgency: he is constantly moving, shifting in his chair, and ready to jump on the next big thing. Lance is the CEO and cofounder of a business that has grown to underpin much of the financial markets. He founded Markit in 2003, to create a credit default swaps (CDS) pricing service for a fast-growing CDS market. Since launching this service to increase transparency in the market and help Markit's customers manage risk he has known nothing but change in building his company to close to revenues of $1 billion in 2013.

His goal for Markit, unchanged from the beginning, is to be an entrepreneurial, employee-led firm that has a real focus on innovation and customers. He leads this entrepreneurial spirit through his attitude of embracing change and a love of learning new things. In so doing he has built a business that started with 6 people and now employs over 3,000. He says, "I like that I have to change as the business progresses through various stages of growth." He believes that the best companies in the world are those where the founder has led them through all stages of growth providing consistent drive for innovation, inspiration, and love of the business.

Through his leadership, the business has a culture of driving change. He says, "We are good at changing—stopping things, changing existing things and starting new things."

"I have empowered 3,000 people globally to think like owners of Markit."

Lance Uggla sees two success factors that launched and propelled Markit on its 10-year growth journey. From the start he shared equity with the small team that started with him in a barn in Hertfordshire, England. As they built their first product—a credit default swap pricing service for financial institutions—he sold ownership to 13 of the largest financial institutions whose pooled data was crucial to the competitive advantage of the product and the success of the company. Since that time the majority of employees has been granted equity from the receptionist to the president. This has meant that Markit has been able to attract extraordinary talent. Acquisitions have fueled half the growth of Markit, and the company has become expert at integrating these firms all under a single brand and company culture. He says, "Equity binds us all together with a single purpose."

"Great firms are constantly innovating."

Lance Uggla believes that Markit cannot rest on its laurels and must continue to be a cutting-edge innovator. In 2012 Markit was named as the Innovation Partner of the Year at the high-profile Canalys Channels Forum—the largest independent channels conference in the Europe/Middle East/Africa region.[6]

Lance says he seeks to break down management layers and bureaucracy that come with a larger business. He doesn't like his managers layering themselves in bureaucracy to protect them from bad decisions. It slows down good decision making and action.

This culture of innovation is enhanced by the cross-business communication and collaboration that occurs in Markit. It is vital so that different parts of the business do not invent the same thing twice. He leads this with his frequent communication across the business including:

- Weekly executive committee meeting (9 people)
- Monthly management meeting (35 people from across the three business units and service functions)
- Biweekly managing directors' meeting (110 most senior people)
- Monthly directors' meeting (500 directors)
- Quarterly Town Hall with all employees

He and his president make sure they never miss a meeting, because it signals something very important to Lance: his accessibility to employees.

"I have no exit strategy."

Lance was awarded the Ernst &Young UK EY Entrepreneur of the Year in 2012 and has no plans to stop. He is aiming for Markit to be in the same market cap as the largest players in the financial services industry. But he is grounded by the values of his parents: the importance of a strong work ethic, good manners, and respect for people.

How Does Lance Uggla Inspire a Sustainable Customer Culture?

Lance Uggla is the epitome of a customer-centric leader who is leaving a legacy embedded in the people in this business. His respect for people and focus on customer-inspired innovation embed this culture in Markit. He loves learning new things and inspires his staff to innovate with and for customers. He creates a collaborative culture in which employees share knowledge, resources, and ownership of the company. His enthusiasm and energy inspire people to follow his vision of the future for their company. He is an example of a leader who creates the future.

Joe Penna may have had Lance Uggla in mind when he said, "Every single person I know who is successful at what they do is successful because they love doing it."[7]

David Thodey, CEO, Telstra, Australia[8]

Agent for the Customer

Born in Perth, Australia, schooled in New Zealand, and 21 years with IBM in customer-facing roles made David Thodey the perfect choice for taking on the daunting task of transforming Telstra to a customer-centered organization. In his first year as Telstra CEO in 2009 there was a lot of angst, and he had to hold his integrity and conviction to do the things he knew needed to be done. Early in his tenure he was asked to define his leadership and differentiate it from the leadership of those who had gone before him. He answered, "I want to be an agent for the customer."

The thing you immediately notice about David Thodey is his respect—the respect he has for people, for his staff, his customers, his competitors, his directors, and shareholders—and the position he holds as CEO of Australia's highest-profile business. As a result he commands respect. As a leader he has an inner belief to do what's right and an inner conviction to follow through. He has a strong faith and also his parental upbringing that acts as his moral compass. He has displayed two personal values he holds as extremely important in business—conviction and honesty—values that have been central to the successful transformation of Telstra.

This fact was recognized in 2012 when he was named CEO of the year by The Australian newspaper and internationally recognized as in the top 10 of the world's leading chief executive officers for their innovative and influential work in the wake of the financial crisis.[9]

"As a leader I am a team player. Success requires good teams around you."

"My 12 members of my senior leadership team are unified around a single purpose," says David. "It has meant that some have had to leave and new ones brought in. Each two weeks they look with their teams at the customer metrics. They are passionate about the customer workshops we conduct. I attend 1 workshop in 10."

David Thodey is open to learning from anyone—his bosses, peers, and subordinates. He looks for the positive in everyone.

"I'm a considered person. I like to get the facts and to get the wisdom of a group of people on an issue. I respect people. I enjoy people."

David is very collaborative by nature. He likes a good, open dialogue with people. Telstra's internal social media system utilizing Yammer has given almost thirty thousand people (and growing) a voice and a forum for commenting on people and issues and for making suggestions. He logs in almost daily and comments on issues raised and gives his perspective. This makes him accessible and transparent to staff and engenders a collaborative spirit. It is also changing the way staff members talk about Telstra. He says that Yammer has revolutionized his life in communicating with staff and hearing their views and ideas.

"I take customer service personally."

David is into his fifth year leading Telstra, Australia's market leading telecommunications company, in a transformation toward becoming a customer-centric business. When asked what keeps him awake at night, he says he is a good sleeper, but he gets upset when a customer has a bad experience with Telstra. As do his other senior executives, David talks frequently with customers—advocates and detractors. He never ceases to be upset when he hears about a bad experience.

This is what drives him to get the message across to all 60,000 employees and contractors to understand that everyone in the business has an impact on customers.

"My aspiration is for Telstra to be the most admired, respected, and trusted telecommunications company in the world."

David says that "what we do is 'touch people's lives'—thousands of them on a daily basis. We can make it a rich experience or a poor one. So, we had to get our people to believe that Telstra can become an admired company."

He says, "We have to all move to the new world together as one Telstra—no matter where in the business we sit.

"We need for all our staff to have confidence at social events to talk with pride about where they work. We implemented an employee referral scheme to enable staff to get direct help for a customer if they have had a bad experience. This enables staff to show that we really care and want to fix a customer's problem."

Creating a New Telstra

"I've always said that customer service is fundamental to Telstra's future," says David. "It's part of the new Telstra we're creating—a company with a service culture and the flexibility to innovate around the customer. What we're creating is a sense of the company as *one Telstra*. By *one Telstra* I'm talking about changing the fabric of the company, creating a company that people can be proud of, and feel good about working for and talking about.

"This has not been hard, because at its best, that's what Telstra has always been—a people company. What we are doing is empowering people to be what they really want to be."

David understands that the transformation of a large, complex, technology-based business like Telstra takes time. But he has already made remarkable strides, which are showing up in revenue growth, profitability, and stock price as well as employee engagement and customer advocacy. He has been able to take the tough decisions and knows that ultimately his team must deliver superior business performance. When you meet him, you know he will finish the job. He just creates that confidence and conviction.

So often it is the personality of the CEO that leads a company, but this is changed when a new CEO is appointed. These then are fads. But one of the challenges is to stay the course. David believes that the company should go on forever without the same CEO; this will mean that a legacy of a sustainable customer culture has become embedded.

How Does David Thodey Inspire a Sustainable Customer Culture?

David gives respect, listens, learns, and takes on board different viewpoints. He is a collaborative team player. He inspires his employees through clarity of vision, values, and strategy and his personal commitment as a role model of customer-centricity. He creates an inclusive environment in which people feel an important part of the company and its future. He demands and gets high performance from his leaders in being accountable and rewarded for customer service and its impact on business performance.

John Stanhope, Chairman, Australia Post[10]

"I do like cars, music and Aussie football,"

John Stanhope's passions for cars, music, and Aussie Rules football—he drives a late-model Mustang, played drums in a rock band, and is a huge supporter and member of the Geelong Football Club—are surpassed only by his passion for business and his family. At first glance, this finance-trained ex-CFO of Telstra, Australia's largest telecommunications business and now chairman of Australia Post (AP), the iconic government-owned mail and parcel carrier, would appear to be a savvy financial expert and director built on traditional lines. After all, his success at Telstra was transforming his 2,500-strong diverse finance and administration group into an effective "value service" organization that inspired an entire transformation of the business taken on by current CEO, David Thodey. His major part in negotiating a major long-term network deal between Telstra and the Australian government worth billions was recognized by his government appointment to the chairmanship of Australia Post. But while all these achievements are true, in some ways these disguise the real John Stanhope to the outside observer.

"When the customer makes you or your business the center of what they do in your solution area, you have achieved customer-centricity."

John is one of the most customer-centric leaders you will meet. He is an innovative thinker who recognized the need for change in large businesses well before anyone else. He is at the vanguard worldwide in advocating new tools for companies to identify, measure, and mitigate current and future marketplace risks based on a customer-centric mindset and culture. He is a master at observing change, asking insightful questions, and listening. He is the first person we have heard to propose that real customer-centricity is achieved when "the customer makes your business the center of his or her world."

John is continually doing personal surveys of customers—his kids, friends, and people he meets—by asking them questions. He is a good listener; for years he had a sign on his desk facing him that said "Be there" to remind him to focus on people he was with and interact in a productive, collaborative way.

He believes people in companies need to do this. The more people, the more shared knowledge and insight.

"I realized at Telstra that the finance function had to become customer-centric. It had to become valued and valuable to the rest of the business by understanding and responding to customer needs."

John's business foundation was formed from a 45-year work life with Telstra, performing almost every function in the organization. He started work as a 17-year-old with the then-combined post office and phone company and soon (with his supervisor) was entrusted with a gun and the weekly payroll that was transported by foot around the inner suburbs of Melbourne where the company had its offices and shops. While he had training with the payroll, there was not much training with the gun. Fortunately he never had to use it. He recounted his experience at the end of the payroll delivery day: going with his supervisor to the pub, putting the gun on the bar, and ordering a glass of milk. In 2004 he was appointed CFO and a director of Telstra's main board, and he set about transforming the finance and administration function.

"The central task at Australia Post is to transform the company into an innovative, customer-centric business that provides a bridge between the physical and digital worlds."

Appointed chairman of Australia Post in 2012, he is working with CEO Ahmed Fahour, who is leading the transformation of this business to a customer-centric organization with a sustainable future at a time when many of the world's government-owned mail services, such as the U.S. Postal Service, are losing millions of dollars and have a bleak future. Part of AP's success is the ability to negotiate changes in public mail services with government and the mail workers union to reduce losses in the mail service while still providing valuable services to consumers. This requires a customer-centric mindset and actions that enable the government and unions to see value from the changes while mail consumers also continue to receive value. John's role in "seeing things from the government's point of view" is crucial. The other element of success is to make the digital transition in its parcel service and other services.

"Disruption is happening everywhere, and I want to be a part of it—either creating it or proactively preempting it."

John's peripheral vision related to the music industry (after all, he was a drummer in a rock band) has taken him into new businesses, such as the small company that enables high-quality video production of music stars' new songs to be produced at a fraction of the cost. The company organizes a competition for fans to produce a video for the singer or band, with a prize going to the selected winner, which costs about 90 percent less than the normal production would. A short list of produced videos is provided to the singer who selects the favorite and uses that one to promote the new song. This is using the concept of "crowds" and "competitive gaming" to create a disruptive competitive model to traditional video production businesses.

Leaving a Legacy

John has worked with three of Australia's oldest companies—Telstra as CFO and director, Australia Post as chairman, and AGL as director. He says: "Wherever I have worked I have been proud of my company—love the brand and reputation. Complaints erode the legacy of a great business. They also erode the financial revenue and performance." John displays great loyalty to the companies he has worked in, to the people he has worked with, and to his many friends. He believes that loyalty should be extended to customers. He goes on to say: "I hate it when customers get bad service and are not kept informed or are promised something with no intention of delivering it—because it is so unnecessary. It comes back to having a customer culture."

By the end of his four-year term as chairman of Australia Post in 2016, John expects to see the transformation complete, the service and cost reduction reforms done, and the company moving toward a strong customer-centric organization. That, he says, will be his legacy. John has unwavering focus, and those who know him well are sure it will happen.

How Does John Stanhope Inspire a Sustainable Customer Culture?

As a professional director he understands the risks and opportunities associated with weak and strong customer cultures and with clear peripheral vision he inspires attention and action through his stories of successes and failures. John clearly explains the links between customer culture and financial performance. He is a very good questioner who helps leaders clarify exactly what they mean and to think about their customers' needs and how they can better satisfy them. He believes that everyone at every level in an organization plays an important role in being customer centric in his or her thinking and actions. His experience in shared services functions, like finance, enable him to clearly explain what is needed to embed a customer service culture. John's parents taught him to be humble, but to take pride in what he accomplishes and inspire others to do the same—particularly for the customer.

Richard Branson, Head of Virgin Group[11]

"Screw it, let's do it."

Most people in business know what Richard Branson has done: a variety of high-profile activities, from circling the globe in a hot-air balloon to creating profitable global businesses under the iconic brand Virgin. From his books we know he is a man of action typified by his phrase "screw it, let's do it." He is also a risk-taker, both personally and in business. But, as John Borghetti, CEO of Virgin Australia, says; "He is a very astute man. The fun-loving side, don't let that fool you. His mind is as sharp as a razor."[12] He is a person to challenge the boundaries, literally as with Virgin Galactic, but also competitively by starting companies to compete with heavyweights in their industries—airlines, banking, and communications.

In some ways he is an enigma—prepared to do publicity stunts to promote Virgin and his philanthropic causes through Virgin Unite while being at heart somewhat reserved.[13] He has gained the status of celebrity with the general public in the countries he visits and with Virgin staff while being able to trust his business leaders and delegate to them the leadership and decision making in their respective organizations. Even in non-English-speaking countries, such as Thailand, Turkey, Lebanon, and the United Arab Emirates, he has generated enormous publicity and interest when launching Virgin Radio in those countries.

Virgin Is a Movement

By any measure he is an inspirational entrepreneur who has created a global brand that will be his legacy. When you meet leaders in the Virgin Group you get a sense that he has created a *movement*, with all the belief and passion that goes with it. We see that in the case study of Virgin Trains, the story behind Virgin Radio, and the leaders of Virgin Unite. As Mark Gilmour told us, the mantra in Virgin is "we don't just play the game, we change it for *good*."

Leaders Should Listen, Delegate, and Support Their Team

Virgin companies now have about sixty-four thousand people in 34 countries. Richard Branson's style of leadership is based around a core set of values of innovation, customer service, community, and environment. Above all, he is people focused, trusts his leaders, listens, and delegates. He takes the view that his senior leaders, who live and breathe the Virgin brand, are there to run their businesses, and he is available to support them and add value where he can. It is their role to recruit and align people with the Virgin culture and to make sure staff and customers are happy. It was recounted to us many times how when he visits staff in Virgin businesses around the world he talks with them, listens, encourages, and involves them in what he is doing. Ian Grace of Virgin Radio says he listens, synthesizes, and then responsively carries out his role to support, for example, the launch of a new radio station. He knows that his staff members need to be properly and regularly recognized for their initiative.

He is a strong believer that Virgin must be set up to run without him. By hiring for the traits that will already make ordinary people culturally "Virgin people," Branson believes the Virgin way will outlive him. He urges his leaders to follow that path, and he is always on the lookout for people who enjoy working with people, are attentive, and smile freely.

Virgin leaders tell us that there is scope for individuality through Branson's style of leadership. He personally regards people as important and wants to enable them to bring out their best. All the leaders in the Virgin businesses have the same mentality and approach to Virgin culture, coming from clear, simple brand values. They say that collective responsibility bonds teams, and having pride in your work is much more effective than a hierarchical culture.[14] Branson believes a business has to be involving and fun, and it has to exercise people's creativity. There are many innovation schemes in Virgin where new ideas are submitted and evaluated and many are introduced. Also top performers are nominated by their peers and regularly recognized.

Leaving a Legacy: "People, Planet, and Profit"

Richard Branson now spends a large chunk of his time on what he calls social entrepreneurship, something he feels is a leadership challenge all businesses need to tackle, and one in which they should get their staff engaged. He sees business as a force for good. He is engaging people across the Virgin Group, through his nonprofit Virgin Unite, to give their time and resources to help their local communities and tackle the big issues facing people on the planet. You now hear people in Virgin talking about *people, planet, and profit.*

He launched the B Team in June 2013, a global nonprofit organization aimed at refocusing business on people, the planet, and the economy. The "team" is made up of a small number of global business and political leaders. With a goal to take the focus off short-term gains, they hope to inspire a Plan B that focuses on business to help solve the world's growing problems of inequality, unemployment, and the unsustainable use of natural resources.[15]

How Does Richard Branson Inspire a Sustainable Customer Culture?

First and foremost Richard Branson is people focused. He genuinely cares about other people and trusts them to do the right thing by customers and by him. He recognizes in people the Virgin ethos and recruits those people by their attitude. He delegates and shows support for people and the business they work in. He gives to people a higher purpose and creates opportunities for them to personally achieve it. He recognizes and requires business performance. All of these characteristics create an enduring customer culture that delivers superior business performance.

Alex Bard, Vice President and General Manager, Salesforce.com, USA[16]

"There was just something about him, something in the way he interacted with all the customers that came through the door, no matter what they were coming in for, that left an impression upon me."

Alex Bard understood the importance of personal interaction from a very young age. He was born in Russia. His parents immigrated to America when he was five years old to live in the Bronx in New York. His mother worked hard as a cashier at a local convenience store, and Alex recalls visiting her often in the store while growing up. He says: "The guy who owned the store was always so friendly, so nice. I remember coming in when I was six years old, and he would give me pennies, and I started to collect pennies. Every time I came in, he would do something just genuine and nice. He didn't just treat my mother and I that way, but you could just see that he had this really great energy, a passion for people in general and his customers in particular. Then I started to appreciate how through a simple interaction you could completely change the relationship that you have with someone."

"Inside of our DNA we will always do the right thing for the customer first—we will think about how would we feel about this happening to us if we were on the other side of this interaction."

Alex has spent most of his professional career since the mid-1990s initiating four start-ups—three out of the four have been in customer service and support. "So being customer-centric is something that I've been forever and I'm hugely passionate about," he says. Three of those businesses he started with two friends from high school with complementary skills who helped them succeed. Alex recalls that "when we started Desk.com the first two people that we hired was our head of customer support and . . . our head of 'customer wow.' So his title actually on his business card is 'VP of customer wow.' So we all understand that customer support is a largely reactive role, but the role of wow was proactive. What could we do, what are the little moments of delight, what are the little surprising things that we could do on behalf of our customers to really blow them away, to see how invested we are in their success?" The proactive role of customer wow was to create unexpected value that resulted in deeper customer relationships. Alex puts down the "wow" factor to the real success of his businesses.

When Alex met Marc Benioff, founder, chairman, and CEO of salesforce.com, who was looking at acquiring Assistly (now Desk.com), they were very much aligned. Alex joined salesforce.com in 2011 when his company was purchased.

"As you grow, to get everybody on the same page you must document what you stand for by being very clear about your values. The first one is—people matter."

Alex believes a company's values are the glue that binds all parts of an organization together, no matter how dispersed around the globe. His view is "we're here to create something special, to have a positive and direct impact, enjoy what we do with who we do it with every day, have fun, smile, bring out the best in one another, trust, dream big, obsess over customers." He says that at Assistly and later at Desk.com, the values were written down.

Now at salesforce.com there are three posters in meeting rooms—a poster of the Holstee manifesto and a poster each of the Desk.com values and the salesforce.com values. They are usually lying on the meeting table or leaning against a wall. These are also used in the recruitment process to reinforce those values when new people join the company.

Leaving a Legacy

From his humble upbringing, Alex knows the value of people and personal interaction. He has already left an impact on people's lives with his entrepreneurial activities that have produced innovative services and unexpected value through customer service. He still has much more he wants to do.

How Does Alex Bard Inspire a Sustainable Customer Culture?

Alex sees the central role of corporate values as the basis for inspiring people to create the "wow" for customers. He also sees them as the foundation for aligning existing and new employees to a sustainable customer culture as organizations grow.

CHAPTER SUMMARY

Changing culture takes effort and persistence, so why would you want to do it? Why do people climb high mountains, sail around the world in small boats, or run a marathon? Not because it is easy—it takes months, sometimes years, of planning, training, and acclimation—but because it is a lasting achievement.

Innate in human nature is the desire to leave a mark, a memory—a legacy when we have moved on. The only real legacy that you can leave in a company or a team is that it endures, it prospers, and the experience, culture, and memory live on in individuals and teams and are replicated as they go on to achieve great things. The products, services, technologies, processes, and physical artifacts associated with a business all change. The short-term fixes and tactics to achieve the quarterly numbers are necessary, but they are not sufficient to leave a mark. But a great, adaptive customer-centric culture can last—and that can be your legacy. That is the legacy of the leaders whose stories are told here.

The only thing that stands between a person and what they want from life is often the will to try it and the faith to believe it's possible.

—Rich DeVos

Chapter 11

Will You Be Ready?

Greatness is not a function of circumstance. Greatness, it turns out, is largely a matter of conscious choice, and discipline.
                                                    —Jim Collins[1]

The future is rushing toward us at supersonic speed. As we said in Chapter 6, there are minor earthquakes bubbling along immediately below the surface just waiting to turn into volcanic eruptions and tsunamis affecting more and more industries.

The major driver is disruptive technologies that change everything. We see it in smartphones and the access to mobile communications by almost everyone on the planet. At last count there were almost 1 billion mobile phones in India, where the cost of a basic mobile phone is $12. We see it in the massive growth in use of social media that has created instant global communications.

What does this mean to your business?

It means that your competitors are global because your customers can increasingly access products from anywhere. For example, a cycling enthusiast can buy carbon-fiber bike wheels directly from China at a third of the price available from major brands in the United States.

It also means that disruptive technology can wipe out your business unless you are closely connected to your customers and can rapidly adapt your business model. For example, digital photography has totally changed the entire value chain that was dominant with film technology. Now digital cameras are being disrupted by smartphones, as consumers increasingly use high-quality smartphones in place of their old point-and-shoot cameras from Canon and Nikon.

It means that tomorrow's customers will be different from those of today. They will be different people or the same people buying in a different way. The demographics of the world's population in the growth economies are shifting fast. For example, banks are now finding they must adapt their offers and ways in which they are delivered and give more convenient access to information to meet needs in a changing demographic population structure.

It means that your changing customer base is being driven by wherever there is smartphone and Internet access. The massive growth of online shopping is changing the face of traditional bricks-and-mortar retailing and how those types of stores must compete—bringing both threats and opportunities.

Companies such as Amazon.com, Google, Apple, Facebook, and eBay, with their huge resources and smart people, are creating and using new technologies that disrupt the way in which industries and businesses currently operate.

As a result, our skills as professionals need to be upgraded as never before, or we become redundant. If you are not creating this culture in your business, you are not keeping up. If you are not systematically developing a sustainable customer culture in your business, you are facing an increasing risk of being wiped out by this onslaught of change.

A customer culture is the only factor in business that is future-proof. If you don't have it, you won't have a future. We are not talking about 10 years. We are talking *now*. So if you don't have it to the level we have discussed in this book, you had better treat it as your urgent number-one priority and act now.

As Jim Collins has found in his research, companies become great by choice. They also decline and disappear when they do not choose to proactively map out their own destiny. The choice is yours.

An Example as a Guide

The following example of a company that supplies capital equipment products to organizations shows you how to start and what you can do. We have not revealed the company name to preserve confidentiality. It used the Market Responsiveness Index (MRI) tool to help it identify where to focus its efforts and resources and which customer culture disciplines to strengthen to support its strategies. A year later it rebenchmarked using the MRI to identify improvements in its customer culture (see Figure 11.1).

The Problem: Slowing Growth

This company had successfully pioneered high-quality capital equipment for hospitals and had no direct competitors. After three years of rapid growth from the successful launch of several innovative new products, the company's growth rate began to fall. The general manager decided to benchmark its customer culture to identify areas of strength and weakness and their implications for strategy.

The Solution: Benchmarking Customer Culture and a Change to Strategy

The resulting MRI indicated that the company had very strong strategic alignment and was very good at understanding and meeting the needs of new customers. The company had focused on getting new customers and had little focus on potential competitors. This was expected. What was a surprise was how poorly it attended to the needs of current customers, reflected in the customer insight discipline of customer culture. This shows customer insight at the 29th percentile in the chart on the left in Figure 11.1 Weakness in this dimension points to a high risk of losing existing customers through dissatisfaction. The general manager realized that current customers could be easily lost to any new potential competitor, and it became clear that this weakness was also retarding the firm's growth rate.

The company serves two types of customers. It sells directly to end users, and once a sale is made these customers generally will not need to repurchase for another five to six years. It was thought that the return on investment did not warrant further investment of time

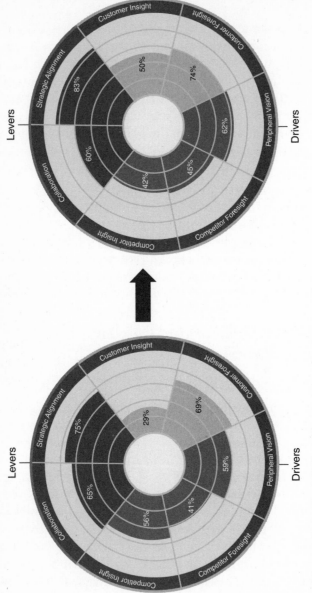

Figure 11.1 The MRI profiles compared, one year apart

and attention in this customer group. But there was a different group that seemed ripe for greater investment toward improved customer insight. This segment of existing customers had the greatest potential for growth and was the most vulnerable to competition.

Private-label customers buy a lot of products, rebrand them, and sell them in the marketplace and are large and frequent customers. But service and responsiveness to these important customers was most often lacking, which was evidenced in the sporadic buying by this group and in the low customer insight score. The company had been growing on the strength of its innovations and development of new market niches, not realizing the potential growth in this customer segment. It didn't have direct resources to focus on this customer group, and the personnel involved kept getting swept away into other projects.

The general manger decided to create a new business unit entirely dedicated to serving the needs of private-label customers. Once designed, staffed, and given a customer-centric mission, it immediately began to engage with private-label customers, understand their needs and involve them directly with new product and service developments. It then provided training for customers on the use of the company's products and marketing resources to help them market to their own customers. Product and service offerings were adjusted to more closely align with their customers' needs. This unit also built a competitive capability by scanning for the most likely new competitors for this market.

The Outcome: Stronger Customer Culture and Regrowth

Customer culture was rebenchmarked 12 months after the initial assessment. As a result of leaders' aggressive actions and focus, the company's level of customer insight almost doubled from the 29th to the 50th percentile. The company had developed and embedded the crucial behaviors necessary to gain deep customer insights. Customer immersion, satisfaction, and feedback systems were implemented, and actions were taken in a proactive rather than reactive manner. Strategic alignment was also stronger, up from the the 75th to the 83rd percentile as clear strategies and value propositions had been developed for the two primary customer segments. These improvements are shown in the chart on the right in Figure 11.1

In a separate survey it was found that private-label customer satisfaction levels had improved dramatically. The observable impact of this improvement on its private-label business has been significant. It grew 20 percent over the year in a rapidly declining capital equipment market environment. In the following year it grew an additional 30 percent.

The benefits have not only accrued to the private-label customers. What the company learned from better addressing private-label customer needs has helped it improve service quality to its direct customers as well.

The general manager summed up the result as follows:

> Because of the MRI and the money we generated from an improved strategy, we didn't have any layoffs. We're one of the very few capital equipment companies in our industry that didn't have layoffs last year, and it was because we grew profitably as our competitors declined.

This company is known for its innovation and its unique products, but in the end, it was not a new product or market that caused its profitable growth to takeoff. Instead, the key to growth and success was simple and something relevant to all companies: a strong understanding and responsiveness to the needs of existing customers enabled by a clear, aligned strategy and focus on delivering superior customer value.

How You Can Start

Start by making a quick assessment of the strength of your customer culture. You can do this by first rating your company, business unit, or function on the questions posed at the end of each of the Chapters 2 to 8. You will see a guide as to how to do the calculations and present your results in Appendix 2.

You can also connect to http://www.marketculture.com/mri.html to do a quick benchmark assessment of where your business stands on customer-centricity and get some guidelines on what you can do, given the assessment of strengths and weaknesses.

There is no excuse for inaction or complacency. The tools are there to make customer culture tangible, measure where you stand, and identify the risks you face in relation to your strategy. You can use proven steps and strengthen relevant customer culture disciplines, based on sound evidence from systematic research, which will drive improved and sustainable business performance.

Whether you are a small or large organization, the same challenge is there. Future-proof your business with a strong, adaptable, innovative customer culture.

Appendix 1

The Research Program

There have been several phases in our research program starting in 2007 and continuing through 2013. Its purpose has been to design, test, implement, and evaluate a customer culture measurement tool that does the following things:

1. It provides a concrete measurement and benchmark of the level of customer-centric behaviors of a company, business unit, function, or team.
2. It includes valid behavioral factors that are linked to business performance outcomes.
3. It indicates which behavioral factors are important to different market strategies.
4. It provides action guidelines for creating or strengthening each of the customer culture disciplines represented by the behavioral factors identified.

Phase 1: Review of Relevant Studies

Beginning in April 2007, we and our research team[1] spent the rest of that year doing extensive research in the field of market orientation, customer experience, customer focus, collaboration, learning orientation, and organizational culture change. In all, over two hundred academic articles, several hundred business articles, and many books were utilized in the research. Many of these included empirical studies designed to identify market orientation and customer focus characteristics and their links with business performance. Each article was reviewed and summarized, and in some cases the original author was interviewed to gain further insights of the studies conducted. While these provided very valuable inputs to our thinking and design, we found that very few had validated models and none were operationalized into a concrete, easy-to-use tool for business leaders. But our synthesis of all this research showed evidence that effective market and customer focus was a corporate culture and it does have positive short-term and longer-term effects on business performance, particularly revenue growth and profit. This encouraged us to move to the next phase: design of a prototype model for pretesting.[2]

Phase 2: Initial Formation and Pretesting of a Survey Tool

From this base of research, combined with the authors' decades of shared experiences in diverse businesses across the globe, we hypothesized a 22-factor model with 102 items designed to measure a market and customer-focused culture. This survey was composed of multilayered cultural drivers starting at its core with seven value factors, then three artifact factors, with six organizational structure factors, and finally six behavior factors.

Qualitative pretesting of this survey was undertaken, with 22 business practitioners working in a variety of businesses in North America. Postsurvey interviews were conducted with all of the participants to determine if the respondents' understanding of the items was clear and as intended. The interviews identified several items where the respondents' understandings were inconsistent, and several items were identified as irrelevant to the respondents' experiences. An overall finding was that the survey as constructed was too long, complex, and unwieldy and would not be completed by business leaders and their teams.

During review of this pretest feedback, it was decided that the survey was far longer than desired, was confusing to participants, and did not present a clear, simple model. The survey needed significant revision, and for the first six months of 2008 every part of the survey was evaluated by the research team and with a small number of business leaders. Research, discussion, and debate followed regarding the content and levels to be included in the survey.

Finally, it was decided that the measurement tool would focus only on behaviors. This is the most visible and concrete element of culture reflecting what people do and how they act. With the growing emergence of the fields of customer experience and customer focus, highlighted by the appointment of chief customer officers in many businesses, it was decided that the most relevant description of what this tool is designed to measure is *customer culture*.

Phase 3: The Foundation Study: Designing and Testing a Tool to Measure Customer Culture Behaviors

By July 2008, a hypothesized nine-factor, 63-item survey was developed for a foundation study that included measures of customer culture on the behavioral level only. This revised survey was pretested with several experts in the field of organizational assessment and found worthy of further research.

This survey instrument, hereafter referred to as the Market Responsiveness Index, or MRI,[3] was designed specifically to assess customer culture. A foundation study was conducted to examine the underlying structure of the instrument and to establish initial reliability and validity estimates. This work resulted in a seven-factor, 35-item final instrument that demonstrates significant predictive validity for several measures of organizational performance. A summary of the conduct of the study, the analytical methods used, and subsequent results follow. A much more detailed description of the study, including the statistical analysis used, is available at http://www.marketculture.com/resourcegateway.html

Foundation Study: Sample

The MRI was designed to be administered to professionals across all industries and at all levels within an organization. The sampling plan was one of convenience and was also designed to represent the diversity of professionals to whom it will be administered in the future. Two methods of sampling were employed in the foundation study. In the first method, the professional contacts of the project team, classes of full-time employees enrolled in MBA programs, and professional distribution lists were used. Individuals were contacted in person or via e-mail by a member of the project team and asked to complete the web-based survey via a link. In exchange for their participation, these individuals were offered a chance to win an Apple iTouch or a $1,000 American Express Gift Card.

In the second method, specific companies or groups within companies were targeted for participation in the foundation study. In exchange for a summary of their results and a follow-up administration and summary in 12 to 18 months, these companies distributed an invitation and link to the web-based survey via e-mail to their employees. All of these efforts resulted in 809 respondents. Individuals with missing MRI data or zero variability on the MRI instrument were removed prior to data analysis, resulting in a final sample size of ($N = 736$).

The sample represents the United States primarily (83.1 percent of the sample), with smaller but significant groups of participants from Australia and Canada. This sample represents diverse industries, including manufacturing (26.1 percent), technology (12.9 percent), wholesale (11.5 percent), and packaging (7.9 percent), among others. The sample represents all levels of the organizational hierarchy, from CEOs and other top executives to hourly employees, and functional diversity with large groups of individuals from marketing, sales, research and development, operations, customer service, and manufacturing.

Foundation Study: Survey Instrument

The pilot instrument hypothesized nine latent factors of customer culture. These were named as follows:

1. Customer alignment
2. Customer insight
3. Customer foresight
4. Competitor insight
5. Competitor foresight
6. P.E.S.T. intelligence (later renamed Peripheral Vision)
7. Cross-functional collaboration
8. Distributive leadership
9. Strategic alignment

Each hypothesized factor was measured by seven items for a total of 63 items. Each item was presented as a statement, and respondents were asked the degree to which they agree with each statement on a 7-point Likert-type scale. In addition, respondents were asked to complete eight items related to the relative performance of their firm to its competitors (namely, profitability, profit growth, sales revenue growth, customer satisfaction, new-product success, innovation, and overall performance). Respondents were also asked to rate two items related to job satisfaction and turnover intentions, respectively. Finally, respondents were asked to report demographic data related to industry, company, job, and personal matters (such as highest level of education attained.)

The survey data was analyzed using several statistical methods. Details on the specifications for each analysis and the results obtained are presented in the sections that follow.

Foundation Study: Results

The foundation study was conducted to examine the underlying structure of the instrument and to establish initial reliability and validity estimates. The MRI instrument was administered to a demographically diverse group of professionals employed in a variety of countries, industries, and companies. This work resulted in a seven-factor, 35-item final instrument that demonstrates significant predictive validity for several measures of organizational performance. The data gathered on the MRI was analyzed to establish it as a unique instrument that demonstrates simple structure, high reliability, and high validity, thus deeming it useful for organizational assessment and prediction. The strong theoretical underpinnings and performance of the instrument in the exploratory, confirmatory, and predictive analyses provides clear support for its continued development and use in practice.

MRI Structure

Although a nine-factor measurement model was proposed for the MRI, a more parsimonious seven-factor model was identified by the exploratory factor analysis and later confirmed by the confirmatory factor analysis procedures. Each factor was labeled according to its conceptual meaning. The seven MRI factors are:

1. **Customer insight:** Understanding and acting on current customer needs and satisfaction
2. **Customer foresight:** Understanding future needs and acting to attract potential customers
3. **Competitor insight:** Monitoring, understanding, and responding to current competitors' strengths and weaknesses
4. **Competitor foresight:** Monitoring, understanding, and responding to potential competitors and future replacement products
5. **Peripheral vision** (formerly P.E.S.T. intelligence): Monitoring, understanding, and responding to external trends and changes in the wider business environment

6. **Cross-functional collaboration:** Interacting, sharing information, working with and assisting colleagues from different work groups and functions
7. **Strategic alignment:** Aligning work to the firm's vision, mission, values, objectives, and strategies

The identification of a five-item-per-factor measurement model was driven, not by methodology, but by practical concerns in that an instrument with equal indicators for each factor was desired. The decisions to include and exclude items were guided by statistical evidence. The resulting seven-factor, five-item-per-factor measurement model demonstrates a good fit. Careful attention was given to avoid overfitting the foundation sample by splitting the sample randomly, building the model on the first split, and then applying or confirming the model on the second split. Multiple indices of fit from different perspectives (absolute, incremental, and stochastic) were used so that a poorly fitting model was not inadvertently identified and confirmed due to statistical artifacts or indicator biases. Additional model estimates, such as factor loadings, item reliabilities, and normalized residuals, were also considered and used to guide decision making.

In the final instrument, all factor loadings are nontrivial and statistically significant, with standardized loadings ranging from .65 to .90. Factor intercorrelations are moderate, ranging from .24 to .66, and demonstrate an expected pattern of relationships. The MRI provides sufficient breadth of coverage for the overall concept, customer culture, as well as good and parsimonious measurement to make it ideal for use. In short, the MRI has a simple measurement structure.

Reliability Evidence

Reliability is a necessary but insufficient condition of validity. One type of reliability, internal consistency reliability, provides an indication of the precision of measurement for a scale. A scale is defined as a set of items that measure the same dimension.

Internal consistency reliabilities are typically assessed by calculating coefficient alpha estimates. It is common practice to use scales with internal consistency reliabilities above .70 in research and to use those with reliabilities above .80 in practice. For the seven scales of the MRI, coefficient alpha reliabilities ranged from .83 to .92. The MRI scales clearly demonstrate sufficient internal consistency reliability for use in practice.

In addition to scale reliability, item reliability is also important to consider. Item reliabilities are calculated by squaring the standardized factor loadings for each item. Item reliability coefficients indicate how much variation in an item's score is attributed to the factor or scale to which it belongs, which is called "reliable variance," and how much is attributed to error or chance, which is called "unreliable variance." Typically, item reliabilities are considered good at .50 or above. The item reliability values for the 35 items on the MRI ranged from .48 to .81, with only three values lower than .50. This suggests that for most items, the item scores are accounted for by a larger proportion of reliable factor variance than by error variance.

The MRI has demonstrated a simple measurement structure and acceptable reliability for use in practice, both in terms of scale or internal consistency reliability and item reliability. This evidence satisfies two preconditions for the determination of validity. Several types of validity evidence are discussed below, including face validity, content validity, construct validity, and criterion-related predictive validity.

Face and Content Validity Evidence

The foundation MRI instrument was designed with face and content validity in mind. Face validity is a subjective judgment that an instrument appears to measure what it is intended to measure—in this case, customer culture and its seven components. Content validity is also a subjective judgment that the breadth and depth of a concept or dimension is represented fully by the items and scales that measure it.

During development, careful attention to the composition of items to measure each hypothesized dimension was given, and dimensions were clearly defined prior to item development. Subject-matter experts reviewed each scale and item to assure that face and content validity were evident. The loss of two factors (from nine to seven scales) and two items (from seven to five items) from each scale does not detract from face or content validity, as the final set of items and factors appears to sufficiently cover the content of the customer culture concept.

Construct Validity

Two types of construct validity were examined statistically. The first, convergent construct validity, provides an indication that items are measuring the constructs intended and that scales are interrelated to measure a higher-order construct, as intended. Convergent construct validity was considered during the exploratory and confirmatory stages of the analyses, though no formal test of convergent construct validity was performed. The MRI factors demonstrate low to moderate correlations (correlations range from .26 to .69), and factors that are clearly related theoretically demonstrate higher correlations than do those factors that are not. For example, competitor insight, competitor foresight, and peripheral vision factors are moderately intercorrelated, while customer insight and strategic alignment are not. In addition, among the second-order confirmatory factor analyses conducted, a single higher-order factor represented the best fit to the data.

The second type of construct validity is discriminant construct validity. Discriminant construct validity provides an indication that each factor is measuring something unique (in other words, that a single second-order factor is insufficient to describe the data). Although all factors should be related to one another in the measurement of the overall concept—in this case customer culture—the individual factors should not be redundant but rather should be discriminant. The factor intercorrelations also provided evidence of discriminant validity because, although the factors are all intercorrelated, the correlation coefficients do not approach or exceed .70, a relatively common criterion for discrimination.

In addition, a specific test of discriminant validity was conducted by comparing the variance extracted by each factor to the correlation between two factors. In this examination, the correlation between a pair of factors should be less than the variance extracted from both factors independently. All pairwise comparisons were made, and only one comparison failed to provide evidence of sufficient discriminant validity, although it approached the level to satisfy the criterion. In sum, sufficient evidence of discriminant validity among the MRI factors was found.

Criterion-Related Predictive Validity

While structural, reliability, and other validity evidence represent necessary conditions for adequate measurement of a construct such as customer culture, evidence of predictive validity is necessary to motivate use of a survey instrument. Although objective measures of business performance were not available for these analyses, subjective measures were used. Subjective measures have been shown empirically to be sufficient indicators of objective measures in the research literature.

A path model with manifest variable equations—bivariate correlation analysis, multivariate regression, and multivariate analysis of variance (MANOVA)—were used to examine the predictive validity of the MRI with this sample. The three types of analysis were complementary, with each one providing support to the findings of the others.

For each of the seven performance outcomes considered (profitability, profit growth, sales revenue growth, customer satisfaction, new product success, innovation, and overall performance), the MRI factors combined to predict between 18 percent and 29 percent of variance in performance ratings. While some factors (such as collaboration and strategic alignment) are predictive of all outcomes, others (such as customer insight and competitor insight) are predictive of several and still others (for example, customer foresight, competitor foresight, peripheral vision) are predictive of only one or two outcomes. Two MRI factors predicted all seven performance outcomes significantly, while the other five factors combined to predict one or more of the performance outcomes. In sum, all of the performance outcomes are predicted by some combination of the MRI factors.

Conclusion

The development of the MRI and the conduct of the structural, reliability, and validity analyses have yielded favorable results for the use of this instrument as a measure of customer culture and a predictor of important organizational outcomes. The development of the idea was based on prior research and the needs of business organizations to assess and implement changes to their organizational culture in a fast-changing world. The development of the instrument, its dimensions and items, was based on strong empirical evidence and guided by the well-established and best practices of academic survey development.

The MRI is a structurally simple instrument that covers the breadth of the customer culture concept. In this sample, the MRI demonstrated reliable and valid measurement, as well as valid prediction of organizational performance.

Foundation Study: Implications

The results of the foundation study of the MRI survey have validated a useful tool. The market and customer orientation construct has a well-established, 20-year history in the academic literature. The conceptual development was strong, and the MRI makes sense to users, as indicated by the underlying structure of their responses and the open-ended feedback they provided to accompany those numerical responses. The development of the MRI and the conduct of several iterations of analysis demonstrate that a customer culture, a high-performance culture based on an external focus, can be reliably measured and demonstrated to predict important organizational outcomes that are of interest to a broad range of organizations, such as profitability, profit growth, sales revenue growth, customer satisfaction, new-product success, and innovation. The MRI represents a reliable and valid measurement tool to assess customer culture and to predict important organizational outcomes.

High performance on the MRI was related to high organizational performance. Organizations with high MRI scores reported superior performance. The MRI dimensions combined to predict between 18 percent and 29 percent of the variance on ratings of the seven performance indicators. Considering how many different things contribute to profitability, for instance, it is quite impressive that the MRI factors combine to predict 18 percent of profitability ratings. One possible implication of this linkage is that managers and organizations that fail to develop a strong customer culture may be handicapped in their ability to perform in each of the seven outcome areas (profitability, innovation, new-product success, and so on). No matter how hard employees work, no matter how efficient an organization is, the organization may fail to perform at the highest possible level if its customer culture is weak. As such, the MRI serves as an early-warning system for future business performance and a gauge of ability to achieve sustainable competitive advantage.

None of the MRI dimensions is related to the performance outcomes in the same way. The MRI dimensions are a set of unique but related indicators of performance, and they combine to predict various performance outcomes differently. Specific culture dimensions can be targeted to achieve specific performance goals. In other words, although an across-the-board increase in all MRI dimensions would bode well for an organization, the tool can also be used to identify the most efficient methods by which gains in a specific performance area can be achieved. For instance, if improving innovation is the goal, improvements in customer foresight, collaboration, and strategic alignment are prescribed. Focusing on performance goals is likely to clarify findings for managers and make prioritizing actions resulting from survey administration to meet their most immediate or important goals.

The sum of the evidence for the MRI is positive, indicating reliable and valid measurement that offers the ability to detect potential weaknesses in an organization for future business performance and identify culture change areas to boost performance in a specific area.

Phase 4: Ongoing MRI: Business Performance Tests

During 2009–2012 we conducted several MRI tests with companies designed to check their MRI levels against objective measures of their business performance. We specifically wanted to test businesses at both ends of the MRI-business performance spectrum—those at the low end and those at the high end. We consistently found that those with low MRI scores showed business performance levels (profitability, profit growth, and sales revenue growth) lower than their industry competitors and those with high MRI scores showed business performance relatively higher than their competitors. These studies add further evidence of the MRI-business performance relationship found in the foundation study.

Phase 5: Longitudinal MRI Studies and Business Performance Improvement

During 2010–2012 we implemented the MRI at least twice with several companies and assessed the actions taken to improve customer culture and the gains made in business performance. The results of these studies are confidential to our clients, but one of these assessments was reported anonymously in Chapter 11. Another, which we have been able to make public, is documented as a detailed case study of a business unit transformation in Telstra Corporation and is available at http://www.marketculture.com/resourcegateway.html

This documents the MRI before and after the first 18 months of the customer culture initiative and the savings, and gains made during that time that could be specifically identified from changes in customer culture disciplines. Gains were shown to be in excess of AUD$15 million (approximately US$14.25 million) per annum and sustainable with continued reinforcement of the customer culture. We are continuing to document these studies with companies to gain more knowledge of the financial and other benefits that are gained from a customer culture transformation.

Phase 6: Development of the Customer Responsiveness Index (CRI) Tool

From our work with a range of large clients we were asked if a specific customer culture measurement tool could be developed for shared service functions such as finance, IT, legal, and HR. For large, diverse companies, where shared service functions are often far removed from external customers, it can be useful for people in those functions to interact with the people they serve within the business as *internal customers*. With the help of John Stanhope (then CFO of Telstra), we developed, tested, and implemented the Customer Responsiveness Index (CRI) in Telstra's Finance and Administration group in 2010. The application of the CRI is described in a Telstra CRI case study available at http://www.marketculture.com/resourcegateway.html

The CRI is a derivation of the MRI tool and is a web-based survey that assesses a support group's cultural capacity for creating superior value for its internal customers. Based on our MRI research and validation, the tool measures customer-centricity and responsiveness in employee behaviors across six customer culture disciplines linked to business performance. We excluded the two "competitor" dimensions (in the MRI) and modified customer foresight to focus only on future needs of existing customers— calling this dimension "customer anticipation." We revisited the "distributive leadership" dimension that was discarded in the MRI foundation study. In further research of studies conducted on employee empowerment, we found that there is an indirect relationship between empowerment and customer satisfaction.

The relationship is empowerment—employee satisfaction—customer satisfaction. We included this in the CRI tool and tested its usefulness with Telstra. As shown in the Telstra CRI case study referenced above, it seems to be particularly useful for shared service functions where at least a part of their role is compliance, but an increasingly important and growing role is that of finding solutions to both internal and external customer problems.

The six behavioral disciplines of the CRI are:

- **Customer insight:** The extent to which employees monitor, understand, and act on current internal customer needs and satisfaction
- **Customer anticipation:** The extent to which employees anticipate emerging internal customer needs, recognize unspoken needs, and take action to satisfy them
- **Peripheral vision:** The extent to which employees monitor, predict, and make decisions in consideration of the emerging trends in the environment that have the potential to impact internal customer needs
- **Cross-functional collaboration:** The extent to which employees interact, share information, work with, and assist colleagues from other work groups
- **Empowerment:** The extent to which employees are empowered to make decisions to solve internal customers' problems, propose new ideas, and control how their work is performed
- **Strategic alignment:** The extent to which employees understand and enact the vision, mission, values, objectives, and strategic direction of the company

Since 2010, this tool has been used for assessing the customer culture of shared service functions by a number of large organizations. We believe it also has application for public service organizations where there are no competitors and there is a need to have a strong customer service culture. In this situation, focus would be on external customers.

Phase 7: Research for This Book

The genesis of this book goes back to 2006 when we were asked by a colleague, "How do you develop a customer focus?" The real research that underpins it was started in 2007. The various phases of research have taken us right through to 2013. The book has taken a year to write, starting in August 2012. This has involved interviews with many business leaders and the development of current case studies and examples that illustrate the seven disciplines of customer culture. It has required an in-depth study of the various phases of customer culture transformation. We have used the MRI tool to help us assess where companies are in their transformation journey as well as personal interviews with the business leaders of those companies. This has been done with the cases provided in Chapter 9: Australia Post, Telstra, Westpac, Virgin Trains, and Starbucks.

Research is ongoing as we learn more from the implementation of the MRI tool and the customer culture transformation journey being undertaken by our current clients.

Appendix 2

Customer Culture: A Leader's Measurement and Action Guide

Take the following steps to get started on the customer culture journey: measure, evaluate, and take action to strengthen.

1. Measure: Estimate Your Level of Customer Culture

Chapters 2 to 8 each include a list of 10 behaviors at the end of the chapter. You can use these to estimate the level of customer culture in your company, business unit, function, or work group. It will be your own assessment and not benchmarked; nevertheless, it will give you an indication of your perception of customer culture strengths and weaknesses across the seven disciplines.

As an example, taken from the page 55 in chapter 2, you can rate each of the following 10 *customer insight* behaviors on a scale of 1 to 10 according to your assessment of the extent to which these behaviors are practiced in your company or team. Use the rating descriptors to guide you.

Rating descriptors: 0 = never; 1 = almost never; 2 = rarely; 3 = occasionally; 4 = sometimes; 5 = regularly; 6 = frequently; 7 = often; 8 = very often; 9 = constantly; 10 = all the time.

☐ 1. To what extent do you and your team understand the needs of current customers?
☐ 2. To what extent do non-customer-facing managers and staff interact with customers?
☐ 3. To what extent do you obtain systematic measures of customer satisfaction?
☐ 4. To what extent do you act on customer problems or complaints?
☐ 5. To what extent do you communicate to customers the actions you have taken resulting from their feedback?
☐ 6. To what extent do you elicit customer insights from all members of your team?
☐ 7. To what extent do you share customer insights with all members of your team?
☐ 8. To what extent do you and your team share insights across other functions and teams outside your group?
☐ 9. To what extent do you publicly recognize individuals who have acted on deep customer insights?
☐ 10. To what extent do you reward individuals who have acted on deep customer insights?

Add together the ratings you have given as an answer to each question, and you will have a score out of 100.

Do the same for each of the other six disciplines. The practices for the seven disciplines are listed at the end of Chapters 2 through 8. You will then have a score out of 100 for all seven disciplines.

Use Figure A2.1 to create a picture of your customer culture strengths and weaknesses. Shade in the areas of each factor on the chart. Each circle represents 0, 20, 40, 60, 80, and 100 from the inner to the outer on a 100-point scale. Any score below 50 should be regarded as a weak customer culture discipline. Any score above 80 represents a strong discipline.

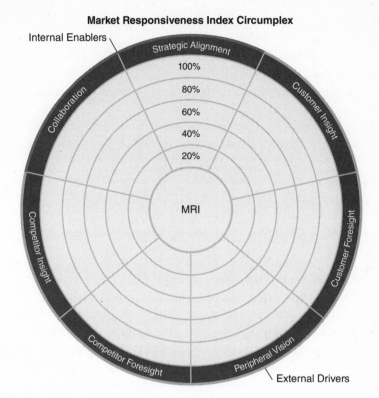

Figure A2.1 Customer culture estimate

2. Evaluate: Assess Customer Culture Strengths and Weaknesses in Relation to Your Strategy

The relative importance of your strengths and weaknesses are related to your strategy. For example, if your market strategy is focused on retaining existing customers and creating advocates, then it is vital that your customer culture be strong in customer insight and competitor insight. If it is focused primarily on acquiring new customers, then customer foresight and competitor insight must be strong. If your strategy is founded on innovation

Disciplines as Drivers	Business Outcomes
Customer Insight	Customer Satisfaction, New Product Success, Sales Revenue Growth, Innovation
Customer Foresight	Innovation
Competitor Insight	Profitability, Profit Growth, Sales Revenue Growth
Competitor Foresight	New-Product Success, Innovation
Peripheral Vision	Innovation
Cross-functional Collaboration	Profitability, Profit Growth, Sales Revenue Growth, Customer Satisfaction, New-Product Success, Innovation
Strategic Alignment	

Figure A2.2 Customer culture drivers of business outcomes

and new products, customer foresight, competitor foresight, and peripheral vision are critical to your future performance.

Whatever your strategy, strategic alignment and cross-functional collaboration need to be strengths so that execution of your strategy is effective and insights are effectively shared across the business. That needs to be done in a way that aligns all teams with the delivery of value that meets current or future customer needs. Figure A2.2 shows the business outcomes that are driven by the customer culture disciplines.

3. Take Action: Strengthen Your Customer Culture

After steps 1 and 2, you may find a need to strengthen one or more customer culture disciplines. Guidelines to action are given by example in the earlier chapters of this book. You can also go to http://www.marketculture.com/resourcegateway.html to see a checklist of actions you can take to strengthen each of the customer culture disciplines.

Notes

Preface

1. Erika Anderson, "11 Quotes from Sir Richard Branson on Business, Leadership, and Passion," *Forbes*, March 16, 2013, http://www.forbes.com/sites/erikaandersen/2013/03/16/11-quotes-from-sir-richard-branson-on-business-leadership-and-passion/.

Introduction

1. The term *customer compelled* was first used by Michael J. Lanning and Lynn Phillips to describe an organization that was driven to give customers anything and everything they want. This is usually impractical and unprofitable and does not allow the firm to focus on the customers it can best serve with superior value.
2. Just before the iPad tablet went on sale in 2010, Steve Jobs showed off Apple's latest creation to a small group of journalists. One asked what consumer and market research had been done to guide its development. "None," Mr. Jobs replied. "It isn't the consumers' job to know what they want." Steve Lohr, "Can Apple Find More Hits Without its Tastemaker" *New York Times*, January 18, 2011, http://www.nytimes.com/2011/01/19/technology/companies/19innovate.html?_r=0.

Chapter 1

1. Stephen R. Covey, *The 7 Habits of Highly Effective People: Powerful Lessons in Personal Change*, New York: The Free Press, 2004.

2. Our thanks to Professor George S. Day, the Geoffrey T. Boisi Professor of Marketing at the Wharton School of the University of Pennsylvania and coauthor with Paul Schoemaker of *Peripheral Vision: Detecting the Weak Signals That Will Make or Break Your Company*, Boston: Harvard Business School Press, 2006. It was Professor Day who first suggested the term "peripheral vision" to describe this customer culture discipline.

3. Interview with Ian Grace, CEO, Virgin Radio, by Linden Brown.

4. Interview with Jason Krieser, General Manager, Allen Medical, by Chris Brown.

5. Jim Collins, *How the Mighty Fall*, London: Random House Business Books, 2009.

6. Reed Hastings, Q3 2011 Letter to shareholders, Netflix, October 24, 2011, 2, http://ir.netflix.com/results.cfm.

7. Interview with Chris Zane, CEO, Zane Cycles, by Chris Brown.

8. This story was told where we were working to instill a customer mindset and behaviors with a large finance and accounting group in an energy utility.

Chapter 2

1. See the full story at http://blogoscoped.com/archive/2007-06-04-n80.html.

2. See http://www.cnbc.com/id/46603589/The_Costco_Craze, also http://video.cnbc.com/gallery/?video=3000086576.

3. You can see the video at the *MarketCulture* blog: http://blog.marketculture.com/2012/10/16/how-knowing-your-customers-improves-your-ability-to-communicate/.

4. Tony Hsieh, *Delivering Happiness: A Path to Profits, Passion, and Purpose*, New York: Business Plus, 2010.

5. Chantal Todé, "Credit Suisse Learns about Customer Experience from Top Down," *Direct Marketing News*, May 23, 2007, http://www.dmnews.com/credit-suisse-learns-about-customer-experience-from-top-down/article/95665/#. See also "Immersing Yourself in Your Customers' World," *Touchpoint Dashboard*, December 19, 2012, http://www.touchpointdashboard.com/2012/12/immersing-yourself-in-your-customers-world/.

6. Geoff Colvin, "How Can American Express Help You?" *Fortune*, April 19, 2012, http://management.fortune.cnn.com/2012/04/19/american-express-customer-service/.

7. Colvin, "How Can American Express Help You?"

8. Barbara Farfan, "Quotations from the Customer-centric Founder and CEO of Amazon, Jeff Bezos," About.com, May 8, 2012, http://retailindustry.about.com/od/frontlinemanagement/a/Amazon_CEO_Jeff_Bezos_quotes.htm.

9. Cynthia Clark, "Increasing Customer Centricity Through Better Listening,"*1to1 Magazine,* August 13, 2012, http://www.1to1media.com/view.aspx?docid=33787.

Chapter 3

1. Aaron Hemmelgarn, "Apple iPad Is an iFailure," *Los Angeles Web Design Blog*, January 27, 2010, http://www.ocwebdesignblog.com/index.php/technology/apple-ipad-is-a-ifailure/.

2. Arik Hesseldahl, "Apple's Hard iPad Sell," *Bloomberg Businessweek*, February 5, 2010, http://www.businessweek.com/technology/content/feb2010/tc2010024_830227.htm.

3. Ken Aaron, "Behind the Music," *Cornell Engineering*, Fall 2005, http://www.engineering.cornell.edu/news/magazine/loader.cfm?csModule=security/getfile&PageID=51779.

4. Dieter Bohn, "Former Palm CEO Jon Rubenstein Joins Qualcomm Board of Directors," *The Verge*, May 6, 2013, http://www.theverge.com/2013/5/6/4306074/former-palm-ceo-jon-rubinstein-joins-qualcomm-board-of-directors.

5. Interview with Mark Gilmour, Virgin Group, by Linden Brown on June 6, 2013.

6. Alan Deutschman, "Inside the Mind of Jeff Bezos," *Fast Company*, August 1, 2004, http://www.fastcompany.com/50541/inside-mind-jeff-bezos.

7. Jeff Bezos Video Talk: http://mindgatemedia.com/lesson/jeff-bezos-talks-about-the-three-factors-to-success/.

8. Mike Dunn, "Yahoo! Finance Partners with 7-11 for Store Pick Ups," *Yahoo! News*, http://news.yahoo.com/amazon-partners-7-11-store-pick-ups-235657161.html.

9. Nathan Mattise, "Easy—Amazon Customers Get Lockers at Staples to Avoid Missed Deliveries," *Ars Technica*, November 5, 2012, http://arstechnica.com/gadgets/2012/11/easy-amazon-customers-get-lockers-at-staples-to-avoid-missed-deliveries/.

10. "The 10,000 Year Clock," The Long Now Foundation, accessed September 14, 2013, http://longnow.org/clock/.

11. Seth Fiegerman, "Jeff Bezos Explains Why He's Building a 10,000 Year Clock," Mashable.com, November 30, 2012, http://mashable.com/2012/11/30/jeff-bezos-10000-year-clock/.

12. Jeff Bezos Video Talk: http://mindgatemedia.com/lesson/jeff-bezos-talks-about-the-three-factors-to-success/.

13. Lance Uggla's story and Markit's remarkable growth over the last decade is told in Chapter 10.

14. Bruce Horovitz, "Starbucks CEO Schultz on Digital Innovation," *USA Today*, April 25, 2013, http://www.usatoday.com/story/money/business/2013/04/24/starbucks-howard-schultz-innovators/2047655/.

15. Howard Schultz, *Pour Your Heart Into It: How Starbucks Built a Company One Cup at a Time*, New York: Hyperion, 1999, 224.

16. Quora, "What Are Some Failed Starbucks Products?" *Forbes*, January 25, 2013, http://www.forbes.com/sites/quora/2013/01/25/what-are-some-failed-starbucks-products/.

17. Janelle Nanos, "The Frappuccino: By the Numbers," *Boston*, December 2012, http://www.bostonmagazine.com/2012/11/frappuccino-by-the-numbers/.

18. Michelle Jones, "What's Brewing with Starbucks Innovation Division" (interview with Mary Wagner, supervisor, Global R&D, Starbucks), Stage-Gate Innovation Summit 2013, February 26–28, 2013, http://www.stage-gate.com/Summit_2013/speakers_starbucks.php.

19. Interview with Jason Yetton, group executive, Westpac Retail and Business Banking, by Linden Brown on May 30, 2013.

Chapter 4

1. Interview of David Thodey, CEO, Telstra by Linden Brown on May 21, 2013.

2. David Roe, "Forrester's Customer Experience Index: The Good, The Bad and the Poor," *CMS Wire*, January 17, 2013, http://www.cmswire.com/cms/customer-experience/forresters-customer-experience-index-the-good-the-bad-and-the-poor-019179.php.

3. Karen Southwick, *Everyone Else Must Fail: The Unvarnished Truth about Oracle and Larry Ellison*, New York: Crown Business, 2003.

4. Ryan Babikian, "Billionaire Larry Ellison Talks Shit and Wages War on Competition," *Elite Daily*, July 26, 2012, http://elitedaily.com/

money/entrepreneurship/billionaire-larry-ellison-talks-shit-wages-
war-competition/.
5. See www.youtube.com/watch?v=tg2d_s1wfcU.
6. The OSS story is first told in Chapter 1, which outlines how the
business began.
7. This story comes from an interview with David Cooke by Chris
Brown, September 2012. In May 2013 David Cooke was appointed
the first non-Japanese managing director of any Konica Minolta
subsidiary outside Japan.
8. "Top Three Netflix Competitors: Who's Challenging the
Industry Giant?" *FierceOnlineVideo*, November 21, 2012, http://
www.fierceonlinevideo.com/special-reports/top-three-netflix-
competitors-whos-challenging-industry-giant#ixzz2TVksXkmx.
9. James B. Stewart, "Netflix Looks Back on Its Near-Death
Spiral," *New York Times*, April 26, 2013, http://www.nytimes.
com/2013/04/27/business/netflix-looks-back-on-its-near-death-
spiral.html?pagewanted=all&_r=0.
10. Interview of Ian Grace, CEO, Virgin Radio, by Linden Brown
on June 12, 2013.
11. Kim Bhasin, "Coke vs. Pepsi: The Amazing Story behind the
Infamous Cola Wars," *Business Insider Australia,* November 3,
2011, http://au.businessinsider.com/soda-wars-coca-cola-pepsi-
history-infographic-2011-11?op=1#the-saga-began-in-1886-when-
john-s-pemberton-developed-the-original-recipe-for-coke-heres-
what-was-in-it-1.
12. "Google's Strategy for Winning the Smartphone Wars: Don't
Fight the Smartphone Wars," *New Statesman*, April 8, 2013,
http://www.newstatesman.com/sci-tech/2013/04/googles-strategy-
winning-smartphone-wars-dont-fight-smartphone-wars.

Chapter 5

1. Gary Hamel and C. K. Prahalad, "How Competition for the
Future Is Different," in *Competing for the Future*, Boston: Harvard
Business Press, 1994, 29–52.
2. Michael E. Porter, Jan W. Rivkin, and Rosabeth Moss Kanter,
*Competitiveness at the Crossroads: Findings of Harvard Business
School's 2012 Survey on U.S. Competitiveness*, Boston: Harvard
Business School, February 2013, 2.

3. See also Steve Denning, "The Surprising Reasons Why America Lost Its Ability to Compete," Forbes, March 10, 2013, http://www.forbes.com/sites/stevedenning/2013/03/10/the-surprising-reasons-why-america-lost-its-ability-to-compete/.

4. Also see Daniel Pink, *To Sell Is Human: The Surprising Truth about Persuading, Convincing and Influencing Others*, Melbourne, AU: Text Publishing, 2012, 128–129.

5. See the story of this transformation in Howard Schultz with Joanne Gordon, *Onward: How Starbucks Fought for Its Life without Losing Its Soul*, New York: Rodale Books, 2011.

6. Oh-Hyun Kwon, "CEO Message" to shareholders, Samsung, 2012, http://www.samsung.com/us/aboutsamsung/ir/ceomessage/IR_CEOMessage.

7. "SWOT Analysis of Samsung," Strategic Management Insight, 2013, http://www.strategicmanagementinsight.com/swot-analyses/samsung-swot-analysis.html.

8. *Analysis of Samsung's Competitiveness in 2012*, ROA Holdings Report No. 012501, 2012, global.roaholdings.com/download/download.html?num=150&type.

9. Interview with Mark Gilmour, head of global brand development and Asia Pacific brand, Virgin Group, by Linden Brown on May 23 and June 6, 2013; interview with Ian Grace, CEO Virgin Radio, by Linden Brown on June 12, 2013.

10. Len Hughes is a retired network engineer who worked in Silicon Valley since its early years in the 1960s and its explosion of technological innovation throughout the remainder of the twentieth century. He has told us many stories of the visionaries and inventors who worked in many of those Silicon Valley companies and how difficult they found it to impart their vision of the future.

11. "Mobile Phone Inventor Dreams of Human Embeds," *Sydney Morning Herald*, March 28, 2008, http://www.smh.com.au/news/technology/dreams-of-human-embeds/2008/03/28/1206207352924.html?page=2.

12. Audley Jarvis, "How Kodak Invented the Digital Camera in 1975: 'Portable' Device Used Cassette Recorder as Memory Card," Techradar.cameras, May 9, 2008, http://www.techradar.com/au/news/cameras/photography-video-capture/how-kodak-invented-the-digital-camera-in-1975-364822.

13. Dean Takahashi, "Widow Speaks about Bob Noyce, Telling the Human Side of the Mayor of Silicon Valley," *VB News*, February 4, 2013, http://venturebeat.com/2013/02/04/widow-speaks-about-bob-noyce-telling-the-human-side-of-the-mayor-of-silicon-valley-video/.
14. Google Glass, http://www.google.com/glass/start/what-it-does/.
15. Cecilia Kang, "Google to Use Balloons to Provide Free Internet Access to Remote or Poor Areas," *Washington Post*, June 14, 2013, http://articles.washingtonpost.com/2013-06-14/business/39983714_1_internet-privacy-balloons-new-zealand.
16. Cadie Thompson, "YouTube May Be Worth $20 Billion by 2020: Morgan Stanley,"CNBC, May 16, 2013, http://www.cnbc.com/id/100743171.
17. Mary Meeker and Liang Wu, "Internet Trends D11 Conference"(presentation), KleinerPerkins Caufield Byers, May 29, 2013, http://www.kpcb.com/insights/2013-internet-trends.
18. Lucy Battersby, "Telstra International Faces Competition from US Giant Verizon," *Sydney Morning Herald*, November 8, 2012, http://www.smh.com.au/it-pro/cloud/telstra-international-faces-competition-from-us-giant-verizon-20121107-28ygp.html#ixzz2FXYcp21A.

Chapter 6

1. George S. Day and Paul J. H. Schoemaker, *Peripheral Vision: Detecting the Weak Signals That Will Make or Break Your Company*, Boston: Harvard Business School Press, 2006, 12.
2. John Naughton, "The End of Everything," *The Deal*, April 2013, 19.
3. Andrew S. Grove, *Only the Paranoid Survive: How to Exploit the Crisis Points That Challenge Every Company*, New York: Random House, 1996.
4. In our discussions with Professor George Day he suggested we call this discipline "peripheral vision." It reflects many of the practices described in his book with Paul Schoemaker: *Peripheral Vision: Detecting the Weak Signals That Will Make or Break Your Company* (Boston: Harvard Business School Press, 2006).
5. Interview of John Stanhope by Linden Brown on March 22, 2013.
6. Andrew Colley, "Borders Bookstores Gone in Rebrand Exercise," *The Australian*, July 31, 2012, http://www.theaustralian.

com.au/australian-it/it-business/borders-bookstores-gone-in-rebrand-exercise /story-e6frganx-1226438888350.

7. Jeremy Greenfield, "Barnes & Noble's Big Problem—and What to Do about It," *Forbes*, February 6, 2013, http://www.forbes.com/sites/jeremygreenfield/2013/02/06/barnes-nobles-big-problem-and-what-to-do-about-it/.

8. David Roe, "Forrester's Customer Experience Index: The Good, The Bad and the Poor," *CMS Wire*, January 17, 2013, http://www.cmswire.com/cms/customer-experience/forresters-customer-experience-index-the-good-the-bad-and-the-poor-019179.php.

9. "2012 Temkin Experience Ratings," Temkin Ratings, accessed September 18, 2013, http://temkinratings.com/temkin-experience-ratings/.

10. Josh Bernoff, "Are You Ready for Digital Disruption?" *Marketing News*, January 2013, 24–25.

11. See Howard Anderson, "Why Did Kodak, Motorola, and Nortel Fail?" *Information Week*, January 12, 2012, http://www.informationweek.com/global-cio/interviews/why-did-kodak-motorola-and-nortel-fail/232400270.

12. See Alexis C. Madrigal, "Paul Otellini's Intel: Can the Company That Built the Future Survive It?" *The Atlantic*, May 16, 2013, http://www.theatlantic.com/technology/archive/2013/05/paul-otellinis-intel-can-the-company-that-built-the-future-survive-it/275825/.

13. See John Davidson, "Intel Victorious over New Chip," *Financial Review*, June 6, 2013, 3, http://www.afr.com/p/technology/digitallife/intel_victorious_over_new_chip_SmFSFbKIjRGYxJI73yQxaM.

14. Interview with Jason Yetton, executive general manager, retail and business banking, Westpac, by Linden Brown on May 30, 2013.

15. Lance Uggla's leadership philosophy and focus on culture is described in Chapter 10.

16. See Michelle Price, "Markit Chief Continues Hunt for Growth," *Financial News*, July 30, 2012, http://www.efinancialnews.com/story/2012-07-30/markit-chief-continues-hunt-for-growth? ea9c8a2de0ee111045601ab04d673622.

17. "FY 2013 Q4 Earnings Release Conference Call Transcript," Investors.NikeInc.com, June 27, 2013, http://investors.nikeinc

.com/files/NIKE,%20Inc.%20Q413%20Earnings%20Release%20
Transcript_v001_u11798.pdf.
18. Mark McClusky, "The Nike Experiment: How the Shoe
Giant Unleashed the Power of Personal Metrics," *Wired*, June
22, 2009, http://www.wired.com/medtech/health/magazine/17-07/
lbnp_nike?currentPage=all.
19. Interview with the CEO and Founder of Executive Next
Practices Institute, Scott Hamilton; see http://www.enpinstitute.com/.
20. Marc Benioff and Carlyle Adler, *Behind the Cloud: The Untold
Story of How Salesforce.com Went from Idea to Billion-Dollar
Company—and Revolutionized an Industry*, San Francisco: Jossey-
Bass, October 2009.
21. Rick Whiting, "Sales Force CEO Benioff: The Cloud Is Passe,"
CRN, June 16, 2011, http://www.crn.com/news/cloud/230800062/
salesforce-ceo-benioff-the-cloud-is-passe.htm.
22. Interview of Alex Bard, senior vice president and general
manager, salesforce.com, by Chris Brown on June 3, 2013.
23. Interview of Grant Ellison, CEO of CommsChoice by Linden
Brown on June 1, 2013.

Chapter 7

1. Juhana Rossi, "Nokia CEO Sticks to Company's Strategy,"
Wall Street Journal, May 7, 2013, http://online.wsj.com/article/SB1
0001424127887323372504578468412034528362.html.
2. Interview with Jason Yetton, Australian Financial Services,
Westpac, by Linden Brown on May 30, 2013.
3. Adam Grant, "Givers Take All: The Hidden Dimension of
Corporate Culture," *McKinsey Quarterly*, April 2013, http://www.
mckinsey.com/insights/organization/givers_take_all_the_hidden_
dimension_of_corporate_culture.
4. Margaret Heffernan, "Ikea's Former CEO on How to
Collaborate," *Inc.*, December 13, 2012, http://www.inc.com/
margaret-heffernan/ikeas-former-ceo-on-how-to-collaborate.html.
5. See Anders Dahlvig, *The IKEA Edge: Building Global Growth
and Social Good at the World's Most Iconic Home Store*,
New York: McGraw-Hill, 2012.
6. The authors worked with Kirsty Shaw and interviewed her on
May 30, 2013.

7. The authors worked with and interviewed Ryan Rampersaud, global client director at BlackRock, in September 2012.

8. David A. Kaplan. "Salesforce's Happy Workforce," *CNN Money*, January 19, 2012, http://tech.fortune.cnn.com/2012/01/19/best-companies-salesforce-benioff/.

9. Interview with Brian Hartzer, CEO, Australian Financial Services at Westpac Banking Corporation, by Linden Brown on May 1, 2013.

10. See "About Us," Virgin.com, http://www.virgin.com/about-us.

11. David K. Williams, "Brad Smith, Intuit CEO: 'How to Be a Great Leader: Get Out of the Way,'" *Forbes*, June 25, 2012.

Chapter 8

1. Interview with David Thodey, CEO Telstra, by Linden Brown on March 21, 2013.

2. For more information on the relevance of business processes to empowerment, see Connie Moore, William Band, Craig Le Clair, et al., "Empower Customers by Transforming Business Processes: A Roundtable Discussion with Forrester Analysts," *Forrester*, August 4, 2011, http://www.forrester.com/Empower+Customers+By+Transforming+Business+Processes/fulltext/-/E-RES60547?docid=60547.

3. This association was found in the Finance and Administration Group of Telstra that had 2,500 people and eight separate functions with a common value of customer service. After a cultural program to build a service culture was implemented only in this function it was found that engagement scores increased significantly compared with the rest of the company. Senior management put this down to strong strategic alignment around service.

4. Cyril Peupion, "Bringing Discipline to Execution," Australian Institute of Company Directors, February 1, 2013, http://www.companydirectors.com.au/Director-Resource-Centre/Publications/Company-Director-magazine/2013-back-editions/February/Opinion-Bringing-discipline-to-execution.

5. Stan Phelps, *What's Your Green Goldfish: Beyond Dollars—15 Ways to Drive Employee Engagement and Reinforce Culture*, Cary, NC: 9 Inch Marketing, 2013; See also "State of the American Workplace: Employee Engagement Insights for U.S.

Business Leaders," Gallup, Inc., 2013, http://www.gallup.com/strategicconsulting/163007/state-american-workplace.aspx.

6. See Adrian Swinscoe, "Employee Engagement Is a Commitment Not a Campaign: Interview with Stan Phelps," *CustomerThink*, May 2, 2013, http://www.customerthink.com/blog/employee_engagement_is_a_commitment_not_a_campaign_interview_with_stan_phelps?goback=.gde_3854012_member_237876024.

7. Makiko Kitamura, "Toyota's President Apologizes for Recall," *Bloomberg Businessweek*, February 5, 2010, http://www.businessweek.com/bwdaily/dnflash/content/feb2010/db2010025_109559.htm.

8. Chris Woodyard, "Toyota Recalls Prius Due to Faulty Brakes," *USA Today*, June 5, 2013, http://www.usatoday.com/story/driveon/2013/06/05/toyota-prius-lexus-hs-recall/2390919/.

9. Interview with John Hooper, CFO of Ergon Energy, by Linden Brown on February 6, 2013.

10. Damon Kitney, "You've Got Mail: Virgin's Kiwi in Flight," *Weekend Australian*, May 18–19, 2013, 23.

11. Ibid, 30.

12. See Virgin Group website: http://www.virgin.com.au/about-us.

13. Interviews with Mark Gilmour, global brand development manager, Virgin Group, by Linden Brown on May 23 and June 6, 2013.

14. Interview with Ian Grace, CEO, Virgin Radio, by Linden Brown on June 12, 2013.

15. Interview with Brian Hartzer by Linden Brown on May 1, 2013.

16. Malcolm Gladwell, *The Tipping Point: How Little Things Can Make a Big Difference*, Boston: Little, Brown and Company, 2000.

17. Interview of Alex Bart, senior vice president and general manager, salesforce.com, by Chris Brown on June 3, 2013.

18. Interview with Tony Collins by Debi Garrod, research colleague of the authors, on December 7, 2012. See also Tony Collins, "Leadership the Virgin Way: Crystal Lecture," University of Wolverhampton, UK, October 2012, video of presentation at http://www.wlv.ac.uk/default.aspx?page=27542.

19. Interview with David Thodey, CEO, Telstra, by Linden Brown on March 21, 2013.

20. Interview with Rachel Sandford, Telstra Cultural Advocacy Program Lead, by Linden Brown on July 26, 2013.
21. Interview with Peter Wheeler, Partner, PwC, by Linden Brown on July 26, 2013.
22. One of the authors, Linden, was studying the Australian pet-food industry at the time and remembers Lyndon Prowse as a "larger than life" figure. Also a reference for this story is found in an interview by George Lewkowicz from the Don Dunstan Foundation for the Don Dunstan Foundation History Project interviewing Mr. Geoff Anderson on the topic of industrial democracy in the 1970s. The interview was held on October 3, 2007, at the Don Dunstan Foundation in North Terrace, Adelaide, Australia, http://dspace.flinders.edu.au/jspui/bitstream/2328/3209/2/ANDERSON_Geoff_Cleared.pdf.
23. "JetBlue: Life as a CEO," YouTube, May 3, 2012, http://www.youtube.com/watch?v=9ma1vQPouYo.
24. David Neeleman, "Creating a Customer Experience," YouTube, May 3, 2012, http://www.youtube.com/watch?v=79iSEB_mnk8.
25. "JetBlue Awarded Seventh Consecutive Customer Satisfaction J.D. Powers and Associates Honor," *BlueTales* (JetBlue blog), June 8, 2011, http://blog.jetblue.com/index.php/2011/06/08/jetblue-awarded-seventh-consecutive-customer-satisfaction-j-d-power-and-associates-honor/.

Chapter 9

1. Nic Cola, director of transformation at Fairfax Media, and Kirsty Shaw, marketing director at Fairfax Media, describe the transformation undertaken in the online businesses in Chapter 8 (from interviews).
2. A detailed case study of Telstra's Finance Group customer-centric transformation can be found at http://www.marketculture.com/resourcegateway.html.
3. There is a rich source of research about the topic of leading organizational and cultural change. John Kotter's eight-stage process is one of the most widely known approaches to leading change. Chip and Dan Heath describe the specifics of what it takes to change in their book, *Switch: How to Change Things When Change Is Hard*. Several stories of how leaders have created

customer-centric organizations have been written by their leaders or their autobiographers. Tony Hsieh tells us the story of Zappos in *Delivering Happiness* and how a customer service culture was built at the center of this online shoe retailer. Howard Schultz tells the story of how Starbucks, after 25 years of growth and profitability, had to be transformed after it lost connection with its marketplace. The Enterprise Rent-A-Car story of how a small firm grew to a national business with customer service at the heart of its culture is another example of building a customer culture from the ground up. Marc Benioff, CEO of salesforce.com, tells his story of the early beginnings and growth of the business with a strong customer culture. The early days of Federal Express and its later growth indicate the level of belief that is necessary to follow a vision and build a customer culture into your business. The inside stories of FedEx are told in two separate books. All of these books and many others provide a sound foundation for planning and executing transformational change.

4. Cooper Smith, "How Social Commerce Is Winning by Going After the Entire Shopping Experience, from Browsing to Sale," Business Insider, September 21, 2013, http://www.businessinsider.com/amazons-letter-to-shareholders-2013-4.

5. This case was compiled from interviews over the period March–June 2013 with the following people at Australia Post: Ahmed Fahour, CEO; Nic Nuske, general manager of sales and marketing; Shane Morris, executive manager; and John Stanhope, chairman.

6. These and other comments are from answers to questions posed by Linden Brown to Ahmed Fahour on June 12, 2013.

7. Interview with Nic Nuske by Linden Brown on April 10, 2013.

8. Patrick Durkin, "Ahmed Fahour: Agent for Change," AFR Boss, June 2013, 24.

9. This case is based on interviews with David Thodey, CEO; John Parkin, NPS program director; and Liz Moore, director of research, insight and analytics at Telstra.

10. See http://www.productreview.com.au/p/telstra-1/2.html for good and bad experiences of Telstra's service.

11. This case is based on an interview with Jason Yetton, group executive, Westpac Retail and Business Banking, by Linden Brown on May 30, 2013.

12. See "Financial Information: 5 Year Summary," Westpac Group, 2012, http://www.westpac.com.au/about-westpac/investor-centre/financial-information/5-year-summary/.
13. See "Westpac Banking Corp," Yahoo! Finance, http://au.finance .yahoo.com/q/hp?s=WBC.AX&a=00&b=29&c=1988&d=06&e=4& f=2013&g=m.
14. This case is based on interviews with Tony Collins and Virgin Trains staff by Debi Garrod, an organizational psychologist who has been working as a consultant over the last five years in Virgin Trains. It is also based on recent articles reporting on the competitive bid for the West Coast Line rail service franchise.
15. Howard Schultz with Joanne Gordon, *Onward: How Starbucks Fought for Its Life without Losing Its Soul*, Emmaus, PA: Rodale Books, 2011, 104.
16. Interview with Arthur Rubinfeld, chief creative officer; president, Global Development and Evolution Fresh Retail, Starbucks, by Chris Brown on May 22, 2013.

Chapter 10

1. Interview with Donald Williamson, leadership coach, on March 2, 2013, Carmel, California.
2. Erika Anderson, "11 Quotes from Sir Richard Branson on Business, Leadership, and Passion," *Forbes*, March 16, 2013, http://www.forbes.com/sites/erikaandersen/2013/03/16/11-quotes-from-sir-richard-branson-on-business-leadership-and-passion/.
3. Interview with Tony Collins, CEO, Virgin Trains, by Debi Garrod on November 30, 2012.
4. The story of what happened in the bid fiasco is described in the Virgin Trains case study in Chapter 9.
5. Interview with Lance Uggla, CEO, Markit, by Chris Brown on March 30, 2013. Markit provides financial information services to financial institutions globally.
6. See infomarkit.eu/blog/?p=142e.
7. Joe Penna, in Nicholas Tart, "Best 101 Entrepreneur Quotes Ever," *14 Clicks*, March 24, 2011, http://14clicks.com/top-entrepreneurship-quotes-ever/#sthash.usH8byrB.dpuf.

8. Interview with David Thodey, CEO, Telstra, by Linden Brown on March 21, 2013. Telstra is Australia's largest telecommunications and information services business, which employs 60,000 staff and contractors.

9. Bianca Soldani, "Best of the Best: Telstra's David Thodey Honoured as a World Top CEO," *Australian Times*, April 10, 2012, http://www.australiantimes.co.uk/news/in-australia/best-of-the-besttelstras-david-thodey-honoured-as-a-top-world-ceo.htm.

10. Interview with John Stanhope, chairman, Australia Post, by Linden Brown on March 23, 2013. Australia Post is a government-owned corporation that provides mail and parcel services to Australian consumers, businesses, and government.

11. Our interviews with Tony Collins, Virgin Trains; Ian Grace, Virgin Radio; and Mark Gilmour at Virgin Group have shed light on Richard Branson as a leader and form the basis of describing Richard Branson's leadership.

12. Jane Kadzow, "Outer Reaches," *Sydney Morning Herald*, June 15, 2013, 15.

13. Interview with Ian Grace by Linden Brown, June 12, 2013. Branson himself says about his high-profile publicity stunts that it doesn't come naturally. Those who know him, such as Ian Grace, CEO at Virgin Radio, say that he spends much more time listening than talking and is able to synthesize the information to make a valuable contribution. In that way he is somewhat reserved.

14. Peter Crush, "Exclusive: Sir Richard Branson Talks to HR Magazine about Leadership," *HR Magazine*, July 12, 2010, http://www.hrmagazine.co.uk/hro/features/1018119/exclusive-sir-richard-branson-talks-hr-magazine-leadership.

15. Alicia Ciccone, "Branson and Friends Hope to Hatch Plan B for Business with New Non-Profit," Brand Channel, June 17, 2013, http://www.brandchannel.com/home/post/2013/06/17/Richard-Branson-B-Team-061713.aspx.

16. Interview with Alex Bard by Chris Brown on June 3, 2013.

Chapter 11

1. This widely used quotation is from Jim Collins, *Good to Great: Why Some Companies Make the Leap ... and Others Don't*, New York: Collins Business, 2001.

Appendix 1

1. Our research group included a powerful multidisciplinary team composed of Sean Gallagher, Lucas Coffeen, Hjalte Hojsgaard, and April Cantwell. Sean interviewed some of the authors of key empirical studies on market orientation and business performance, most notably Stan Slater, who was a coauthor of two of the seminal studies in this field. He also discussed our thinking with professors George Day (Wharton), Rohit Deshpande (Harvard), and John Kotter (Harvard). Sean also provided access to business leaders who participated in the early testing and implementation of what became the MRI tool. Lucas conducted all of the literature review of research, synthesized it, and managed the entire project. Hjalte gave us access to European connections for feedback during testing and provided conceptual and modeling skills to the development process. April provided her expertise in quantitative analysis, sampling, item selection, and wording. She gave valuable practical advice on survey design, implementation, and analysis of results.

2. A bibliography of the most relevant studies and papers can be found at http://www.marketculture.com/resourcegateway.html.

3. During the research phase this survey tool was called the Market Culture Benchmark (MCB). After completion of the foundation study and commercialization of the tool for use by companies, we changed its name to the Market Responsiveness Index (MRI). We see the MRI as equivalent to a business health scan, where we are aiming to measure the customer culture heartbeat of the organization. To avoid confusion, we have used MRI to describe the tool throughout the foundation study.

Index

NOTE: Boldface numbers indicate illustrations.